Forever Girls

Forever Girls

Necro-Cinematics and South Korean Girlhood

Jinhee Choi

Oxford University Press is a department of the University of Oxford.
It furthers the University's objective of excellence in research, scholarship,
and education by publishing worldwide. Oxford is a registered trade mark of
Oxford University Press in the UK and in certain other countries.

Published in the United States of America by Oxford University Press
198 Madison Avenue, New York, NY 10016, United States of America.

© Oxford University Press 2025

All rights reserved. No part of this publication may be reproduced, stored in a retrieval system, transmitted, used for text and data mining, or used for training artificial intelligence, in any form or by any means, without the prior permission in writing of Oxford University Press, or as expressly permitted by law, by licence or under terms agreed with the appropriate reprographics rights organization. Enquiries concerning reproduction outside the scope of the above should be sent to the Rights Department, Oxford University Press, at the address above.

You must not circulate this work in any other form
and you must impose this same condition on any acquirer

Library of Congress Cataloging-in-Publication Data
Names: Choi, Jinhee, author.
Title: Forever girls : necro-cinematics and South Korean girlhood / Jinhee Choi.
Description: New York : Oxford University Press, 2025. |
Includes bibliographical references and index. |
Identifiers: LCCN 2024044185 (print) | LCCN 2024044186 (ebook) |
ISBN 9780197685792 (paperback) | ISBN 9780197685785 (hardback) |
ISBN 9780197685808 (epub) | ISBN 9780197685822
Subjects: LCSH: Motion pictures—Korea (South)—History. | Girls in motion pictures.
Classification: LCC PN1993.5 .K6 C484425 2025 (print) | LCC PN1993.5 .K6 (ebook) |
DDC 791.43095195—dc22
LC record available at https://lccn.loc.gov/2024044185
LC ebook record available at https://lccn.loc.gov/2024044186

DOI: 10.1093/9780197685822.001.0001

to my mother,
who is, to me, forever a girl

Contents

Acknowledgments	ix
List of Figures	xi
Notes on Korean Romanization	xiii

Introduction	1
1. Reference Girls: The 1970s	23
2. Girls Who Disappear, Girls Who Remember: From the Writing to Speaking Subject	54
3. Death of a Girl: Necro-cinematics and Bong Joon Ho's Girl Trilogy	80
4. Directing Girls: Korean Indie Women Directors and Girlhood	103
5. Idle Girls: *Sunny* (2011), *Miss Granny* (2014), and *Queen of Walking* (2015)	140
Afterword	162

Notes	165
Selected Filmography	187
Bibliography	191
Index, complied by David O'Hara	201

Acknowledgments

My "girl book" took longer than I expected. I started working on girlhood as a sensibility some time ago but began writing more extensively on South Korean girlhood after I had published with Oxford University Press (OUP) the edited volume on the Japanese director, Ozu Yasujiro in 2018. Then, of course, there was the COVID-19 pandemic. I appreciate the patience and encouragement of the acquisitions editor at OUP, Norman Hirschy, with whom I worked on both the Ozu volume and the girl book; and the project editor, Rachel Ruisard, who thoughtfully assessed my manuscript from the first page until the last. As I redirected the focus of my scholarship to South Korean girlhood, I immediately faced challenges in its scope and felt a need for an overarching framework that would encompass the questions I raise on girls' labor, sensibility, sexuality, and their frequent deaths on and off screen. I thank the two anonymous reviewers of this book manuscript and hope I at least provided a historical and theoretical trajectory that enables girls to be removed from the historical and social mores of death and trauma and to move toward a hope—a major reason that I end this book with "idle" girls.

Throughout this long, delayed process, I have received enormous support from the colleagues in Film Studies, and in return earned the responsibility of being the head of the Department of Film Studies at King's College, London. I am grateful to my colleagues at King's with whom I could frankly share my challenges over drinks or meals, and those who suggested invaluable theoretical frameworks that I was able to incorporate in the book. Research and publication grants from the Arts and Humanities Faculty at King's as well as invitations from South Korea also allowed me to make several research trips to Seoul. Jennie Carlsten has been my go-to person to have several versions of the book proposal and the entire draft of manuscript proofread prior to my submission to the press. So was my colleague Michele Pierson on shorter pieces of writing. I presented chapters of this book at Cornell University, the University of Southern California, Wesleyan University, and the Annual Conference of the Society of Cinema and Media Studies in the United States; the University of Warwick, the University of Edinburgh, the University of Salford, the University of Sheffield, and the School of Oriental and African Studies in the UK; the University of Tubingen and Goethe University Frankfurt in Germany; Keimyeong University and Yonsei University; as well as A Century of Global Korean Cinema in Korea. There must be places that I have missed here, but the audiences' feedback there enabled me to reconsider some of the questions that I had been trying to answer in my book. I would also like to extend my thanks to scholars in Korea with whom I had discussed my initial thoughts about this book and who invited me to have a short, intensive course on this project in one winter—Professor Baek Moon-im and Professor Woo Miseong and Professor Rhee Suk Koo at Yonsei University—and to my students, who enrolled in my Asian Popular Cinema and Korean Cinema at King's—showing much enthusiasm for the topics that I presented to them, including girlhood. And finally, there are colleagues, scholars, friends, and curators who looked forward to the book's publication: Jinsoo An, Una Beck, Aga Baranowka, Mark Betz, Steve Choe, Jihoon Kim, Irene Hee Seung Lee, Sangjoon Lee, Daniel Martin, David Martin-Jones, Michele Pierson, Chi-yun Shin, and Seunghye Sun. I am grateful to them.

I dedicated my first monograph to my late father, from whom I said I got my "supposed brains." And this book should be to my mother, from whom I inherited exceptional memory—she remembers everything with great detail—and of course, her talent for cooking. I appreciate my big brother's secret monitoring of my well-being, regularly checking on my Instagram to make sure I eat well. His family in Seoul I also miss. With my second brother, I could have big laughs occasionally; we share a similar sense of humor. Last, my two cats: my sweet girl Fiona died in September 2021; I had cherished her companionship every day since 2013. And Larissa whom I adopted from the London Inner City Kitties (LICK) Cat Rescue Charity after Fiona had gone. Larissa steered me away from my desk by sitting on the keyboard of my computer to make sure I took proper breaks, but the typos are all mine.

Figures

I.1	*Sonyeo* statue (photo by the author, 2015).	2
1.1	Jeong-a's gaze lands on the space under the overpass with a cast shadow—an empty sign of modernity (*Crazy for You*, Moon Yeo-song, 1977).	31
1.2	Mun-hui makes a plea to stop body searches (*The Maiden Who Went to the City*, Kim Soo-yong, 1981).	37
1.3	In-yeong momentarily looks more feminine after having spent a night with Bak (*A Woman Like the Sun*, Lee Man-hui, 1974).	40
1.4	But she soon returns to her regular clothing of a sailor shirt (*A Woman Like the Sun*, 1974).	41
1.5	Yeong-ja's glance over the train track (*Yeong-ja's Heydays*, Kim Ho-sun, 1975).	44
1.6	Yeong-ja enters the brothel in the far background (*Yeong-ja's Heydays*, 1975).	45
1.7a-b	Hyeon-ju's bike ride in the present and past (*Night Journey*, Kim Soo-yong, 1977).	49
2.1a-b	When the Headmistress asks Ju-ran to stare at the projector, what she sees is a blank sun disk (*The Silenced,* Lee Hae-young, 2015).	60
2.2	An overhead shot of the station (*Spirits' Homecoming*, Cho Jung-rae, 2016).	71
2.3	Jong-bun looks over the cover of *A Little Princess* (*Snowy Road*, Lee Na-jeong, 2015).	76
2.4	Over-the-shoulder shot of Yeong-ae, which mirrors that of Jong-bun (*Snowy Road*, 2015).	77
2.5	Yeong-ae, who poses as a volunteer to work in the Labor Corps, glances at herself in a photograph (*Snowy Road*, 2015).	77
3.1	A-jeong's dead body is on display (*Mother*, Bong Joon-ho, 2009).	85
4.1a-c	After a heated debate, Ha-na is about to cry, feeling frustrated. When Ha-na begins to cry, Yu-mi enters the shot to sit next to her. The camera then cuts for a slight reframing to show Yu-jin joining the two, with all three girls crying together (*The House of Us*, Yoon Ga-eun, 2019).	117
4.2	A shot composition of the three girls resembles the shape of an island in the far background (*The House of Us*, 2019).	118
4.3	Do-hui drinks milk with a meal at Yeong-nam's (*A Girl at My Door*, July Jung, 2014).	128

xii Figures

4.4a–b Do-hui drinks milk defiantly in the investigation room in contrast to an earlier shot of her drinking milk at Yeong-nam's. As she slides the glass slightly, she looks in Yeong-nam's direction (*A Girl at My Door,* 2014). 129

4.5 Mi-so is seen repeatedly cleaning the window throughout the film (*Microhabitat*, Jeon Go-woon 2018). 138

4.6 Mi-so's isolation as a sign of her symbolic death (*Microhabitat*, 2018). 138

5.1 A poster of *Sunday Night and Monday Morning* (1970). 141

5.2 Girls fight against the backdrop of police suppressing a political demonstration (*Sunny*, Kang Hyeong-cheol, 2011). 145

5.3 When Na-mi and Sang-mi struggle with their heads down, their initial difference is less discernible (*Sunny*, 2011). 146

5.4 Su-ji's self-reflection on the glass panel further underscores the gap between the idolized self and the violent reality (*Sunny*, 2011). 146

5.5 One of the fan signs in the middle says, "Bling Bling Hwang Dong-hyuk" (*Miss Granny*, Hwang Dong-hyuk, 2014). 161

Notes on Korean Romanization

Throughout the book, I follow the Revised Romanization of Korean issued by the Ministry of Culture in 2000, except for proper names that had already earned currency in public—especially directors, actors, and actresses such as Bong Joon-ho (instead of Bong Jun-ho). In the main body, for the work published in Korean, authors' names maintain their usual order—surnames followed by given names, respecting their preferences for the insertion or omission of a hyphen between syllables of the given name—while for English publications, in the order of first then family name.

Introduction

In *Factory Complex* (*Wirogongdan*, Im Heung-soon, 2014), an artist film that won the Silver Lion at the Venice Biennale, women factory workers and employees in various service sectors and affective industry—including flight attendants and customer service staff—are interviewed, reflecting on their working experiences and involvement in labor unions and movements from the 1970s and '80s to the present. Their interviews are interspersed not only with historical footage and photographs of the past but also with shots of girls in blindfolds. The blindfolded girls roam the forests or appear in urban spaces such as the rooftops of low-wage workers' dormitories or in the middle of union protests. The juxtaposition of the interviewees' personal experiences with these fictional segments—footage that sometimes reinforces or illustrates the interviewees' testimonies, and sometimes provides a counterpoint—underscores the existence of a gap between the workers' ideals and aspirations and the historical reality. In the film, girlhood is a stand-in, suggestive, reference image that was dreamed of but neither existed nor was appreciated throughout the developmental history of South Korea [hereafter Korea] as a nation-state.[1] Girlhood, like the mysterious figure in Im's film, could be seen as a floating signifier or "reference image" that hovers above or below one's depicted wishes or despair. My use of the term "reference image" here is inspired by Genevieve Yue's work on "China girl"/"girl head"—an actual piece of footage of a woman or women found or inserted in film strips and used to provide a reference that guides Hollywood filmmakers and lab technicians to control image quality. According to Yue, the girl head as reference image is "operative" not mimetic.[2] The function and connotation of the reference image that I tease out in the Korean context differ but retain the premise that gender (or image of gender) is an operative concept that (mis)guides representation.

Girl (*sonyeo*) image is not tied to a single demographic group, often extending beyond childhood or adolescence; nor is it associated with a set of fixed traits. At one end of polarized images of girlhood, one can find a strong association between girls and the victimhood of national traumas, past

---

Forever Girls. Jinhee Choi, Oxford University Press. © Oxford University Press 2025.
DOI: 10.1093/9780197685822.003.0001

2 Forever Girls

and present. In 2011, a peace statue of a girl in Korean traditional costume (*sonyeosang*) was erected on the street just across from the Japanese embassy in Seoul (figure I.1). It is a reminder of the hardships of Korean military sex slaves ("comfort women [*wianbu*]") under Japanese colonial rule (1910–1945) and commemorates their survival. Some were in their early teens when

Figure I.1 *Sonyeo* statue (photo by the author, 2015).

they were recruited under a false promise of employment in Japan and other occupied territories, or abducted and/or forced to provide sexual labor for imperial soldiers in military bases during World War II.[3] Whenever political tension between Japan and Korea escalates, touching on the colonial past, and the demand for compensation for survivors resurfaces, the idea of victimhood is strongly inscribed in the image of the girl. Girls' victimhood extends the atrocity of World War II; girls' bodies are the prime sites where victims endured national traumas such as the 1980 Gwangju pro-democracy movement, where thousands of civilians were killed during their protests. Girls have been exploited as low-wage employees and stigmatized as sexual laborers.[4] At the other end of the spectrum are the Korean girl groups of the K-pop music business who have become the apparently lively yet disposable commodities in the entertainment industry: after undergoing several years of training without being adequately paid, most of their contracts do not get renewed. Some of the famous band members, such as Gu Ha-ra and Sulli, prematurely terminated their lives in 2019.[5]

Conflicting remembrance and construction of girlhood—from factory workers to military sexual slaves to Korean pop idols—also permeate contemporary Korean (commercial and art) cinema, performance art, and artist films. Girls have often appeared as the victims of national traumas, sexual violence and oppressive institutions. *A Petal* (*Kkotnip*, Jang Sun-woo, 1996) revolves around a girl who suffers from post-traumatic syndrome after having lost her brother and mother in the Gwangju Uprising, a 1980 pro-democratic movement. In the performance piece *Sex Education in the 21st Century* (2002) by US/Germany-based artist Mirae kh Rhee, Rhee herself is dressed as a pregnant high school girl in downtown Seoul as a way to expose the lack of adequate sex education in Korea.[6] Im's *Factory Complex* (2014), mentioned above, provides a contemporary Korean history of women's labor movements based on interviews with former and current employees in the various manufacturing and service sectors. A recent surge of Korean films with girl protagonists further complicates the picture. These include popular horror film franchises such as the *Whispering Corridor* series (*Yeogogoedam*, 1998–ongoing) and the box office hit *Sunny* (*Sseoni*, Kang Hyeong-cheol, 2011), not to mention recent indie films such as *A Girl at My Door* (*Do-huiya*, also spelled as [a.s.a.] *Dohee-ya*, July Jung, 2014); *The World of Us* (*Urideul*, Yoon Ga-eun, 2016); *House of Hummingbird* (*Beolsae*, Kim Bora, 2018); and the flower trilogy starring Jeong Ha-dam (*Wild Flowers* [*Deulkkot*]; *Steel Flower* [*Seutil peulawo*]; and *Ash Flower* [*Jekkot*], Park Seok-yeong, 2014–2016).

Due to the ambiguity of "girl" as a term and its malleable association with various demographic referents, throughout the history of Korean cinema

4 Forever Girls

it has encompassed diverse character types, from schoolgirls to low-wage employees such as factory workers, domestic helpers, bus conductors, and sex workers.[7] Throughout this book, girl is not approached as a specific character type but more as a social imaginary and a site that embodies contradicting attributes and moral values. Focusing on girl's sexuality, labor, leisure, and freedom, I foreground how the "reference girl" established in the 1970s continues to operate and control the representation of gender in contemporary Korean cinema. I further examine girl protagonists in contemporary Korean cinema, as the principal subject that remembers the past, experiences the present, and envisions the future, and I further tease out their cinematic significance. My work on girls nicely counterbalances and complements the existing scholarship in English that has focused on the crisis of masculinity in Korean cinema under the past military dictatorship and contemporary economic crises.[8]

Korean Feminism and Girl Culture

Straddled between industrialization and democratization, two major forces that have driven and shaped contemporary South Korean society, the portrayal of girls in contemporary Korean cinema should further be examined in the light of changing discourses on girls. I will briefly situate the emerging significance of girl culture within the contemporary climate of feminist discourses on girls, both in the West and Korea, with an eye particularly on generational tensions. There were precedents of commercially successful films with girl protagonists, such as *My Sassy Girl* (*Yeopgijeokin geunyeo*, Kwak Jae-young, 2001) and the aforementioned horror series and films featuring girls (*Whispering Corridors* [1998] and *A Tale of Two Sisters* [*Janghwa, Hongryeon*, Kim Jee-woon, 2003]), all of which were ranked high in the domestic box office. But *Sunny* (2011) marked another turning point in the South Korean film industry. Ranked in the top three in the domestic box office of that year with 7.3 million admissions, it not only showcased the commercial viability of a group of girls as protagonists but also appeared to depart from the conventions of girl protagonists as victims of the sexual violence and national trauma of the 1980s.[9] Na-mi (played by Shim Eun-kyung), after having run into her high school friend, Chun-hwa, at a hospital, traces their five mutual friends from high school. Together, they had formed the "seven princesses" (often a euphemism for a gang of girls that bully and dominate a school). In order to fulfill Chun-hwa's wish for a reunion, Na-mi locates the former members of the gang one by one, with the film alternating between the 1980s and the present day. While the 1980s were and still are commonly represented as the decade during which many political activists, student protesters, and workers faced torture, disappeared, and died, *Sunny* presents girls as being preoccupied solely with their solidarity, power struggles, and desires for new consumer goods.[10] In one scene, a lavish fight between two rival gangs of girls takes place on the street against the backdrop of policemen suppressing the students' political demonstration.

The film is set during a brief period in which government policies on school uniforms were suspended: a tracking shot of the girls' shoes and bags reminds the spectator of the frenzy to acquire Western brands. A cultural history of the 1980s, which is often sidetracked or dismissed in Korean films set in the 1980s, is recalled with a nostalgic tone in *Sunny*. The temporal co-existence of two different generations—the girl protagonists in the 1980s and their children's generation in the present—raises an interesting question with regard to the current status of Korean feminism. Although the film is set in the 1980s, it is well tied to the post-feminist sensibility and contradictions. The film's moral essence resembles more that of the 1990s, when girls were able to mobilize the trends of popular culture as active consumers. The agency of girls to propel and sustain such culture resulted from the establishment of the democratic government in 1993, after a period of military dictatorship and government lasting over three decades (1961–1992). Hee Jeong Sohn characterizes the film *Sunny* as a "make-over" fantasy film, focusing on the female leads' transformation of their appearance, once they are summoned back to the present.[11]

Girl protagonists in Hollywood counterparts such as *Clueless* (Amy Heckerling, 1995) or the protagonists in "girly" television series such as *Sex and the City* (1998–2004) demonstrate similar traits: the preoccupation with looks and appearances without serious political commitment. Both Kathleen Rowe Karlyn and Hilary Radner examine romantic comedy as a site where the desire for a new femininity is fantasized. In films such as *Clueless* and *Mean Girls* (Mark Waters, 2004), the absence of the mother is a precondition for the establishment of a liminal time and space between childhood and adulthood where girls rule: a "girl world."[12] Even when the mother is not completely absent, the girls' bond with their fathers more than with their mothers. These works tap into the ideals of post-feminism, "a rebellious pursuing what they want, with or without the approval of their mothers."[13] In her discussion of *Romy and Michele's High School Reunion* (David Mirkin, 1997), Radner claims that "girlhood represents a version of femininity that is neither that of the spinster nor that of the mother, offering a notion of agency, in particular the capacity for change, that is specifically feminine but not yet aligned with the normative behaviors associated with womanly roles."[14] An apparent striving for distinctive personality through a preoccupation with the body and fashion in Hollywood romantic comedies of girlhood seems to be less salient in the Korean context. Instead, romantic comedies focusing on newlyweds, such as *Marriage Story* (*Gyeolhoniyagi*, Kim Ui-seok, 1992) and *My Love and My Bride* (*Naui sarang naui sinbu*, Lee Myung-se, 1990), present the "new woman" and the presence of "unruly" women that invite the reconfiguring of gender traits.[15]

Scholarship on the prominence of girls in both the Western post-feminist and Korean context has not been necessarily celebratory, underscoring the gap existing between the second wave of feminism and its contemporary transformation. Rosalind Gill critiques the contradictory nature of post-feminist discourses and ideals: the girl's individual identity and sense of entitlement utilize the achievement of feminist movements and practices advocated and promoted by the second wave of feminism of the 1970s, but it is viewed as dated and irrelevant to the immediate environment. As Gill notes, "Feminism is not ignored or even attacked . . . but is simultaneously taken for granted and repudiated."[16] Individual agency in girl culture is presented as free from any external pulls that would curtail one's own desires and wishes, yet the choices made end up reinstating the heterosexual normativity.

A similar tension has been detected within the Korean context. Prominent feminist sociology scholar Cho Haejung states,

> In the 90s, we find ourselves at a loss. Women of the younger generation who are eager to separate themselves from their mothers . . . and who are free from the Utopian ideologies of the 1980s, find a way out in the "Global postmodern culture." The roles and images of women were transformed without accompanying change in the deep structure of sexism.[17]

This ambivalent, and even contradictory, relationship between different generations of feminism has been characterized through that between mother and daughter; "daughters of the second wave of feminists derive significant pleasure from reading chick lit."[18]

Gill, who characterizes post-feminism as a sensibility, delineates a new type of femininity endorsed by girls and young women in the 1990s and 2000s. In popular post-feminist media forms, such as chick lit and popular romantic comedies and television series (such as *Bridget Jones Dairy* [Sharon Maguire, 2001] and *Sex and the City*), girls and young women make their own choices about appearance, partnership, and sexuality, through which their individual identities are expressed and a sense of empowerment is garnered.[19] Rather than shying away from pursuing sexual pleasure, women protagonists actively seek it, and their financial independence further provides them with opportunities to embody the desired standard of beauty. What results from such media forms and discourse is the preoccupation with the female body. Gill and Elena Herdieckerhoff claim, "Femininity is defined as a bodily property rather than a social structural or psychological one."[20]

Unlike the female protagonists in Hollywood cinema who are preoccupied with bodily image and beauty, Korean girls' subjectivity and energy in 1990s popular culture was expressed through their fandom, directed at popular idol bands and singers. Girl fans asserted their limited agency by looking out and sometimes attempting to have an impact on the path and fate of their favorite bands. Girls' fandom gained media attention, along with the immense popularity of the first generation of boy bands in the 1990s, which lasted until the early 2000s: Seo Taeji and Boys (Seotaejiwa aideul, 1992–1996); H.O.T (1996–2001); Sechs Kies (1997–2000); Shinhwa (1998–2006); and g.o.d (*jiodi*, 1999–2005).[21] The female fandom has been pejoratively called *ppasuni* in Korean, preoccupied with extreme enthusiasm toward the object of their fandom, with the syllable *suni* explicitly connoting its gender as in "*gongsuni*" (factory girls). Yet their agency, however limited, certainly sparked media attention and was noted by some Korean scholars, as when the girls publicly protested against censorship when a song by Seo Taeji and Boys was banned, or when the fandom "disapproved" the breakup of such bands as H.O.T and g.o.d.[22]

One of the apparent and perhaps key differences between the "girl world" in Hollywood films and "girl fandom" in the Korean media context, is the collective identity of the latter. The first generation of girl fandom coincided with the emergence and demise of the first generation of idol bands (late 1990s through early 2000s, ending with the breakup of g.o.d in 2004). Their fandom is characterized by their overidentification with band members as well as fans' collective visibility.[23] Their attendance at idol bands' concerts and live television music programs was visually and spatially identifiable and demarcated by the color of balloons they displayed when cheering for their idols, and the sections of the auditorium allocated for the fans of a popular band. Some Korean feminists forge an interesting genealogy of girls' collectivity, from that of girls' fandom to "candlelight girls" (*chotbul sonyeo*), whose presence was palpable in Korean public rallies for various political causes, including the series of protests against the government's deregulations of US beef imports in 2008.[24]

It was not until the 2010s, however, that girl culture and fandom appeared as the subject matter of Korean popular culture. Korean television drama series such as *Reply 1997* (*Eungdaphara* 1997 [July–September, 2012]) and *Reply 1994* (*Eungdaphara* 1994 [October–December, 2013]), both of which aired on the cable network tvN in 2012 and 2013, comically portray girl fandom toward the first generation of idol bands. In the *Reply 1997* series, two best friends, Si-won [also spelled as (a.s.a. hereafter) Shi-won] and Yu-jeong [a.s.a. Yoo-jung], end up cheering for two rival boy bands, H.O.T and Sechs Kies, and face off against one another as members of two different fan bases. In *Reply 1994*, one secondary character named Yun-jin is able to sneak into the auditorium of a broadcasting company to see a live performance of Seo Taeji and Boys, accomplishing this by abandoning her identity as a fan and instead queueing with adult fans of a different performer, just to have a seat allocation.

The prominent girl culture of the 1990s registers some of the post-feminist contradictions. The overall trajectory of both the *Reply 1997* and *1994* series (and in fact, of the last installment of the series, *Reply 1988*) revolves around a romantic rivalry that runs through the series and would not be resolved until the concluding episodes, inviting the audience to guess who the spouse of the female lead would be. Despite the divergent approaches taken to characterize and demarcate the culture and discourses surrounding the contemporary girl culture—be it post-feminism, neo-feminism, popular feminism, and in the Korean context, fandom—the underlying assumption is that this is a culture shaped and cultivated by a neo-liberal capitalist ethos, where girls' identities, either individualistic or collective, and their apparent agency are shaped and constructed by the culture and entertainment industry. Sarah Banet-Weiser, in her book *Empowered: Popular Feminism and Popular Misogyny*, observes that popular feminism can be examined in the light of visibility and accessibility within capitalist commodity culture. Banet-Weiser claims, "[The] historical context of commodity feminism provides a backdrop for the expansion of popular feminism into other capitalist, consumerist realms."[25] As Gill notes, the obsession with appearance and desire for the body for the sake of one's own pleasure (not for men) are constantly monitored and disciplined by the consumerist logic through which popular feminist ideas and politics are branded. In a similar context, the Korean girls culture emerged in the 1990s when girls were recognized as key consumers; idol bands' CDs, memorabilia, and other goods incessantly lured the girls into opening their wallets. The inputs of the girl consumers on the path of idol bands create a kind of feedback loop, but the market is primarily constructed for corporate profits and managed by marketing strategies.

In post- and popular feminism, the significance of the second wave of feminism is both acknowledged and disavowed, turning feminism into a consumer trend or a sensibility; as Karlyn notes, "Postfeminism is a sensibility that has characterized contemporary, popular understandings of gender, and the broad discursive field that frames both Girl Culture and the Third Wave."[26] In contrast to post- or popular feminism, the third wave of feminism is often considered more self-reflexive in its critique of the limits to second-wave feminism's ideals and practice, which had been based on class privilege and ethnicity: the "white feminism" of middle-class women of the baby boom generation.[27] Yet, such characterization escapes the new generation(s) of Korean feminists, given that the emergence of Korean feminist movements in the 1970s and '80s (as discussed in the first chapter) was very closely tied to the labor movements of the working class, and girls and young women were instrumental in forming the unions for factory workers.[28]

Another significant historical connection to be made to the 1990s, especially for this book, is the relationship between the Korean feminist film criticism that evolved in the early 1990s and the emergence of women directors, who were exposed to such discourses and scholarship. The thirtieth anniversary of Korean cine-feminism was marked in 2019, tracing the movement's foundations back to the 1989 formation of the Korean women's filmmaking association *Bariteo*, followed by the introduction of feminist scholarship to academia and film culture.[29] Emerging in the 1990s, the "first generation" of Korean feminist film scholars such as Kim Soyoung, Yu Jina, and Joo Youshin turned their eyes on Korean cinema, both classical and contemporary, offering sharp criticisms of gender representation. Laura Mulvey's "Visual Pleasure and Narrative Cinema" was translated into, and published in, Korean in 1993, along with the work of Tania Modleski and Jane Gaines in the same volume.[30] Many of the women directors active in the industry from 2010 onward were educated and trained in film schools. They were certainly beneficiaries of the feminist discourses and scholarship advanced in the 1990s and after, and they were exposed to Korean "young feminism" of the 1990s and 2000s and were active on the internet.[31] Girlhood, for them, would not remain a passive concept, and the subject of girlhood has been taken up by many filmmakers of diverse genders, avoiding gender essentialism. A brief historical contextualization of Korean girlhood immediately following nonetheless helps situate both the continuity and transformation of girlhood represented.

Reference Girl

Although the main focus of this book is on contemporary Korean cinema, in particular from 2010 onward, for the history of girls' subjectivities, I locate the "reference girl" in the 1970s, when the relationship of the girls' sexuality and labor is more palpable within single films and across oeuvres. The significance of the 1970s is sociological as well as cultural and cinematic. As Ruth Barraclough notes, the significance of factory girls in the 1970s not only lies in their contribution to industrial development and social change through cheap labor, but further in the social construction of their persona as "a disturbing and powerful mix of the political and the sexual."[32] "Factory girls" could be translated as either *yeogong* (female factory workers) or "*gongsuni*," the latter being a more pejorative term. Their literature, according to Barraclough, enjoyed two prominent moments in history: one in the 1920s and '30s, and the other in the 1970s and '80s.[33] In the earlier period, the proletariat literature movement considered both industrial and demographic changes: the movement of society from agricultural to industrial, and the movement of girls from the countryside to ports and cities. In the latter period, during which Korea accelerated its industrialization, "factory girl literature" emerged alongside the labor literature movement (*nodong munhak*) that thrived in the 1980s.

Girl characters are not completely new to the 1970s and my aim is not to mark the 1970s as a rupture. In the golden era of the 1950s and '60s, as Soyoung Kim summarizes, three prominent female character types—wife, widow, and domestic helper (*sikmo, hanyeo*)—dominated and limited gender representation in Korean cinema.[34] In the 1970s, girl protagonists proliferated beyond the golden era's prevalent character types of domestic helpers or sisters. With the emergence of the teen picture as a profitable genre, high school had become the primary backdrop for both boys and girls; and thanks to its popularity, girls appeared not merely as supporting characters—daughters and sisters—in family dramas but became the subjects who drove the narrative. The high school series mirrored the cycles of youth films (*cheongchun yeonghwa*) of the mid-1960s but featured a new, younger generation of both male and female stars, such as Lee Seung-hyun (from the *Prankster* [*Yalgae*] series, 1976–77) and Im Ye-jin (of the *Really Really* [*Jinjja jinjja*] series [1976–1977]). These popular cycles were followed by short spinoffs featuring the female lead, maximizing the popularity gained from the boys' high school series, starring Kang Ju-hie (*The House Where the Sun Rises* [*Haegatteuneunjip*, Seok Rae-myeong, 1980]; *My Name Is Maya* [*Naeireumeun maya*, Kim Eung-cheon, 1981]). Not closely tied to the necessity to work for a living, as were domestic helpers or factory workers, the schoolgirl protagonists were, by virtue of their lifestyle, able to depart from the representation of sacrificial sister (*nui*) of the previous eras or schoolgirls (*yeohaksaeng*) of the colonial era (1910–1945), who were burdened by their responsibilities for family or the lost nation.[35]

The appearance of the Korean term "*sonyeo*" in 1970s film titles further underscores their diverse social status: *Confession of a Girl* (*Eoneu sonyeoui gobaek*, Park Jong-ho, 1970), *Girls' High School Days* (*Yeogosijeol*, Kang

Dae-sun, 1972), *A Woman Like the Sun* (*Taeyang dalmeun sonyeo*, Lee Man-hui, 1974) and *Girls from Scratch* (*Maenjumeokui sonyeodeul*, Kim Yeong-hyo, 1976). These films feature protagonists ranging from student to casual laborer to factory worker. Yet what is intriguing about these "girls," particularly in the latter two films, is that regardless of their social positions, they undergo the arc of downward mobility and even face death: real, symbolic, or virtual. They share a similar arc with the most popular film cycle of the 1970s—hostess (*hoseuteseu*) bargirl films. A representative of the cycle is *Yeong-ja's Heyday* (*Yeongjaui jeonseongsidae*, Kim Ho-sun, 1975), which topped the domestic box office that year.[36] Yeong-ja's journey to the city involves working initially as a domestic helper (sexually violated by the scoundrel son of the hosting family), then briefly as a low-wage worker at a sweatshop and as a bus conductor (losing her arm in a traffic accident while working), and last as a sex worker. A parallel or virtual downward mobility is found in two films released around the same time: *Crazy for You* (*Jinjja jinjja joahye*, Moon Yeo-song, 1977), one of the "girl" film cycle mentioned above; and *Girls from Scratch* (1976). Although temporary and virtual, the female protagonists, Ji-yeong and Nam-suk, respectively, find themselves in a situation where they must decide whether they will resort to using their sexuality or sexual labor for financial returns. In fact, such an arc is brief even in *Yeong-ja's Heyday*; the majority of the film is dedicated to the predicament that Yeong-ja faces as a sex worker in the present, her lost girlhood only glimpsed in the flashbacks. If girlhood is associated with Yeong-ja's past, the sexuality of Ji-yeong and Nam-suk, is associated with their immediate future—as a potential object of exploitation and means for financial earning, regardless of their social status.

Girls provide a fascinating entry point for the discussion of gender in contemporary Korean cinema due to their acute embodiment of contradictory values. Park Hyun Seon notes that female characters of the golden era oscillate between legitimate members of society (and family) and disposable commodities (women on the street) who become the object of monitoring and surveillance.[37] The latter convention develops into what she calls the "body (*yukche*)" series of the 1960s and well into the "hostess" films in the '70s.[38] Oh Young Sook characterizes '70s girl protagonists as, borrowing the Korean filmmaker Ha Gil-jong's words, "frivolous, chirpy and flapping like an eel thrown on snow."[39] Ha criticized his contemporary but older generation auteur Lee Man-hui's gender representation, in particular Baek-hwa in Lee's *The Road to Sampo* (*Sampo ganeungil*, 1975), as lacking any psychological depth. Oh further observes that the female lead often forges a May–December relationship with an older man who is unable to protect her, reflecting a pessimistic moral view of the era. This may be an adequate characterization of the '70s girl, but

I am wary of over-generalization. Rather, by examining how certain tropes and images were taken and transformed by the female leads of the 1960s and '70s (and even up to the present), I show that these female protagonists have shared limitations, lacking any full agency to choose otherwise.

The girl characters of the 1970s certainly appear younger than the female leads of the golden era—although Yeong-ja, for instance, does not identify her exact age when asked by Chang-su (played by late Song Jae-ho), a male factory worker—and they may lack the strong persona found in their 1960s counterparts. Joo locates both the liminality of and the spectatorial ambivalence toward Sonya, the female protagonist in *Flower in Hell* (*Jiokhwa*, Shin Sang-ok, 1958), played by the legendary Korean actress Choi Eun-hee. For her moral transgression—the seduction of a younger brother of her lover, who smuggles goods from a US military base—Sonya is narratively punished, facing death in the end. Yet, as Joo notes, Sonya's character remains fascinating to the spectator due to her charisma and competence in adopting Western culture, competence gained through her profession as a sex worker in the sprawling camp town that accommodates the various needs of GIs from the nearby US military base.[40] The contradictory moral values attributed to, and embodied by, a character like Sonya could help the spectator be more acutely aware of social contradictions. The 1970s girls, be they low-wage employees or students or bargirls, whose initial aspirations have been thwarted and who had to resort to other means, may be able to expose a similar kind of contradictory developmentalism as an ideology; economic growth piggybacked on low-wage laborers in light industry and manufacturing, who are still not included as legitimate members of society with equal value. Whether girls' characters in the 1970s could exert even momentarily the same level of autonomy as Sonya requires a more in-depth discussion of individual films, which I undertake in this book. But the popularity of these films in the 1970s further invites us to consider the exploitation of girls' sexuality both on and off screen.

My discussion of 1970s girls provides historical and theoretical grounds for the discussion of contemporary Korean girlhood. Their relevance to the discussion of contemporary girlhood is critical, as the "reference girl" still operates and guides the cinematic rendition of girls. It complements the existing English-language scholarship on Korean cinema, which has so far been focused on the golden age of 1950s and '60s.[41] Although girls' labor is acknowledged as a significant factor in national development, it often takes a back seat, shown only briefly or completely omitted. Even films that feature low-waged young women employees, such as the typist Eun-mi in *Madame Freedom* (1956) and the titular character in Kim Ki-young's *The Housemaid*

(*Hanyeo*, 1960), constantly portray their presence as a threat to a modern nuclear family in which masculinity is jeopardized by the modernity imposed from above on an aspirational middle class.[42]

Despite the fact that the cheap labor of female low-wage workers, in both the public and domestic spheres, remained integral to Korean economic development in the 1960s and 1970s, that labor does not occupy much screen time, merely remaining in the backdrop. As Kim notes, the representation of dorm rooms and music hall in *The Housemaid* is completely unrealistic.[43] In the pre-credit sequence of the film, Kim's family is shown in their family room; Dong-sik, the husband, reports a newspaper article about a "trouble" [*sageon*] between a maid and her hosting family, and further discusses the importance of the maid's labor in their own home. After the credits, the film cuts briefly to the factory, the vast site of which is filled with rows of machines being operated by women workers. The camera tracks to show more closely several machines running; it stays with two workers, Kyeong-hui (a.s.a. Kyung-hee) and Seon-yeong (a.s.a. Seon-young), as the machine stops, then follows them as the two exit. The two character types—a maid mentioned in the pre-credit sequence and factory workers shown here—are immediately connected with the low-wage labor they offer. Moreover, Myeong-suk (a.s.a. Myung-sook), who thereafter begins to work for Kim's family, used to work in the same factory as Kyeong-hui and Seon-yeong. What we witness throughout the film is not the labor of female workers (as a student of mine pointed out, the wife of Kim's family, who is the breadwinner and works from home, is busier than the maid) but their sexuality, presented as both threatening and fatal. The relationship between sexuality and labor (sexual or otherwise) attributed to girls is one of the key threads that runs throughout this book. In more recent Korean films, girls' bodies still remain to be violated and their sexual labor serves as a means for their meager living; in *Mother* (*Modeo*, Bong Joon-ho, 2009) and *Girl* (*Sonyeo*, Choi Jin-seong, 2013), girl characters perform sex work in exchange for rice.

If the women pioneers of the golden era were preoccupied with depicting widow and wife—Park Nam-ok and Hong Eun-won made films about the titular characters of *Widow* (*Mimangin*, 1955) and *A Woman Judge* (*Yeopansa*, 1962)—girls have been a fascinating theme revisited by women directors from the 1980s until recently. Regardless of whether women directors choose the subject matter out of their personal predilections or due to an industry bias that does not allow women directors to explore high-budget genres, girls provide a site for the observation of Korean society and of personal as well as national histories.[44] Lee Mi-rye directed two films starring girls with very contrasting personae; *My Daughter Rescued from a Swamp* (*Sureongeseo geonjin naettal*, 1984) and *0Shim* (*Yeongshimi*, 1990), a juvenile delinquent and a middle-class high school girl, respectively. Although her work provides an interesting lineage for the work of women directors who followed, Lee's work has often been omitted or dismissed as lacking a critical edge, in contrast to the women directors who debuted over a decade later, such as Jeong Jae-eun and her critically acclaimed *Take Care of My Cat* (*Goyangireul butakhae*, 2001).[45] Only five women directors, including Lee, made feature films in the commercial industry prior to its liberalization in the 1990s. In an interview, director Yim Soon-rye, who debuted in 1996 with her feature *Three Friends* (*Sechingu*), differentiates herself from predecessors such as Lee Mi-rye, who was trained under the traditional apprentice system in the Korean industry.[46] Yim first garnered critical attention through her short film *Promenade in the Rain* (a.k.a. *Walking in the Rain, Ujung sanchaek*, 1994), which was awarded the Grand Prize and the Press Award at the first Seoul Short Film Festival sponsored by a Korean conglomerate, Samsung. Her short film observes the boredom and fantasy of a low-wage female worker selling tickets at a small local theater. The 1990s saw a group of women directors such as Yim herself, Byun Young-joo (the *Murmuring* documentary trilogy [1995–1999]) and Lee Jeong-hwang (*Art Museum by the Zoo* [*Misulgwanyeop dongmulwon*, 1998]), receive either critical attention or moderate commercial success.

Through girlhood as reference image, I hope to establish contemporary Korean cinema's connection to, as well as its shift from, the oeuvre of golden era women directors. *Daughter-in-Law* (*Minmyeoneuri*, 1965), directed by the legendary actress-turned-director Choi Eun-hee, is a period piece, but it provides an interesting transition to the 1970s films. It foregrounds the domestic labor that the female protagonist Jeom-sun must offer as a (newlywed) "girl." Following the Korean custom of child marriage, *minmyeoneuri*, she must marry a child-husband; Choi herself starred as the wife and is a lot more mature than her pre–school age husband, who calls her *saeksi* in Korean—a term often used to refer to a newly married wife. Although visually and narratively Choi does not comfortably fit the appearance or character of a girl— born in 1926, she must have been in her late thirties when she was filming and starring in the film—her character, Jeom-sun, is interestingly subtitled by the Korean Culture Center UK, in English, as "girl." In a fascinating montage sequence, she performs a series of domestic chores, moving back and forth between the kitchen and front yard. The sequence ends with the mother-in-law dropping a pestle into a large mortar (*jeolgu*). If Jeom-sun's subjugation and role within the family is underscored in her repeated lateral movements, her mother-in-law's authority is manifest through her vertical posture and movement of the arm. Jeom-sun falls sick due to the enormous amount of work demanded by her mother-in-law and returns home to rest and possibly for medical treatment. Jeom-sun's own mother aptly characterizes the custom of child marriage as a pretext for a girl/wife to offer unpaid domestic labor to the married family; the mother laments that she would not have had Jeom-sun undergo such hardship if their family had been able to afford a decent living. Although spatially and temporally displaced to the pre-modern period, the daughter's move to a new home for her marriage and her sacrifice for her family indeed parallels and anticipates the common narrative trope of the 1970s, where girls move to the cities to earn and send money back to their homes. The young husband, with the help of his father, tricks his mother; convinced that Jeom-sun will help the husband and family thrive (a fake shaman's verdict requested by the father-in-law), the mother-in-law visits Jeom-sun and persuades her to return to the marital home. The film ends with an ambiguous "home-coming," Jeom-sun stranded in a space between the two households.[47]

Throughout this book, girl or girlhood is not strictly defined in terms of age but as a trait or a site where conflicting values are attributed to sexuality and labor, both desired yet exploited. I further situate and explore girls' sensibility as uncomfortably sitting between the two: sexuality and labor. Various genres and cycles, including horror, have foregrounded girls' interiority and sensibilities. In such films as the *Whispering Corridor* series and *A Tale of Two Sisters*, girls' interiority and their limited agency are externalized through mise-en-scène. High school horror films or house horror provide important aesthetic precedents, to be explored in the films revolving around girls' experiences during the colonial era or post-war Korean society that would be discussed in this book.

Necro-cinematics

Korean cinema is still gendered; so is the scholarship on Korean cinema. "Hard men" remain as the focal site in many Korean films and box office hits released in the 2010s, such as *Nameless Gangster: Rules of the Time* (*Beomjoewaui jeonjaeng*, Yoon Jong-bin, 2012), *New World* (*Sinsegye*, Park Hoon-Jung, 2013) and *Asura: The City of Madness* (*Asura*, Kim Sung-su, 2016). Even where films feature women or girl protagonists, they are part of an "ensemble" cast, or their rendition is a simple reversal of gender traits rather than careful reflection on gender representation.[48] English-language scholarship on classical and contemporary Korean cinema has been celebratory; an explicit critique has rarely been leveled. The scholarship continues to

16 Forever Girls

focus heavily on the works of male auteurs—Shin Sang-ok, Han Hyeong-mo, Park Chan-wook, Kim Ki-duk, Hong Sang-soo, and Bong Joon-ho—omitting rather than critiquing the work of a certain bent and orientation.[49]

Nam Lee, in her recent monograph on Bong Joon-ho, does discuss the mother figure in some of Bong's work, but the numerous deaths of girls in Bong's films remain unaddressed. Lee notes, for instance, the significance of water or rain as an atmospheric and historical signifier in Bong's films; that is, the rain "in *Memories of Murder* reminds the audience of the terror of the 1980s . . . while heavy rain conjures up the traumatic history of the Kwangju [Gwangju] Massacre in *The Host*."[50] Instead of the motif of water as part of Bong's authorship, I pay closer attention to the girls' deaths or survival in Bong's films: how their deaths become a device for creating a moral dilemma for, and rivalry among, male characters. The schoolgirl that Detective Seo (from Seoul) got to know in *Memories of Murder*, for instance, serves as a means to raise a moral question for both of the male cops— Seo and Bak (a.s.a. Park)—acutely conveyed through the killer's gaze that oscillates between the schoolgirl and Bak's nurse partner Kwok. Both the film's narrative resolution and the national development rely on the death of girls or, possibly, are achieved *at the expense* of female subjects' deaths. Focusing on the idea of "at the expense of"—in contrast to the discourse of "for the sake of" national developments—I intend to further advance the necro-cinematics that operates within contemporary Korean cinema and Bong's unofficial "girl trilogy" (*The Host* [*Goemul*, 2006], *Snowpiercer* [2013] and *Okja* [2017]), or even the death of Jessica in *Parasite* (*Gisaengchung*, 2019).

In her discussion of military sexual slaves ("*wianbu*"), Jin-kyung Lee characterizes the disposability of their sexual labor during the colonial era by employing the concept of "necropolitics" advanced by Achille Mbembe; the exploitation of sexual labor is premised on the possible or eventual death of laborers.[51] Mbembe associates such politics with the state of exception where the sovereign exercises control over the life of the marginal or subjugated, manifest in such historical contexts as Nazism (concentration camps), colonial imperialism, and racism (slavery), where the survival of the subjugated is "coextensive with the sovereign right to kill."[52] Lee finds a parallel between military sexual slaves during the colonial era and the Korean women's prostitution for US military clients, where "'selling sex' exists in an inherent continuum with sexual violence, which always carries the risk of death."[53] Contemporary Korean films that depict girls during the colonial era, which are discussed in the second chapter, register such historical conditions: *The Silenced* (*Gyeongseonghakgyu: Sarajinsonyeodeul*, Lee Hae-young, 2015), *Snowy Road* (*Nungil*, Lee Na-jeong, 2015), and *Spirits' Homecoming* (*Gwihyang*, Cho

Jung-rae, 2016). In these films, girls are paired: one (or both) of the pair faces death in each film, during their investigation of another girl's death in the first, and during their struggle to escape a military base in the latter two.

Such a narrative logic extends, however, beyond the films set during the colonial era, mentioned above, to govern films with wider historical and political remit. This narrative and aesthetic convention and logic I term "necro-cinematics" in order to differentiate from and compare to "necropolitics" as conditions. In Lee Chang-dong's *Burning* (*Beoning*, 2018), the relationship between a young woman, Hae-mi, and two men, Jong-su and Ben, unfolds. In the second half of the film, after Hae-mi's disappearance, the male rivalry escalates. Jong-su, a working-class man and aspiring writer, retrieves Hae-mi's traces as he tails Ben, an idle rich man. Despite the narrative ambiguity with regard to Hae-mi's disappearance—which may be actual or imagined—Hae-mi becomes a "collectible" like the various female items that Ben has hoarded in the cabinet of his bathroom, and her elimination is equated with the arson of an abandoned barn that Ben spots in the countryside. She is "disposable," reflecting her importance only as a device to trigger a battle between the two male leads, as in Lee's earlier film *Green Fish* (*Chorokmulgogi*, 1997)

Even among films in which girls are salient, acting as more than mere devices instrumental to narrative development, the girls die, either literally or symbolically, so that it is impossible to sustain the female friendship that has initially been formed. In *Sunny*, mentioned earlier, Chun-hwa is the only character able to have a successful career and financially independent life, but the narrative trajectory is set in motion by her impending death, concluding with the reunion of her friends at her funeral. Independent cinema, regardless of the gender of directors, incessantly relies on the death of girls: to name a few examples, *Han Gong-ju* (Lee Su-jin, 2013), *Jamsil* (*Nuechideon bang*, Lee Wanmin, 2016), *After My Death* (*Joemanheun sonyeo*, Kim Euiseok, 2017), and *Second Life* (*Seon-huiwa Seul-gi*, Park Young-ju, 2018).

In her discussion of the representation of suicide in Hollywood and world cinema—specifically, *The Virgin Suicides* (Sofia Coppola, 1999) and *Paradise Now* (Hany Abu-Assad, 2005)—Michele Aaron distinguishes "to-be-dead" from "dead-already"; if the former embodies the necessity of death for the sake of the erotic economies and visual pleasure of Western culture, the latter registers the necropolitical conditions of an occupied territory and the imperialist logic whereby sovereignty is enforced through the terror and death of the subjugated and the marginal. Aaron observes, "*Paradise Now*'s imperialist economy pertains to the Palestinian experience but also cinema more broadly. In this way, the dead-already figure is to be revealed as a condition of both film and colonialism and the *correspondence* between them" (my italics).[54]

The distinction between the two categories is certainly insightful, yet the category of "dead-already" deserves a nuanced discussion, subject to both the specific historical contexts depicted and production circumstances. The death of a girl has been claimed to embody the status of occupied nation-state during the colonial era and/or the victim of authoritarian rule in Korean and other East Asian contexts, yet such an equation has also been criticized as a cliché— a symptom of gendered construction of the national ethos, which excludes the subjectivity of girls or women to excuse the nation-state's inadequacy or patriarchal nature.[55] A more important question to consider would be: what do films achieve *at the expense of* the death of a girl (or girls)? I find the initial observation that guides Aaron's essay quite useful here, though: "Films about suicide tell us little of the emotional and psychic realities that give rise to and result from the act, [but] they tell us a lot about cinema, and ironically, what makes it tick."[56] When and why, then, do girls in contemporary Korean cinema become disposable? I echo Aaron's questions, raised in her book *Death and the Moving Image*, in order to articulate necro-cinematics: "Who dies? Who suffers or survives? Who recovers? Who saves? Who kills? Who watches? What belief systems are being challenged, confirmed or reinforced through the image or narrative of dying, and what audience is it targeting?"[57]

If the narrative pleasure of mainstream or independent cinema is produced or achieved *at the expense of the death of a girl*, such a structure could be comparable to the conditions of necropolitics that Mbembe locates in imperial, colonial, and postcolonial societies where sovereignty "means the capacity to define who matters and who does not, who is disposable and who is not."[58] Aaron describes such a logic manifest in cinema as "mortal economies": "the structuring logic or systems of exchange or encounter, underwritten by life's worth, and by its, albeit imaginary, capacity to dictate who may live and who must die."[59] Yet "dead-already" and "to-be-dead" are not automatically mapped onto necropolitics and necromanticism. Ethical significance and the aesthetic rendering of deaths should further be weighed in each category. In her recent book, *The Force of Non-violence*, Judith Butler associates the unequal worth of lives with their unequal grievability.[60] Lives of the marginal and the non-human are deemed unworthy, and their deaths and loss remain unnoticed, not to mention being inadequately grieved. Grievability, then, could be factored into the examination of narrative logic and ethical consequences within a film.

My aim here is not to overgeneralize the values and ideologies associated with the death of a girl as a capitalist logic, nor do I wish to ascribe it as a major characteristic specific to Korean national cinema.[61] The death of a girl functions differently in each film; subsequently, the analysis in this book focuses on each individual death. As discussed in the first chapter, girlhood, romantic longing, and sexual desire were represented in the 1970s as elements that could potentially impede the nation's development. More recently, women directors' works, and some independent films, have drawn a slightly different picture of girlhood, defying the narrative conclusion of necro-cinematics sketched earlier in the chapter. In her directorial debut *Crush and Blush* (*Misseu hongdangmu*, 2008), the woman director Lee Kyonug-mi features a girl who is capable of exposing the hypocrisy of the adult world. In a similar vein, Yoon Ga-eun critiques the manner in which the girls' world replicates the social hierarchy and power relations in her own directorial debut, *The World of Us* (*Urideul*, 2016).

Drawing on Yue's idea that a reference image is operative rather than mimetic, chapter 1 locates the "reference girl" of Korean cinema in the 1970s, whose image exposes the contradictory nature of the military government's developmentalist ethos, an ethos that relies on girls' labor yet expels their bodies. A girl's narrative outcome is determined by her potential contribution to the economic development of the nation-state. Regardless of the girls' social positions, their sexuality is seen as a commodity. Bae Kyeong-min notes that the male subject in the teen films, such as the *Pranksters* (*yalgae*) series, is constructed as both an individual and collective subject. In such a process, Bae observes, a female character often functions only as an obstacle—a threat to the male collectivity necessary to becoming a "legitimate" adult citizen in the future.[62] The first chapter redirects the focus from the adolescent masculinity in the teen films to the girlhood represented. I examine the *Really Really* (*Jinjja jinjja*) series—in particular, the first and third installments, *Never Forget Me* (*Jinjja jinjja itjima*, Moon Yeo-song, 1976) and *Crazy for You* (*Jinjja jinjja johahae,* Moon Yeo-song, 1977), and their construction of male and female subjectivities in relation to their respective contribution to the modern nation-state. In addition to schoolgirls, who are most frequently tied to girlhood, I further examine girl protagonists with different social positions: a bus conductor in *Girls from Scratch* (1976) and a carefree girl in *A Woman Like the Sun* (1974), focusing on the girls' viability as a potential labor force or lack thereof. In the latter half of the chapter, I turn to Korean male veterans' work: *Yeong-ja's Heydays, Insect Woman* (*Chungnyeo*, Kim Ki-young, 1972) and *Night Journey* (a.k.a. *Night Voyage, Yahaeng*, Kim Soo-yong, 1977)—how the girlhood glimpsed in each film underscores the social forces that constantly pull the female characters away from where they once belonged or place where they hope to move forward.

The next two chapters loosely correspond to the distinction between "dead-already" and "to-be-dead" in relation to girl protagonists. Throughout the two chapters, however, I hope to complicate the distinction. Girls have been employed in contemporary Korean cinema as victims of historical trauma, as seen in such films as *A Petal*, which features a girl protagonist mentally distraught after the Gwangju democratic uprising. In a similar vein, in *Peppermint Candy* (*Bakhasatang*, Lee Chang-dong, 1999) factory worker Sun-im is the object of the male protagonist Yeong-ho's longing for the innocent past—a period untainted by his experience of historical, political, and economic turmoil that spans more than two decades. Yet girls or young female protagonists have rarely been presented as films' subjects, unable to embody or remember the modern history of Korea.

In the second chapter, entitled "Girls Who Disappear, Girls Who Remember," I turn to the colonial and post-war eras where girl victims remember, share, and write the history of their predicaments. *The Silenced* (2015), *Snowy Road* (2015), and *A Werewolf Boy* (*Neukdae sonyeon*, Jo Sung-hee, 2012) all present girls as the "writing subject" who asserts her limited agency by writing, literally or figuratively. The three films nicely complement one another in terms of their historical settings; *The Silenced* and *Snowy Road* are set in the 1930s and '40s under Japanese colonial rule, while *A Werewolf Boy* is set during the post-war period of dictatorship. Personal writing, such as in diaries and letters, has been a practice integral to girls' culture since the 1920s and '30s and has become a persistent trope in girls' fiction and cinema. I examine how the personal writing provides the marginal subject in the three films mentioned, with a perspective that allows communication between girls and the sharing of personal experience. As a coda, I briefly discuss the film *I Can Speak* (*Ai kaen seupikeu*, Kim Hyun-seok, 2017). *I Can Speak* transforms the female protagonist, whose past includes working as a sexual slave during the colonial era, from a writing to a speaking subject. As Hyunah Yang observes of the former military sex slaves, "The survivor feels guilt, but she also exhibits courage and a desire to speak out about her experiences."[63]

In the third chapter, I first advance necro-cinematics by analyzing two comparable scenes from *The Gangster, the Cop, the Devil* (*Akinjeon*, Lee Won-tae, 2019) and *Memories of Murder* in which a girl is murdered to stage a male rivalry and/or to create a moral dilemma for male characters. Through the comparative analysis of *Mother* (*Madeo*, Bong Joon-ho, 2009), *Poetry* (*Si*, Lee Chang-dong, 2010), and *Han Gong-ju* (Lee Sujin, 2013), all of which depict and trace a similar sexual crime, I argue for the need of necro-cinematics: the function of Korean girl protagonists' deaths could converge in historical, colonial conditions (necropolitics, examined in the previous chapter) and in the present situation. Necro-cinematics would help to critically engage with the gender manifest in Bong's girls films: *The Host* (2006), *Snowpiercer* (2013), and *Okja* (2017), which the Korean media unofficially names as a trilogy. Gender has been hardly at the center of the existing English-language scholarship on Bong, and necro-cinematics will help to show the girls' fates rendered instrumentally within the South Korean and global film industry.

In the next chapter, focusing on women directors' indie films that feature a girl as the female lead—in particular, *The House of Us* (*Urijip*, Yoon Ga-eun, 2019), *A Girl at My Door*—I explore the extent to which women directors may offer an alternative to the necro-cinematics that still dominates the Korean film industry. The Association of Korean Independent Film and Video (founded in 1998) defines it in broad terms, citing "indie" film's artistic aim that "encourages the audience to see the world in a new way, to dream of a better self and believe in a better society."[64] I question and explore the extent to which indie films directed by women directors mark a significant departure both from commercial cinema and within indie cinema. I highlight some of the continuities and transformation between reference girl and the girl protagonists of indie cinema, focusing on the insularity of the girlhood. The idea of "shelter writing" developed in Susan Fraiman's book *Extreme Domesticity*—a sense of security obtained by the marginal subject through creating a personal space or domestic routines—further provide me to redirect the discussion: from how the homosocial relationship is formed in films with girl protagonists to how female camaraderie is manifested through the (im)possibility of creating a shelter.[65] *Microhabitat*—although the protagonist Mi-so is hardly a girl demographically speaking—squarely resonates with the '70s reference girl in her desire to pursue leisure. A chance of her pursuit of leisure without affecting her personal relationship and friendship, however, seems to be slim, resulting in social isolation rather than the liminal freedom granted in *A Woman Like the Sun*.

The last chapter engages with a possibility to allow cinematic idleness for girl protagonists. Singing, dancing, or other leisure activities have been presented as a possibility to grant a girl protagonist limited freedom. The regional hits *Sunny* and *Miss Granny* (*Susanghan geunyeo*, Hwang Dong-hyuk, 2014) present themselves as an interesting case study to analyze in relation to the notion of leisure and idleness and their respective moral values. Both were domestic box office hits—the latter of which was directed by Hwang (*Squid Game* [*Ojingeo geim*] *Season I*, 2021)—and yielded numerous adaptations in the region. To this pair, I add *Queen of Walking*, an independent Korean film also starring Shim Eun-kyung, who played Na-mi in the film *Sunny* and the young granny in *Miss Granny*. I examine the way in which *Queen of*

Walking grants "idleness" that the girl protagonist deserves, as a form of moral freedom.[66] From the examination of girls' cinematic death to their seeking of shelter, then idleness, this book concludes with a positive note or even a wish: envisioning of a possibility for them to appreciate and enjoy the moral freedom of being *forever girls*.

1
Reference Girls

The 1970s

Signaling the beginning of the teen romance production cycle of the 1970s, *Never Forget Me* (*Jinjja jinjja itjima*, Moon Yeo-song, 1976) ignited the stardom of Lee Deok-hwa and Im Ye-jin. Romance blossoms between high-schoolers Yeong-su and Jeong-a (also spelled as [a.s.a.] Jeong-ah), but the couple must separate when Yeong-su's family moves to Seoul for his higher education. Yeong-su returns to his hometown, a seaport town Mokpo, three years later with the hope that he can now resume and consummate his love for Jeong-a as an adult. On the train, he imagines Jeong-a running to embrace him and promising to be his lovely wife. However, when he reaches Jeong-a's home, her sister and father greet him instead, informing him that Jeong-a has passed away due to an illness.

This conventional teen romance of unrequited love, however, has a visually and viscerally shocking epilogue. After having paid a visit to the shrine where Jeong-a's family memorialized her death, Yeong-su slowly walks by himself, following the train track while recalling his memories of Jeong-a; he then sees an apparition of an adult Jeong-a with permed hair, different from the short, bobbed style of her high school days, seen throughout the film. As she runs toward the screen foreground (in the direction of Yeong-su), a train moves from the foreground to background, running over her, and crushing even his wishful imagination. This ending seems to exceed the conventional sad ending, casting the teen romance and adolescent sexuality as insubstantial and unproductive; it is a fantasy to be eradicated in order for Yeong-su to move forward to be the national male subject expected.

In her discussion of the 1970s South Korean "hostess" (*hoseuteseu*) bargirl films, a journalistic term coined to refer to then-popular films that foregrounded and exploited female sexuality, Molly Kim underlines the in-corporeality of tragic female protagonists.[1] Some of the primary film texts—such as *Heavenly Homecoming to Stars* (*Byeoldeului gohyang*, Lee Jang-ho, 1974) and *Yeong-ja's Heydays* (*Yeongjaui jeonseongsidae*, Kim Ho-sun, 1975), each of which topped the domestic box office rankings upon its release—rely

Forever Girls. Jinhee Choi, Oxford University Press. © Oxford University Press 2025.
DOI: 10.1093/9780197685822.003.0002

on the construction of the female protagonists to be deprived of the national subjectivity expected of the male subject. Drawing on the feminist scholarship around Hollywood films advanced by Christine Gledhill, Linda Williams, and Janet Steiger, Kim observes how the female protagonist's bodily and personal integrity are constantly fractured and often recalled from male protagonists' perspectives. Female bodies are repeatedly displayed throughout the films, yet their existence in the present or future is ultimately denied by being excluded from the public sphere and pushed to the margin.[2]

Never Forget Me is not a bargirl film, but the similarity in narrative trajectory and outcome is striking. Like *Heavenly Homecoming to Stars*, *Never Forget Me* is framed through the flashback of the male character, Yeong-su, who is on the train and on his way to his hometown after having moved to Seoul to further his education. During the courtship between Yeong-su and Jeong-a, Yeong-su is willing to prove himself as a "disciplined" man to Jeong-a's father, who used to work in the military and fought in the Vietnam War. At his household, the national flag hangs ominously on the wall. Both the beginning and ending of *Never Forget Me* help to construct the kind of masculinity desired of Yeong-su as a male adult. The surprising ending signifies that there is no room for the titillating adolescent sexuality or girlhood to fit into the envisioned state-led modernity, an incompatibility between liminal girlhood and national development as a whole.

There is an important intersection and overlap between the bargirl cycle and other films that feature girls as protagonists. My interest in the 1970s, especially 1970s girlhood, however, departs from the existing feminist scholarship on the former in terms of both modality and temporality. Since the 1990s, there has been a growing number of oral labor histories published on woman workers—even more from the 2010s onward. These include, to name a few, *Class Struggle or Family Struggle*; *They Are Not Machines; I, Woman Laborer* [*Na yeoseong nodongja*], a collection of interviews with nine women labor activists; *Women, Speaking of Labor* [*Yeoja, nodongeul malhada*]; and *Women in the Sky*.[3] Further scholarship emerged to consider the representation of working-class subjects, including factory and sex workers, such as *Factory Girl Literature* and *Service Economies*.[4] The 1970s marks an important reference point in these texts, as low-wage women laborers' working experiences and conditions were reflected and re-examined within the changing discursive and scholarly contexts.

I revisit the 1970s girls as "reference girls" to look back to, and to guide my approach to, the contemporary cinematic rendering of girls' sensibility, sexuality, labor, and leisure; many facets of girlhood manifest in various modalities and temporalities, continuing to resurface in, relate to, and be transformed in the present. The aim of this chapter is neither a historiographical nor a linear tracing of the representation of girlhood; rather, it shows how the girl figures of the 1970s still have a certain currency and resonance, affecting both the filmmaking and the spectatorship of the present. In her discussion of 1940s Hollywood women's films, Mary Anne Doane references a film industry figure's claim that "[the motion picture] leaves behind it a residue, or deposit, of imagery and association."[5] Throughout this chapter, I underscore historical and cinematic residues and deposits, by tracing parallels, connections, and continuities between the 1970s girls and contemporary counterparts.

The 1970s provides another important point of reference for this book; some of the actresses who had portrayed distinctive girlhood and female sexuality in the 1970s, such as Moon Sook (a.s.a. Mun Suk), Youn Yuh-jung (a.s.a. Yun Yeo-jeong) and late Yoon Jeong-hee (a.s.a. Yun Jeong-hie), all sojourned abroad—whether briefly or for a longer period—after their marriages in the 1970s. Informed by their stardom, I hope to articulate their performances in contemporary cinema within a broader historical and cine-matic context. These performances, some of which will be examined in this chapter and which continue to serve as a reference in the remaining chapters, include those of Moon (*A Woman Like the Sun* [*Taeyang dalmeun sonyeo*, Lee Man-hui, 1974]); Youn (*Insect Woman* [*Chungnyeo*, Kim Ki-young, 1972]); and Yoon (*Sunday Night and Monday Morning* [*Ilyoilbamgwa wolyoil achim*, Choi In-cheol, 1970]; *Night Journey* [a.k.a. *Night Voyage*, *Yahaeng*, Kim Soo-yong, 1977]; and *Poetry* [*Si*, Lee Chang-dong, 2010]).

Some of these actresses are still associated with, and reminded of, their performances in the 1970s. After Moon's return to screen, through her appear-ance in the film *The Beauty Inside* (*Byuti insaideu*, Baek Jong-yeol, 2015) as a supporting character, a newspaper article title read "Has Fallen Ill for 40 years and Woken Up . . . A Girl Who Fell in Love."[6] Moon's portrayal of In-yeong as a flaneuse—"[an] individual keenly attuned to the creative potential of the city and the liberating possibilities of a good walk" —in Lee Man-hui's *A Woman Like the Sun* makes a great contrast with Mi-so (a.s.a. Miso) in *Microhabitat*, which will be discussed in chapter 4: the two share the aim of being idle and pursuing leisure, but with different consequences.[7] After Youn won the Oscar for Best Actress in 2021 for starring as a grandmother in the American in-dependent film *Minari* (Lee Isaac Chung, 2020), numerous retrospectives of her filmic career—from the 1970s to the contemporary scene—were organ-ized both at home and abroad. A revisit to her filmography, such as the roles she played in the Korean director Kim Ki-young's *Woman of Fire* (*Hwanyeo*, 1971) and *Insect Woman*, helps one to map her contemporary work in a new way; in particular, her post-2000 performances as a matriarch with explicit command of sexuality, in such films as Im Sang-soo's *Good Lawyer's Wife* (*Baramnan gajok*, 2003) and *The Taste of Money* (*Donui mat*, 2012). Also remarkable is her performance as the aging sex worker in *The Bacchus Lady* (*Jukeoya saneun yeoja*, Lee Je-yong [a.s.a. E J-yong], 2016). Yoon's character Mi-ja in *Poetry*, discussed in chapter 3, embodies both girls' sensibility as well as female sexuality as a virtual commodity, the latter of which is a primary theme in the 1970s.

For the girlhood discussed in this book, 1970s girls do not provide a character type or a single, fixed "image" but rather provide varying references for subsequent films to engage and be in dialogue with. My use of the term "reference girl" is to pay attention to its perfunctory nature and functionality both within the South Korean national(istic) discourses and, more importantly, in relationship to contemporary Korean cinematics and spectatorship. Genevieve Yue carefully advances a materialist feminist film history, writing of the "girl head" or the "China girl"—a material image on film strip used in Hollywood film labs and other national film industries to calibrate color, skin tone, and other minute details.[8] She claims that women's bodies, which are associated with materiality, are not only "cut up (in representation) but more importantly cut out (in formal procedure)."[9] Yue's scholarly intervention lies in her critique of material history of cinema as gendered, even "below representation."[10] Her feminist scholarship deserves an in-depth discussion, but that is beyond the scope of this book. Nevertheless, her idea of the "reference image" as operative rather than mimetic helps me locate the "reference girl" within the South Korean context in the 1970s.[11] From Jeong-a's apparition in *Never Forget Me*, briefly discussed here, to the blindfolded girls in Im's *Factory Complex* mentioned in the introduction, and to the many girl subjects in contemporary Korean cinema explored in this book, girlhood is a denied form of subjectivity, having been excluded from the national as well as cinematic history.

In this chapter, I focus on the multiplicities of girlhood, examining the girl protagonists of diverse class backgrounds and social positions: *Crazy for You* (*Jinjja jinjja joahae*, Moon Yeo-song, 1977), the last installment of the *Really Really* series; *Girls from Scratch* (*Maenjumeokui sonyeodeul*, Kim Yeong-hyo, 1976); *The Maiden Who Went to the City* (*Dosiro gan cheonyeo*, Kim Soo-yong, 1981); and *A Woman Like the Sun*, none of which has been discussed extensively in Korean or English language scholarship. These films demonstrate the inclusive nature of girls' referents: schoolgirl, bus conductor, and a flaneuse. Some of the leads in these films may embody girlish characteristics within slightly older heroines of the same period: naiveté, childishness, cheerfulness, and immaturity.[12] Nonetheless, they depart from the female protagonists of the popular bargirl films of the 1970s, and their characterization and values cannot be reduced merely to the negative, inconsequential roles allotted within the contemporaneous nationalist developmental ideology and social mores. The second half of this chapter concerns the glimpses of girlhood that are manifest in the Korean veterans' works—*Yeong-ja's Heydays*, *The Insect Woman*, and *Night Journey*. Regardless of the subject of flashback—be it a male or female character—the girlhood of the female leads in these films is portrayed in the past tense, yet repeatedly resurfaces to direct the narrative trajectory as well as determine their actions and social positions in the present.

Three Girls

Ji-yeong, a Schoolgirl

Under the military dictatorship led by Park Chung Hee (1961–1979), the self-sustaining economy was the top priority, over and above democracy, the welfare system, and national security.[13] The existing Korean language scholarship positions the then-popular genres, such as the prankster (*yalgae*) series and the bargirl cycle, as manifestations of the gendered nature of state-led modernity. With a focus on adolescent masculinity, Bae Gyeong-min views the high school in the prankster series as the principal site where masculinity and male collectivity were to be envisioned, negotiated, and reproduced under the national development ideology.[14] In order for male adolescents to become desired members of the society, he argues, girls' characters in the series are often relegated to subsidiary roles, whose significance relies on the extent to which they may function as threats to the male camaraderie and community to be formed.[15] Yu Jina, a Korean feminist scholar, contextualizes the proliferation of the "female body genre"—such as the bargirl films of the 1970s and erotic costume dramas of the '80s—as a result of changes in both social and business practices. As illegal service industries such as prostitution, facilitated through coffee shops and salons, increased and became integral to business practice, the female body in this genre is exploited as a site where a voyeuristic, scopophilic desire is projected onto the excessively sexualized body.[16]

Paying attention to the trans-media, discursive context on girl [*sonyeo*] across 1970s' novels, music, and cinema, Oh Young Sook notes that many female characters are constructed to embody girlishness (*sonyeoseong*) as a sign of immaturity.[17] In contrast to female protagonists of 1950s and 1960s melodrama, such as *Flower in Hell* (*Jiokhwa*, Shin Sang-ok, 1958) and *Homebound*

(*Gwiro*, Lee Man-hui, 1967), the 1970s heroines are visibly younger. Actress Im Ye-jin, who was born in 1960, played the female lead in the *Really Really* series (1976–1977) when she was still in her teens; when Moon (b. 1954) auditioned for Lee's *A Woman Like the Sun*, she was twenty years old. Oh claims that other female protagonists, including the leads in such films as *Heavenly Homecoming to Stars*, *Yeong-ja's Heydays*, and *Winter Women* (*Gyeul yeoja*, Kim Ho-sun, 1977), are no longer adolescents but fall under what she characterizes as "parameters of girlhood"—naiveté, childishness, cheerfulness, and immaturity.[18] The aforementioned scholarship helps to situate the relationship between popular genres and the national specificity, but one should further be sensitive to the multiplicities of girlhood as well as spectatorship. The three films discussed here certainly present different modes or experiences of girlhood, with very few films granting or hinting at any liminal freedom outside home, education system, or workplace.

With the popularity of *Never Forget Me* (1976), its second installment, *I Am Really Sorry* (*Jinjja jinjja mianhae*) quickly came out in the same year. *Crazy for You* (1977) is considered the last installment of this *Really Really* (*Jinjja jinjja*) series, and shares the cinematographer, Yi Seok-gi, with the second installment.[19] Unlike the first two installments, which star Lee and Im as a romantic couple, *Crazy for You* casts instead Kim Hyun as the male lead while the role of Ji-yeong (played by Im), the girl protagonist, is more foregrounded. It is interesting to observe how a reversed gender role in the last installment fails to deliver the national subjectivity expected of both male and female subjects. The narrative unfolds against the changing urban scape of the modernizing nation, with Ji-yeong playing tennis. The male lead Jin is a marathon player, and the two "meet cute" during his practice. Throughout the film, we see Jin running against the backdrop of highways, river, and park, as if he symbolizes the future of the nation. The track coach quickly takes a back seat in the narrative development, once Ji-yeong begins to help Jin to improve his record; the costume colors of the coach and of Ji-yeong—red and blue (the major colors of the Korean national flag)—visually associate both to the national ethos. However, Jin falls ill near the date of the race. Against the advice offered by the doctor and the coach, he enters the competition. Close to the finish line, he collapses and is unable to complete the race.

Despite the reversed gender role, Ji-yeong, the girl protagonist, is constrained by the patriarchy that governs both her school and her home. As Jin is unable to pay for the treatment he needs, Ji-yeong decides to take on the financial burden herself. Her status as a student is not visually foregrounded until after Jin is brought back to the hospital for the second time. Unlike Jin, who occasionally wears his school uniform even as an eager trainee, Ji-yeong is not seen in her school uniform until halfway through the film. This first glimpse occurs, ironically, while she walks down the hospital's corridor, not at her school. This is shortly after she asks for money from her father, who declines, as he is unaware of the reason behind her request. She falsely promises a photographer that she will pose in the nude, but instead steals his camera to pawn it. But she is caught when the pawnshop owner reports her to the police.

Ji-yeong's interaction with her family members is mostly with her younger brother, and later with her father during the school's processing of her suspension. Nevertheless, the cinematographer Yi incessantly uses aperture framings to capture various characters throughout the film either by placing objects in the foreground or through natural or artificial apertures, to the extent that the style becomes self-reflexive and even witty.[20] When Ji-yeong is surrounded by her family members after she has been suspended from her school, a strange oval-shaped object in the foreground accentuates the apparent unity of her family. But the look of family unity is completed only when her younger brother enters the shot, claiming that he is no longer ashamed of his sister. This scene, although it slightly diverges, in terms of staging, from a previous scene in the principal's office, mirrors the idea that Ji-yeong is to be disciplined and confined in the institutionally sanctioned, otherwise domestic spaces as both a student and a girl. In both scenes, the visual balance is achieved through the entrance of a male character, first the father in the principal's office and the younger brother at home, further taking away the agency of the girl.

The newspaper article that features Ji-yeong's story is only mentioned by several characters (including Ji-yeong's younger brother and In-su, who is a roommate of Jin) rather than shown to the spectator. Such storytelling creates another gap in the range of knowledge between characters themselves and the spectator, leaving unanswered the extent to which the newspaper article is faithful to the actual event or merely titillating to make it appear more scandalous. Ji-yeong's subjectivity is excluded from the official (or journalistic) record of her action and its consequences, pushing her further to the margins—a repeated trope that I will revisit in chapter 3 in my discussion of *Han Gong-ju* (Lee Su-jin, 2013). As we will see in chapter 2, girls' personal writing (the telling of their own stories) is not only a persistent trope in the girl culture that has continued from the colonial era, but it is also a device to reveal their interiority and to attribute an agency to them, however limited.

If the girl's sensibility and potentiality are denied in both home and school, what is foregrounded is her adolescent sexuality as a virtual commodity. Prior to the mentioned scene at the photographer's studio, Ji-yeong wanders from her home to the studio; she later finds herself in the police station for the theft. Her journey parallels on a smaller scale the trajectory of downward mobility manifest in the bargirl films. When she enters the photo studio and is greeted by the photographer, whom she met earlier in the film, she passes a framed photo of a female torso with bare breasts, and she sits between this and another photo that is a close-up of a woman's eyes. Ji-yeong literally sits between two possibilities: of recourse to the girl's sexuality as a commodity or being subject to social surveillance. Although she fails, she attempts to avoid the first possibility by outwitting the photographer. She asks the photographer to give her some privacy to get undressed, but prior to that, her glance has already landed on the professional camera hanging on the wall; in a rack focus shot, first the photographer in the foreground comes into view, then the camera in the background. She did not intend to pose for him; rather her hesitation is a ploy to steal the camera.

Unlike Jeong-a in *Never Forget Me*, the first installment of the series, Ji-yeong does not face her own death. Nonetheless, her girlhood ends up being seen as unproductive and even futile. In the last scene, Ji-yeong returns to her normal clothing—the pink shirt—associated with neither her student status nor the future of the nation (the red and blue seen earlier in the film). She takes a walk in the woods after she has been discouraged by Jin's track coach from continuing her relationship with Jin. Her walk is intercut with her memory of Jin running; yet her strolling is soon to be interrupted by the news of Jin's death: he has fallen down the stairs in the hospital after she left the scene. Here is an interesting reversal of the subject of a melodramatic fall (down the stairs): from the usual female protagonist of women's films to the male protagonist in this film. Throughout the film, Jin's increasingly "sick" body—also a sign of his class background that yields an unhygienic environment—has become more visible to the eye due to his infection, leaving marks on his face and hands. Death as an ultimate form of exclusion awaits the injured male body that does not contribute to the nationalistic ideology of progress and development.[21]

Ji-yeong's initial, apparent agency in *Crazy for You* is manifest through her physical mobility and spirit; we first see her play tennis in the opening sequence and especially in the montage sequence of Jin's training. But her sexual innocence and moral integrity can be neither sustained nor appreciated. The girl's "unproductivity" does not lead to a liminal freedom but instead is associated with futility. Earlier in the film, while she is waiting for Jin, Ji-yeong glances at the overpass, followed by its shot with the cast shadow (figure 1.1). This cutaway may hint at the tragic outcome of her burgeoning romance with Jin but, more importantly at the futility of the schoolgirl's unproductivity. In

Figure 1.1 Jeong-a's gaze lands on the space under the overpass with a cast shadow—an empty sign of modernity (*Crazy for You*, Moon Yeo-song, 1977).

the same scene, she is approached by the photographer mentioned earlier, whose offer she initially turns down. In need of money later in the film, she visits his studio. When her romantic desire is about to blossom, it is tempered by her sexuality as a virtual commodity.

Next to the bargirl cycle of the 1970s that topped the domestic box office, teen films, including the *Prankster* and the *Really Really* series, constituted the popular production trends that guaranteed reliable box office returns. The main target audience of the *Really Really* series was claimed to be high school girls.[22] Thanks to the popularity of the series, *Crazy for You* opened in Danseongsa, which was one of the top tier first-run cinemas in downtown Seoul.[23] It proved, however, to be less successful at the box office than the first two installments. With the increased population and traffic in Seoul, cinema-going in the 1970s was a less affordable leisure activity for many audiences on low incomes; traveling to central Seoul to see a film was not cost-effective, given the ticket prices and the time needed to travel.[24] The distribution history of the teen films further helps to confirm the multiplicities of girlhood both in its representation of experience and its consumption. Teen films were not even re-distributed in the second-run theaters in the industrial districts such as Yeongdeungpo gu, where many factories were located; female audiences there could not relate to the everyday experience of high school students. For the low-wage women factory workers, many of whom migrated to Seoul from rural areas and whose "peers were attending secondary schools while they sweated in factories," the teen romance may not be the subject that immediately appealed to them.[25]

Nam-suk, a Bus Conductor

According to the labor historian Hwasook Nam, the term "factory girls" (*gongsuni*) was widely used by the early 1970s, but in a derogatory sense. Female factory workers were often associated with being "lower class, uneducated, and thus socially unworthy young women whose exposure to the factory environment made them unfeminine and made their morality suspect."[26] With the rapid industrialization and export-driven economic growth, there was an enormous migration from the countryside to the metropolis with the lure of modernity and employment. Women workers' cheap labor in both the light manufacturing and service industries was integral to the emerging economy and modernity envisioned. According to Nam, between 1960 and 1975, about 6.86 million migrated from the countryside to cities and, in the latter half of 1960s, approximately 600,000 per year.[27] Bus conductor (*beoseu annaeyang*) became one of the occupations that girls from working-class families or villages often turned to, as it did not require any professional skills. The term "bus girl," introduced in the 1920s, disappeared after the liberation in 1945, and was reintroduced as bus conductor when the government replaced male conductors with women in 1961 in order to present the role as a key profession within the service industry. With such a change, it was hoped to create a more "pleasant" environment for commuters. The number of bus conductors was over 30,000 in 1971 and reached over 50,000 by the mid-1970s.[28]

There were several reports of deaths of bus conductors throughout the 1960s and '70s due to the lack of adequate labor laws and safety measures. A report in 1975 shows that, on average, bus conductors worked 18.5 hours per day; their maximum monthly salary would be around 15,000 KRW in 1974.[29] A complete body search of bus conductors was common, in order to discourage transportation employees from stealing bus fares to compensate for their small monthly salary. Deplorable conditions were reported and shared in bus conductors' essays, submitted to various platforms and forums. The ministry of labor also published and awarded bus conductors' essays, part of the effort to present the role as a worthy and modern profession in the service industry.[30] With the introduction of gadgets to replace bus conductors, such as bell buttons and fare boxes, the role was already in decline by the early

1980s; it became extinct in 1990 when the legal requirement of the presence of a bus conductor was eliminated.[31]

Several female leads or supporting characters in the 1970s films temporarily land on transportation occupations; as a bus conductor in *Yeong-ja's Heydays*, or as a tour guide on an express coach in *The Midnight Sun* (*Yeongsi*, Lee Man-hui, 1972). *Girls From Scratch* is one of the few films that is dedicated to presenting the life of a bus conductor, although its coda slants toward a didactic message. Nam-suk, the female lead, helps her family in the village with her income earned as a bus conductor. With her father having passed away, she has given up the opportunity to further her education and sacrifices her future to support her family. With passion, she cares for her co-workers and studies in her spare time to earn a high school certificate.

Girls from Scratch, however, embodies a series of revisions to bypass the state's censorship.[32] Song Areum traces how the film's title changed several times, first following the title of the source novel, *The Land that Shakes* (*Heundeulineun ttang*, Hong Seong-won, 1975), which was adapted by Kim Seung-ok. Kim was by then already established as a novelist and screenwriter, with his novel *A Journey to Mujin* (*Mujingihaeng*, 1964) adapted into the film *Mist* (*Angae*, Kim Soo-yong, 1967). The script of *The Land that Shakes* underwent a complete re-write in 1976; then was renamed *A Distant Station* (*Ajikdo meon jongchakyeok*), alluding to the award-winning essay by a bus conductor, Lee Mae-sun (1976), for the sake of passing the censors. But it kept the original story line that had been censored, and the script was finally adapted into *Three Maidens, Off Duty* (*Bibeonalui secheonyeo*, scripted by Kim Seung-ok), which earned the scenario its final seal. Song claims that its title was changed one last time, back to the original *Girls from Scratch*, released as an almost new stand-alone piece, faithful neither to the source text nor to the original scenario submitted.[33] *The Maiden Who Went to the City*, which is closer to the original scenario adapted and submitted in 1976, came to fruition only in 1981, after the veteran director Kim took up the director role.

Girls from Scratch departs from both the source novel and several versions of re-writes that followed; it has the conventional narrative trajectory of a village girl's plight upon moving to a city. It begins with an upbeat tone to celebrate women's labor, similar to the American documentary *The Life and Times of Rosie the Riveter* (Conie Field, 1980), which depicts the experience of women workers in the heavy industries during World War II. Like Ji-yeong in *Crazy for You*, Nam-suk, the lead, undergoes a downward mobility. While Nam-suk stays at the company's dormitory, she is a model, compassionate citizen; she diligently works as well as studies during her spare time to earn an education certificate. But she learns that her family must move out of their home, as the friend of her late father—a benefactor of her family—urgently needs to sell their house. With her small salary, she is unable to provide her family with the money needed and turns to a better paying job; she decides to work as a bargirl alongside her friend (played by late Kim Su-mi), in exchange for an advance with which to help her family. After Nam-suk's co-workers and line manager (played by a legendary actress from the 1960s, Do Geum-bong) learn of her predicament and realize the reason behind her disappearance from the company, they collect money to help Nam-suk, although the collection falls short of the amount needed to pay back the advance. With the company's support through a hardship fund, Nam-suk can safely return to her old job.

As Lee notes, there might be a "structural linkage" among various types of low-wage professions that working-class women had to turn to and move between: "domestic service work, sex works for both domestic and foreign clientele, and other kinds of sexualized and nonsexual service labor."[34] In the film, however, Nam-suk's turn to sex work is prevented by the introduction of a moderate welfare system within the company, presenting it as a form of familism. The film's didactic ending not only promotes the profession as a safe environment but further underscores the family enterprise ideology as integral to the national development ethos. In his speech to Saemaeul leaders in 1977, then-president Park Chung-hee states,

> Thereby complete harmony between employees and employers would be made possible, and on this basis efficiency and productivity can be promoted. . . . [T]herefore, this movement, as the labor-capital cooperation movement uniquely developed in our country, will become a driving force to build up national strength.[35]

Barraclough, however, casts a critical eye on such a "development myth of 'Confucian capitalism' "; that is, that "factory girls could be protected by the company, living *en famille* in the dormitories, while profit was extracted from them."[36] Whenever working-class women were presented as a threat, they were often intimidated into giving up their political rights by thugs hired by the company, even by their co-workers and the police. Such a contradictory rhetoric and image, Barraclough concludes, aligns with the society's perception of women factory workers' economic and sexual independence as disturbing.[37] Labor historian Seung-kyung Kim also notes how women workers' daily experiences revolve around and are more directly affected by "various types of unequal relations": many tiers of hierarchy based on gender and seniority (line manager—under manager—line leader—worker) rather than a simple binary of the capital versus laborers.[38]

A pairing of *Girls from Scratch* with *The Maiden Who Went to the City* (*The Maiden* hereafter) would be useful here; both films' protagonists, Nam-suk and Mun-hui, manifest what Barraclough calls "the factory girl virtue"; but if the former feeds the predicament of low-wage worker into the conventional narrative trajectory of downward mobility found in the bargirl cycle, the latter helps to show the harsh working environments of the "model" worker.[39] The latter film features three "girls" (Mun-hui, Yeong-ok and Seong-ae) with different backgrounds and experiences. *The Maiden* alludes to *Girls from Scratch*, by casting the actress Lee Yeong-ok, who played the lead, Nam-suk, in the latter. However, as critic Kim So-hui puts it, *The Maiden* pays attention to "in-between moments of labor instead of labor per se."[40] Within their busy daily schedules and overwork, bus conductors were unable to eat properly and endured sexual harassment. Many stole bus fare to supplement their inadequate salaries and were exposed to humiliating body searches by company managers who monitored the amount of bus fares collected. There were several reports of suicides of bus conductors motivated by shame, including the death of Kwon Hui-jin in 1966 and that of Kang Mi-suk in 1978.[41] Mun-hui, one of the three leads in *The Maiden*, jumps off a building after a complete body search.

The revisionist, feminist labor history on women factory workers in the 1970s increasingly argues for the need to reconfigure the relationship between the female subject and the nation-state. Unlike male workers, who could claim more managerial roles and move up in both ranks and salary, women workers occupied "low-skilled" temporary positions with tenuous prospects of promotion, and the possibility of reaching only half of men's salaries.[42] Similar to other low-wage professions, there were prevalent rumors that questioned bus conductors' moral integrity; they were often sexually involved with and violated by male co-workers.[43] In one scene of *The Maiden*, Mun-hui is mistreated by a driver during the whole day and summoned by him after work. She agrees to meet up with him to resolve their conflicts. He takes her to several places, including the entertainment park, then eventually to a shabby "love motel," intending to sexually violate her. As she kicks him and escapes from the scene, she is ironically posed against a recruitment advertisement. The horrified look on her face is juxtaposed against the misleading advertisement with a slogan that reads "Earn your way through school; earn your way to success," while the line below specifies working conditions and salary: "Flexible working hours; 100,000 KRW per month; welcome the earning of sports and other certificates." As the ad is torn, it is unclear what kind of profession it is, but the close-up certainly points to the striking gap between the ad/hoax and the salary that Mun-hui earns in the film.

Instead of approaching the relationship as binary—low-wage workers versus capitalism or victims versus the state—Barraclough observes, "Factory girls found themselves caught between class and gender ideologies that saw them as neither real workers nor properly feminine."[44] Women workers' lives should not be discussed or dismissed as one homogenous entity under the idea of victim.[45] The more important and relevant question to raise, according to Barraclough, is the subject of writing or the author of representation. As she poses the question, it is not only how factory or low-wage workers are represented, but more important, "how [literary] representation substitutes the political representation of working-class women."[46]

In 1977, the South Korean government began to implement some measures to accommodate workers' educational aspirations. Night classes (*yahak*) sponsored by employers were used as "a device to recruit, retain and control workers."[47] In *Girls from Scratch*, we see Nam-suk study to earn a diploma while working on the bus. In the experience of many low-wage workers, education was a distant aspiration as they gave up their own chance of education to further that of their male siblings. Mun-hui in *The Maiden* also attends the night classes offered, which soon close due to the lack of government or company support.

We can interrogate, as with *Crazy for You*, the relationship between representation and audience. It is ironic that *The Maiden* did not stay long in the cinema; public protest by bus conductors and an appeal by a customs union pulled the film from the cinema only three days after its release, despite the fact that the protagonist Mun-hui calls for the ethical behavior of both bus conductors themselves and the transportation companies.[48] In her examination of the censorship of the film, Song notes that censors asked for a shortened duration of the scene in which the male bus driver is beaten up by his peers after the company finds out that he attempted to sexually violate Mun-hui; they further advised that the scene of Mun-hui's body search should avoid too much revelation of her body.[49] In the version currently available on the Korean Classic Film channel on YouTube, some of these scenes have been simply erased and replaced with white screen, while the voice and sound from the scene continue. Nonetheless, Song concludes that the immediate cancellation of its screening may have had more to do with a fear of its impact: its capacity to mobilize public protests and demonstrations, when political protests were severely suppressed and filtered by the press in the early 1980s. The government was concerned that the public protests would lead to social unrest.[50]

The Maiden invites various readings. Some find that the film does not quite offer a radical social critique and that the moralistic position advocated by Mun-hui—that bus conductors should stop stealing customers' bus fares to stop the company from requiring body searches—renders the issue as one of individual choice—to stay away from unethical behaviors—rather than a structural issue.[51] Nonetheless, the rooftop protest by Mun-hui, asking for both the company's suspension of body searches and for co-workers' solidarity, resonates with the imagery of female protestors summoned up in the revisionist labor history of women workers and protests (figure 1.2). Nam begins her study with "a woman-in-the-sky," a female rubber factory worker, Gang Juryeong (a.s.a. Kang Churyong), who had protested while sitting on the rooftop and refusing a wage cut at her company in 1931; she traces through the female factory protestors in the 1970s at Dongil textile company and then examines Kim Jin-sook's "sky protest" in 2011—her sit-in protest on a crane for 309 days.[52] After Mun-hui's jump from the rooftop, which is censored and again filled with a white screen, the camera immediately cuts to the automated fare counting machine, followed by a shot of Mun-hui walking with a medical crutch, assisted by her boyfriend. Instead of reading this as a compromised ending, it can be seen as an allusion to the uneven economic development achieved *at the expense of* girls' cheap labor. The film ends with a view of the heavy traffic in modern Seoul seen from above the Namdaemun Gate, one of the four gates that surrounded the old capital, Hanyang, of the Joseon dynasty.

Figure 1.2 Mun-hui makes a plea to stop body searches (*The Maiden Who Went to the City*, Kim Soo-yong, 1981).

In-yeong, a flaneuse

If Ji-yeong's student status gets in the way of her financial security, In-yeong, in Lee's *A Woman Like the Sun*, enjoys her liminal freedom, embodying the then-nascent youth culture (wide jeans and long curly hair) and pathos. In-yeong hitches a ride in Dong-su's car on her way to Dongdaemun station to join her friends, who are already enjoying their vacation on the beach. But all the money she carries is stolen. In-yeong meets Dong-su again at the police station, where he pays a court fine on her behalf. The film pairs two characters—In-yeong as a girl, and Dong-su as a criminal—to associate their liminality: In-yeong claims that she has failed her college entrance exam twice, and Dong-su, in his forties, is on the run after shooting a man with whom his wife had had an affair. The mobile camera as well as the physical agility of In-yeong further point to the freedom she enjoys as a girl. Although her pursuit of the boy who has stolen her money fails when she falls and the petty crook escapes, her mobility signals the freedom she temporarily embodies. In the film's coda, Dong-su promises In-yeong that he will return with the money she needs, yet Dong-su's arrest for the murder he has committed keeps him from rejoining In-yeong in the park. Instead, she circles a fountain by herself, suggesting that her physical mobility (and consequently her liminal freedom) will stay intact for just a little while longer.

A Korean film scholar, Oh, notes how the prevalent May-December relationship manifest in the 1970s films transmits a sense of defeatism and pessimism.[53] The "immaturity" of a female protagonist serves as a narrative premise to justify the male protagonist's guilt over his inability to "protect" the girl protagonist and her frailty. Oh characterizes such guilt as a form of 1970s melancholia, a product of authoritarianism under which various state-imposed cultural restrictions (such as night curfews, or the banning of long hair for men) curtailed individual freedoms. Such a mood or attitude manifested on screen could be seen as a way to cope with, and even to resist, the state's authority.[54] The social standings of male characters—college students, artists, daily laborers, or even (former) convicts—who themselves fall short of being privileged, even aimless, could be viewed in the context of the young generation's refusal to grow up, not fully engaging with the masculinity and productivity demanded of them by the state. *Road to Sampo*, director Lee's next film with Moon, also portrays such a relationship; Baek-hwa tags along with the two elder men on their journey to Sampo. And despite her desire to stay with the younger of the two, Yeong-dal, she is abandoned in a railway station when the two men decide to resume their journey without her.

Although Oh does mention Lee's *A Woman Like the Sun* as following this form of gender pairing, it is unclear (at least to me) whether In-yeong is portrayed as a figure in need of protection by Dong-su.[55] Dong-su is drawn to her because of her carefree nature, her relentless pursuit of leisure and fun, which he lacks. When he tries to borrow from a friend the money In-yeong needs, Dong-su describes her as cute. As Sharon Kinsella notes, the aesthetics of cute, which proliferated between 1970 and 1990 in Japan, is a manifestation of consumer culture, where a girl (*shōjo*) has been "transformed into an abstract concept and *a sign of consumption* in the Japanese mass-media and modern intellectual discourse."[56] After Dong-su has paid In-yeong's fine at the police station, they embark on a shopping spree, with Dong-su buying her a new pair of shoes, then eating snacks and having more drinks at Dong-su's apartment. She is oblivious of her initial aim to join her friends on the beach, even after she earns enough money from signing a modeling contract. Instead, she uses all of her money to throw an extravagant birthday party for Dong-su, ordering food and inviting the strangers that she encounters in the streets and apartment hallways.

Prior to In-yeong's accidental reunion with Dong-su at the police station, she tries to make up the money she has lost. In-yeong is willing to subject herself to situations where she could be exploited by her male companions. She herself appears to become a figure who embodies virtual downward mobility (from working at a beer hall, visiting a hotel to spend an "innocent" night with a writer, and having to pay a fine for violating the law—she claims that she is mistaken as a prostitute). Yet throughout the film, she is willing to earn money only under her terms and conditions. When she in fact goes to the hotel to "inspire" the writer, she kicks him off her body and escapes the hotel room when she learns exactly what he expects from her companionship. On the street, she is mistaken for a sex worker by a drunkard, but she dares him by demanding an exorbitant fee, which makes him leave her alone. The soundtrack by the Korean rock band star Shin Jung-hyeon further accentuates the nascent youth culture, while the actress Moon's performance as In-yeong is particularly free and natural, as when, within the diegesis, her test footage as a model is projected on the studio wall. During the screening of the footage in the film, she is not merely a soon-to-be commodity but takes the position of the viewing subject as well, enjoying watching her own footage with other staff members. Her position is self-regarding, if not narcissistic.

Whether Dong-su and In-yeong have consummated their love after the lavish birthday party remains ambiguous. After having spent the night together, they are seen in several discontinuous shots of the two embracing and kissing on the stairs of a building. In-yeong is seen in a blue dress, with a

Figure 1.3 In-yeong momentarily looks more feminine after having spent a night with Bak (*A Woman Like the Sun*, Lee Man-hui, 1974).

more feminine, mature hairstyle, her tasseled frizzy hair tidied with hairpins on both sides (figure 1.3). But In-yeong's costume soon changes to her usual sailor shirt and a pair of jeans, as if the previous sequence is a mere fantasy of womanhood that is expected of her (figure 1.4). Whose fantasy it is remains unclear.

Hilary Radner, while characterizing the appeal of girlishness and, by extension, neo-feminism in contemporary Hollywood cinema, states, "[Girlhood offers] a notion of agency, in particular the capacity for change, that is specifically feminine but not yet aligned with the normative behaviors associated with womanly roles."[57] If female sexuality is constructed for the girl protagonists in *Crazy for You* and *Girls from Scratch* as an either-or choice, mapped onto either complete abstinence (girl) or excess (bargirl), In-yeong's sexual desire oscillates between the two, presenting as well as exploring sexual possibilities she encounters or she herself creates. As Radner notes, the term "girl" evokes the idea of a woman in a continuous state of *becoming*, who is empowered by her ability to sexualize herself for her own pleasure.[58] In-yeong appears to remain to be liminal even if Dong-su is unable to turn up at the end. Her off-screen romance with director Lee, begun during the film's shooting, was short-lived; Lee passed away during the post-production stage of their last film together—his posthumous film *Road to Sampo*—and *A Woman*

Figure 1.4 But she soon returns to her regular clothing of a sailor shirt (*A Woman Like the Sun*, 1974).

Like the Sun might be seen as Lee's last cinematic granting of Moon's liminal freedom.[59] Moon emigrated to the United States shortly after his death in 1975, and her return to the screen in 2015 has earned her small supporting roles since; but her girlish persona is repeatedly referenced.[60]

Despite the varying nature of girlhood in the three films discussed so far, the girls are indeed presented as, to borrow Lee's term, "virtual sexual commodities," either willing or unwilling. My subsequent analysis of girlhood in contemporary South Korean cinema—girls as writing subjects to reveal their interiority, and girls' use of diaries and letters as well as their "shelter writing" to cope with their extreme (domestic) conditions—is guided by, and supplements, the discussion of 1970s girlhood in this chapter.[61] Despite the rise of teen films or films with young working-class protagonists, the girls' liminality is rarely granted, constantly denied as being un-conducive to the modernity envisioned by, and dictated through, the national developmental ethos.

Glimpses of Girlhood

Among the bargirl films of the 1970s, *Yeong-ja's Heydays* is at the center of many discussions of female subjectivity (or lack thereof), sexual labor, and modernity. Ranked at the top of the domestic box office in 1975, the film revolves around the titular character, Yeong-ja (played by Yeom Bok-sun), who undergoes the hardships of several low-wage professions, to which girls from the countryside often turned, prior to eventually landing in the sex industry. The film begins when Yeong-ja, now a sex worker, is arrested during a police raid on the district. Her encounter at the police station with her old suitor, Chang-su (played by late Song Jae-ho), triggers a flashback to her turbulent employments since her first job in the city as a domestic helper. Chang-su, who was hired at her boss's factory, pursues Yeong-ja but is soon drafted to serve his military duty. She loses her job shortly after she has been sexually violated by the scoundrel son of her boss. With the low income she earns at a sweatshop, she can neither make a living nor support her family, who live in the countryside. She quits to become a bus conductor, working briefly as a bargirl in-between. After losing her arm in a traffic accident, Yeong-ja ends up in a brothel.

For Jin-kyung Lee, the film's source novel, written by Choi In-ho, well demonstrates the mechanism of necropolitics. Lee observes that prostitution, domestic or military, is a profession in which "the possibility of (physical) death is an integral part of prostitution as an occupation."[62] The ending of the source novel, from which the film departs due to state censorship, well illustrates her point; Yeong-ja and her co-workers die of an accidental fire in the district.[63] She claims, "The surplus of young female labor that could not be absorbed into the usual occupations would be produced as a new 'social-sexual' category of working-class women, that is, as prostitutes on the margins of rapidly industrializing South Korean society."[64] In contrast, the film's coda instead briefly visits Yeong-ja who is now married to a disabled man. Yeong-ja and her husband (played by Lee Sun-je) run a small restaurant by a construction site. Barraclough appreciates the film's non-sentimental ending: "Rather than showing them [Yeong-ja and her husband] as exemplary objects of pity or charity, the movie depicts them as a normal, scarred working class family."[65] Film scholar and critic Kim notes instead the hovering face of Yeong-ja in the last shot of the film. The film's revised ending showcases an instant male bonding formed between Chang-su, the suitor of Yeong-ja throughout the film, and Yeong-ja's husband, whom Chang-su just met.[66] While we see them leave together on their bikes side by side, a close-up image of Yeong-ja is superimposed in the air. Kim argues that even if Yeong-ja escapes death, she remains in the margins of society (both class-wise and spatially), and her body is denied a corporeal reality, hovering only as an image.[67]

I concur with the problems that the existing scholarship brings forward through their respective analyses of *Yeong-ja's Heydays*: the cultural relationship of the film or novel to the national specificity of South Korean authoritarianism at the time. Although fully informed by the social and political mores of the 1970s, I shy away from offering a generalization of the female leads of the bargirl cycle, of which Yeong-ja is representative. Many female leads' struggles or even deaths are seen against the backdrop of the modern icons and industrial landscapes, but their functions or significance in each film should be treated individually, not as though they are all alike. I pay closer attention to the textual specificity of each film, which renders the protagonist's death different: thematically, narratively, and stylistically.

Yeong-ja's Heydays tricks the viewer with a false ending. Prior to the film's coda, we see the train passing by from a high angle, followed by a shot of Yeong-ja crying on a bridge. Although Yeong-ja's exact location in relation to the running train is unclear, the high angle shot of the train is associated with the gaze of Yeong-ja. The scene signals her impending death, as it is the last place that her aimless strolling of the city reaches, after she has even been solicited for sex work by an old woman at the train station.[68] This false coda could suggest an impasse to the possibility of a romantic relationship with Chang-su, as the sequence of her walks has been crosscut with Chang-su searching in vain for Yeong-ja, who has left the district; but more important, this apparent ending points to the dead-end of Yeong-ja's migration to the city.

Train tracks have been repeatedly associated with her movement toward the city. In an earlier flashback in black and white footage, we see Yeong-ja on the train leaving her hometown. She is about to send her mother all of the monetary benefits she has received after losing her arm while working as a bus conductor, one of her in-between jobs prior to landing in the red-light district. As she struggles to write a letter that will accompany the money she is about to send home, her voice-over recites the letter for a volunteer (a male student) who helps write it. While the voice-over continues, the camera cuts back to the station where we see Yeong-ja's mother running after a train. As the camera pulls back, we see Yeong-ja in the rear seat of a train, looking at her mother; followed by a shot of Yeong-ja's family receiving her letter and money. It is a montage that combines several temporalities: Yeong-ja's leaving her hometown in the past, her voice-over in the present, and her family's receiving and reading the letter in the near future (or in the past).[69] The sequence spills over to the present, now back to color, where Yeong-ja attempts to kill herself by standing in front of an oncoming train. She fails, as the train stops in front of her.

Another scene of train track appears between her several visits to a clinic to receive treatments for a sexually transmitted disease (STD). As the doctor advises her to stay away from any sexual intercourse during the treatment, she tries to avoid sexual contact with one of her regular customers. After a shot of Yeong-ja getting an additional injection for her treatment, we see the empty train track stretched from the foreground right to the center of the background, followed by a shot of Yeong-ja looking off-screen. When the camera cuts back to the train track, this time we see several children playing in a circle in the background (figure 1.5). The image of children playing becomes blurry, as if it is Yeong-ja's subjective shot, reminiscing about or missing her younger siblings. She then sits by the train track and plays a children's game, *gonggi-nori* (with ball stones), by herself.

In the two scenes described—Yeong-ja's departure from her hometown, and her reminiscence of childhood—her girlhood is absent. She is the eldest of a low-income family without a father, and her migration to the city does not let her earn sufficient wages to support her family and educate her siblings. She is pushed farther and farther away from her home as well as from the initial goal that may have motivated her to leave home in the first place. The camerawork of the train scene described above mirrors an earlier scene, when she is fired from her first employment. When her boss sees Yeong-ja flirting with the employer's son, she accuses her of having seduced him. As Yeong-ja is told that she is fired, there is a cut to show an exterior shot of the house with the camera placed inside a car; then Yeong-ja is revealed, sitting in the back seat and looking back at the house. The delayed revelation of Yeong-ja in these two scenes underscores the social forces that repeatedly pull Yeong-ja away from both her home and employment opportunities to be financially independent, instead driving her to less desirable workplaces with fewer opportunities.

Throughout the film, Yeong-ja constantly flaunts the collective complicity or individual sympathies, even at times that from Chang-su. The performance

Figure 1.5 Yeong-ja's glance over the train track (*Yeong-ja's Heydays*, Kim Ho-sun, 1975).

style of Yeom Bok-sun, who plays Yeong-ja, constantly keeps the spectator from discerning specific emotions. In many close-up shots of Yeong-ja that punctuate emotionally charged scenes, it is unclear what kinds of feelings she is experiencing: are they fear, desperation, remorse, sadness, or anger? Yeom may lack the self-reflection of the female lead reflected in the mirror in such films as *Heavenly Homecoming to Stars* or *The March of Fools* (*Babodeului haengjin*, Ha Gil-jong, 1975): a stylistic marker for the character as well as the spectator to register a moment of self-recognition and possibly see their sincerity underneath the apparent cheerfulness or girlishness.[70] But through the few perceptual alignments with Yeong-ja just mentioned, her absent girlhood and lost aspiration can be glimpsed.

Yeong-ja's eventual departure from the district is closely tied to her increasing internalization of the state's perspective, subjecting herself to what Antonio Gramsci terms the ideological state apparatus. Yeong-ja's date with Chang-su after their first visit together to the clinic is cut short, as she is afraid of passing a police station. They part and each meanders through narrow alleys; the camera follows Yeong-ja walking down the street. As she turns around a corner, the camera cuts to show her opening and closing the door to the brothel where she works; staged in depth with an iris on the door, the camera makes it look as if she is absorbed into the void, a space of nonexistence and/or possible death as in the source novel (figure 1.6).

After her last treatment for STD, Chang-su invites Yeong-ja to give her a full bath in the public bathhouse where he works as a masseuse. During the bath, she confesses to him that she is increasingly concerned with other people's perception of her and has begun to feel ashamed. This confession is followed by a shot of one street of the red-light district, shot similarly to the jerky mobile

Figure 1.6 Yeong-ja enters the brothel in the far background (*Yeong-ja's Heydays*, 1975).

46 Forever Girls

camera movement seen in the opening scene of a police raid of the district, searching for illegal sex workers.[71] But this shot is framed around Yeong-ja. Instead of going home, she returns to the basement of the public bathhouse, where Chang-su lives with an old man who is in charge of its heating system. Yeong-ja claims that she could not return to the brothel. The mobile shot mentioned has marked her beginning to feel "shame." In the many narrow alleys and passageways around the prostitution district, Yeong-ja and other sex workers are constantly pushed around and chased like moles looking for a place to hide, whenever there is a police raid.

If the glimpses of Yeong-ja's girlhood underscore its absence, in the other films, *Insect Woman* and *Night Journey*, the girlhood portrayed is more pronounced and repeatedly resurfaces to dictate the protagonists' decisions. In *Insect Woman*, the father of Myeong-ja (a.s.a. Myung-ja, played by Youn) dies during her high school days, and this event is recalled several times at critical points in the film. In *Night Journey*, the female lead's sexual frustration and desire are in constant contrast with her sexual experience with her teacher in the past, even though the exact nature of their relationship remains obscure as to whether it was consensual. In these films, the female leads' actions, desires, and frustrations pivot around the events associated with their girlhood.

Similar to Kim Ki-young's earlier film, *The Housemaid* (*Hanyeo*, 1961), *Insect Woman* is presented as a *mise-en-abyme*. Framed within a story of a middle-aged man, Dong-sik, visiting a hospital because of his sexual impotence, the main story revolves around his evolving relationship with Myeong-ja, and her eventual death. Dong-sik's violation of Myeong-ja helps him to regain his sexual virility; Dong-sik's entrepreneurial wife eventually allows their affair and even pays Myeong-ja a monthly stipend. As long as Myeong-ja follows the wife's rules, they can "share" him; during the day he spends time with Myeong-ja, and at night he is with his wife. One rule says that there should be no children between Dong-sik and Myeong-ja. They move into a house of their own, where strange things happen: a baby is brought to the house from nowhere, then disappears, and dies; there are repeated intrusions of rats— director Kim's motif continuing from his previous film, *The Housemaid*. As Dong-sik wishes to abandon their relationship, Myeong-ja kills him, and then, during the police investigation of the murder, takes her own life.

The main story of *Insect Woman* interestingly begins with Myeong-ja as a schoolgirl. The opening scene takes place at her high school, and we soon learn that her father has recently passed away. As she returns home to ascend the stairs that lead to her flat, a high-angle shot of the empty stairs is overlapped with the voice of her late father, calling her name. Myeong-ja's mother suggests that her daughter work as a bargirl to support the family, including her elder brother, as the mother hopes to further his education. Much-repeated stories of familial "sacrifice" imposed on girls deprive Myeong-ja of opportunities to finish or further her education. With the absent father, the family unity or "unit" can only be maintained *at the expense of* the daughter's sacrifice.

The two families make opposite choices in trying to avoid a complete disintegration of the family: Myeong-ja's family "lets go of" her, while Dong-sik's family accepts her as a pseudo-family member. In contrast to the staging of Dong-sik's family, Myeong-ja's family is staged in a tighter circle in a small *anbang* (master bedroom).[72] Such a staging ironically accentuates the rigidity of the patriarchal burden imposed on Myeong-ja, rather than her family's intimacy or unison; the dynamic of her family appears as suffocating as the cramped room in which both Myeong-ja and her mother quickly break down emotionally. Similar to a comparable scene in *Crazy for You* (analyzed earlier), in which Ji-yeong's agency is taken away after her failed attempt to pay Jin's hospital bill, the unity of the family in Kim's film can be secured only *at the expense of* the girl's sacrifice and—as in *Yeong-ja's Heydays*—*through* her (eventual) absence.

This common and conventional narrative gets a twist when Myeong-ja both defies and exploits the patriarchy. Although her father lived with Myeong-ja's family, he was not legally married to her mother. Myeong-ja's devastation at losing her father to his legitimate family leads her to form her relationship to Dong-sik in a peculiar way; she is both insolent to Dong-sik's wife and family and desperate to hold on to him. The initial image and the shot of empty stairs are repeated throughout the film, signaling the eventual "fall," both literal and metaphorical, that awaits her. Within the reversed gender role in a middle-class family with a breadwinner wife and an effeminate husband, Dong-sik becomes a mere object to be exchanged between two women, his wife and Myeong-ja, whose relationship increasingly takes a form of contractor versus sub-contractor.[73] The two women's rivalry over Dong-sik is further circumscribed by Myeong-ja's conscious effort to avoid finding herself in the same situation as with her father, losing the male guardian figure (her father or male partner) to others. Her trauma at losing her father creeps in. The shot of the stairs that lead to her family flat repeatedly punctuates the key moments of disintegration of Myeong-ja's family.

The film reminds the spectator of Myeong-ja's girlhood trauma one last time. During the police re-enactment of the crime scene, the razor blade that Myeong-ja thought was lost after she slit the throat of Dong-sik, mysteriously reappears. The scene of her ending her own life, with the shout that "youth is a rebellion," a motto that she learned on her last day of school, is interspersed with the shots of her father carried down the stairs. In the montage sequence of Myeong-ja by the stairs in the household that she has built with Dong-sik, the temporality of the present and past is merged. The subject and object of her gaze becomes one—Myeong-ja, herself—when the shot of her looking down the stairs in the present is followed by one of her looking up in her school uniform. What is removed by killing Dong-sik or Myeong-ja herself is not the unfair relationships that surround her but the clear line between subject and object. While actively defying the patriarchal system, Myeong-ja's failure to keep afloat within the system and her subsequent paranoia lead to the collapse or near-collapse of her own logic, resulting in her death.[74] Youn's character in *Insect Woman*, or even *Woman of Fire*, takes advantage of, and even exploits, the middle class's hypocrisy, yet her actions increasingly push her to the bottom tier of the system. Youn's contemporary film, *Bacchus Lady*, deserves a brief comparison here. As an old sex worker who solicits her customers on the street and charges a minimal fee—the "Bacchus" in the title alludes to an energy drink—she is driven to the margins and ends in prison for assisting the euthanasia of her old customer/acquaintance; she can leave prison or end her sentence only with her own death.

In *Night Journey*, there are repeated flashbacks to Hyeon-ju's sexual experience during her high school days. Hyeon-ju (played by late Yoon) works at a bank and although legally unmarried, she lives with her male manager, Bak (a.s.a. Park). *Mist* and *Night Journey*, both directed by late Kim Soo-yong, showcase reverse journeys. *Mist* revolves around the male lead's short visit to his hometown village, while waiting for a decision by his company's board of directors; *Night Journey* is concerned with Hyeon-ju's visit to her home during her annual vacation. Her everyday life is already filled with habituations and frustrations; cooking, eating, sex, and leisure all have become automatic and unsatisfying to Hyeon-ju. Unaccompanied by Bak, she reminisces about her sexual relationship with her high school teacher, who was about to depart to Vietnam for the war. Dressing for a bike ride with her younger sister, she tries on her high school uniform. We see Hyeon-ju on the bike by the beach, with her sister running after it. As the camera cuts closer to her, signaling the start of a flashback to her high school days, she increasingly becomes both the subject and object of her desire. In the flashback, Hyeon-ju is seen at first with the teacher holding the backseat of the bicycle to help her balance on the bike. She falls and the teacher becomes sexually intimate with her. The scene alternates between the present and the past, with Hyeon-ju's teacher holding the bike for her in the past, as described, and as she holds a bike for her younger sister in the present; her imagination becomes self-regarding, replacing the glance of her teacher in the past with her own. A graphic match is formed between

Hyeon-ju holding the backseat for her younger sister and the now absent, deceased teacher, blurring the subject and object of their glances; Hyeon-ju is both the desired and the desiring in the present (figure 1.7a–b).

Some critics characterize the scene with the teacher, along with a later scene, as sexual assault; the initiation of sex does not seem consensual at first and appears to be even more disturbing given that the male teacher is seen in his military uniform. It may recall the masculinity expected under the military dictatorship of Park Chung-hee. Yet Hyeon-ju's reminiscing about her past is repeatedly associated with, and reflective of, her present desire for a lawful relationship with her partner Bak. The flashback to the beach in the past is followed by a scene of Hyeon-ju and her teacher in Korean traditional wedding costumes. This subjective reconstruction of her sexual relationship with him may be a result of her mother's or her own wish for a marriage in the past as well as the present. However, Hyeon-ju in the present is fully aware of a disparity existing between her own and others' perception of her past.

Figure 1.7 a–b Hyeon-ju's bike ride in the present and past (*Night Journey*, Kim Soo-yong, 1977).

Shortly after, we learn through her conversation with her mother, and later with a man with whom she is on a blind date (possibly with an eye to an arranged marriage), that the gossip about her and her teacher had spread, and this eventually forced her to leave her hometown.

On the last day of her vacation, we see her spending a night with a stranger at a hotel.[75] Again, whether this is consensual rough sex or sexual assault is debatable, but in the scenes at both the beach and the hotel, female desire for, or pursuit of, a satisfying sexual relationship is "censored"— ironically, the film has been notoriously censored due to the explicit portrayal of sexuality. Earlier in the film, while Hyeon-ju is strolling in the city by herself, she sees a young man handcuffed by a policeman; Hyeon-ju is also handcuffed when she is dragged by the stranger to a hotel, where she and the stranger are seen having sex. Their affair is further intercut with the aforementioned imaginary wedding scene of her and her teacher. According to the film script submitted for the censors, the scene in the present (with a mysterious man) is shot as a scene with the teacher, although the male actor is barely visible.[76] The film remains ambiguous as to whether her affair with the stranger is real or imagined. But the film hints that it is at least partially grounded in reality, as the next day the chain of her watch remains broken; a close-up of the damage to the chain was shown during the previous scene at the hotel.

Yoon plays the high school girl in the flashback and Hyeon-ju in the present. Hyeon-ju even puts on her high school uniform when she arrives at her mother's place to re-live her memory. While Yoon would not easily come across as a girl in terms of appearance (she was near thirty when the film was shot in 1973, although it was released in 1977), the repeated flashbacks foreground the interiority of both the girl's own past and her current sexually frustrated desires.[77] Through the modernist gesture toward character subjectivity and interiority in both sequences analyzed here, Hyeon-ju is clearly the subject of her imagination and longing, as if it is a form of self-regarding imagination, a characteristic of girlhood. Her gestures and performance are very much posed or even sculpted to signal her gradual satisfaction or frustration while her partner(s) remain off-screen or blocked.[78] After she returns to Seoul, she takes two entire days to pursue leisure—bowling, visiting arcades, having her nails done and facials. Although solitary, she can afford such leisure pursuits and fully appreciates them all, which may lead the viewer to infer that the night with a stranger is the product of her own imagination, or an actual encounter with a stranger that marks the end of a series of leisure activities she enjoyed during her annual leave. I will return to Hyeon-ju when I discuss Yoon's earlier film, *Sunday Night and Monday*

Morning (1970) in which she portrays another "office lady," who aimlessly strolls around the city by herself, while she waits for her boyfriend to finish his work. As the female flaneuse, like Hyeon-ju, she visits various sites in the city (such as the cinema, park, coffee shop) but is unable to fully enjoy them. The film, however, certainly renders her as the subject of desire, sexual or otherwise.

Conclusion

In *Never Forget Me*, with which I opened this chapter, scenes taking place on trains serve not only as framing devices for Yeong-su's reminiscing about his relationship with Jeong-a but depict a space where Jeong-a's and Yeong-su's mutual attraction and sexual desires increase for each other. On one morning, on a crowded communal train, his hat is blown off by the wind while he protects her from falling from the train. He holds her from behind and their reaction shots accelerate, along with the speed of the train; the scene is indirectly rendered as sexual, given the moaning and facial expressions of Jeong-a. Throughout the film, although the two leads fight off their desire to further engage sexually, they remain innocent. Yet the rumor has already spread about the possibility of their sexual misconduct. Jeong-a's death is almost a punishment for their burgeoning adolescent sexuality. The fact that Jeong-a dies from pneumonia further links her death with their last moment together alone at Yeong-su's place. The night before Yeong-su is to leave town, Jeong-a visits his home one last time. Unable to express or act on their desire, Jeong-a runs out of the room in the pouring rain in her bare feet. Jeong-a's sister later informs Yeong-su that Jeong-a died shortly after his family had moved away. If her physical condition that led to her death was a consequence of their last moment together, it is linked to the adolescent female sexuality forbidden by the patriarchy, represented throughout the film by Yeong-su's brother. The coming-of-age story of Yeong-su is *at the expense of* Jeong-a's death. In the 1970s, girlhood, when it involves sexual activity, functions as a form of exclusion. In the girl protagonists' films such as *Girls' High School Days* (*Yeogosijeol*, Kang Dae-sun, 1972), and the earlier analyzed, *Crazy for You*, girls are expelled from, or suspended from, their schools due to rumors. Girls' sexuality, when active, is deterministic, setting the path of the female lead's downward mobility or even immobility (and death), regardless of the girls' varying intentions and agencies, as in other box-office hits of the 1970s. In another box-office hit, *Winter Woman*, Ihwa becomes sexually "philanthropic," as if that's the only option available other than exclusion or death, once her stalker (and suitor) kills himself at her rejection.

The immateriality of the female body has been at the center of many feminist film scholars' research both in English and Korean language scholarship. Karen Redrobe [Beckman] traces the practice and motif of the vanishing lady exemplified across different media and style, from the nineteenth-century magic shows that led to some early cinema to Hitchcock's *The Lady Vanishes* (1938): a tendency in Western art and culture where male agency, be it in the form of a magician, a filmmaker, or the nation-state, is often set against the vanishing female body.[79] If death is a form of permanent vanishing or disappearance, many girl subjects to be discussed in this book, including Jeong-a just mentioned, do fall under the spell of eventual vanishing.

Nam asks, "Where did all those *yogong* [*yeogong*] go, and what are they doing now? Yogong who were in their late teens and early twenties in the mid-1970s and who continued to labor as wage workers were middle-aged and older women in their late forties, fifties, and sixties in the first decade of the twenty-first century."[80] Barraclough answers: "While Korean factory girls may have disappeared from literature, they have not vanished."[81] As if answering these queries, Im Hoong-sun's artist film, *Factory Complex* (2014), begins with the oral histories of factory workers in the manufacturing industry who share their experiences in the 1970s, and extends its scope to include the casualized laborers in service sectors, such as flight attendants and those who are working at large retailers and call centers. Im's film foregrounds the shared nature of their employment in the past and now: precarity. So does the recent work of some women directors: Boo Ji-young's *Cart* (*Kateu*, 2014), a fictionalized rendering of a strike organized by women workers at a large retailer; and Shin Su-won's *Light for the Youth* (*Jeolmeuniui yangji*, 2019) and July Jung's *Next Sohee* (*Daeum So-hui*, 2022), which feature a male and a female protagonist, respectively, working in call centers.

In the South Korean context, girls' bodies in the 1970s are treated in conflicting ways; as the reservoir of cheap labor with their desires and adolescent sexualities to be suppressed, silenced, or punished. My approach to '70s girls in this chapter could be considered the restorative or recuperative feminist methodology, as termed by Yue, from which she carefully differentiates her own materialist approach: "either to fill the gap in the historical record, as with feminist scholarship concerned with restoring women to a history they had been written out of, or to further bury the traces of the woman's body in the formulation of an aesthetic theory (in art history and film theory)."[82] In subsequent chapters, I further forge a relationship between the 1970s girls and contemporary girlhood, in the light of revisionist historians' work on female labor, sexuality, and even death, and I explore their shared functions as sites to register the conflicting forces of coloniality, postcoloniality, and late modernity, and the extent to which cinema could grant girls' liminality and freedom.

2

Girls Who Disappear, Girls Who Remember

From the Writing to Speaking Subject

The year 1937 marks the beginning of the last phase of Japanese colonial rule in Korea (1910–1945), during which period the policy of *naeseon ilchae* (*naisen ittai* in Japanese) strengthened Japanese rule and transformed the everyday life of Koreans. Due to its geographical proximity to the Japanese war front, Korea was exploited for "total mobilization," gaining new significance as a strategic military base for the Japanese cause. Korean men were drafted to serve in military camps, factories, and mines, and many young girls and women were further subjected to work as sex slaves.[1] Censorship became more severe in both Japan and Korea, with the Japanese language being taught and spoken more widely in Korea. The title of this chapter, "Girls Who Disappear, Girls Who Remember," is inspired by both the original title of the film *The Silenced* (Lee Hae-young, 2015)—*Gyeongseonghakkyo: Sarajin sonyeodeul* (literally translated, *Gyeongseong School; Girls Who Disappeared*)—and Janet Poole's insightful book on this period and its literature, *When the Future Disappears: The Modernist Imagination in Late Colonial Korea*. The idea of "disappearance" aptly characterizes this historical moment, when the Korean people saw the nation's future and their own prospects eclipsed. In this chapter, I examine the representation of girls as writing subjects, even as their rights to write in Korean were denied and their subjugation and sacrifice escalated in late colonial Korea.

The mid-2010s saw many well-established male auteurs, commercially viable or critically acclaimed, plunge into rendering various historic events of the colonial period on screen: *Assassination* (*Amsal*, Choi Dong-hoon, 2015); *The Last Princess* (*Deokhyeongju*, Hur Jin-ho, 2016); *The Handmaiden* (*Agassi* [also spelled as [a.s.a.] *Ahgassi*], Park Chan-wook, 2016); *Dongju: The Portrait of a Poet* (*Dongju*, Lee Joon-ik, 2016); *The Age of Shadows* (*Miljeong*, Kim Jee-woon, 2016); *Love, Lies* (*Haeeohwa* [a.s.a. *Haeuhhwa*], Park Heung-sik, 2016); *Anarchist from Colony* (*Park Yeol*, Lee Joon-ik, 2017); and *The Battleship*

Forever Girls. Jinhee Choi, Oxford University Press. © Oxford University Press 2025.
DOI: 10.1093/9780197685822.003.0003

Island (*Gunhamdo*, Ryoo Seung-hwan, 2017). This cycle was followed by another, although of a much smaller scale, in 2019–2020: *A Resistance* (*Hanggeo*, Choi Min-ho, 2019) and *Bicycle King Uhm Bok-dong* (*Jajeonchawang Eom Bok-dong*, Kim Yu-sung, 2019). Women directors appeared, with *Snowy Road* (*Nungil*, Lee Na-jeong, 2015) and *Malmoi* (Eom Yu-na, 2019), both directorial debuts.

These two cycles of films coincided with historical changes in the circumstances of South Korea. In 2015, the Japanese and Korean governments re-negotiated and reached a bilateral agreement on compensation for the victims and survivors of atrocities, despite the survivors' objections of the inadequacy of such compensation. In the same year, Japan campaigned to have Gunkanjima (known as Battleship Island) recognized as a world heritage site for its contribution to the modernization of the region, with no acknowledgment that the colonized were exploited to work on this very island. The historic March 1st independence movement against Japanese colonial rule in 1919 marked its centennial in 2019.[2] Some of the films mentioned above achieved commercial success while others were criticized for their aggressive distribution strategy, historical inadequacy, or lack of character depth.[3] With a few exceptions—such as the crime-thriller *The Age of Shadow* (set in the 1920s) and Park Chan-wook's *The Handmaiden* (an adaptation of Sarah Waters's 2002 novel *Fingersmith*, which does not specify the exact period of its setting)—many of the films listed here are partially or entirely set in late colonial Korea, with characters who do not survive to witness the end of colonial rule.[4] In the biopic, *Dongju*, the titular Korean poet Yun Dong-ju (a.s.a. Yoon Dong-ju), known for his lyrical poems (*seojeongsi*), is seen incarcerated in a Japanese prison. The poet dies only six months prior to Japan's defeat in August 1945. A horror film, *The Silenced* is set in a girls' boarding school in 1938; in *Snowy Road* and *Spirits' Homecoming* (*Gwihyang*, Cho Jung-rae, 2016), both of which depict survivors of military sexual slavery, the characters experience the abrupt end of the colonial era.

The films about colonialism feature female characters as part of an ensemble cast (*Assassination*) or as the principal protagonist (*The Last Princess*; *A Resistance*), and some do avoid the representational pitfall for the protagonist of being a victim of sexual crime or threat, one point of the triangulation that Kim allocates to colonial cinema: nationalistic protagonist, complicit antagonist, and female victim.[5] Nonetheless, the narrative significance of the female characters is still assessed in terms of their alignment with either of the two forces that propel the male characters of late colonial Korean films. For instance, in *Assassination*, set in 1933, the female identical twins, Ok-yun and Mitsuko (both played by Jeon Ji-hyun), follow the contrasting paths adopted by their parents: that of the mother, who helped the independence fighters, and of the father, who collaborated with the colonial government.

In his study of the representation of colonialism in post-war Korean cinema, Jinsoo An observes that films rarely "mobilize the historical investigation of colonial problem[s] from the present viewpoint. Instead these films begin and end in the colonial period."[6] Further, in the latest case studies from the 2000s, he notes that the nationalist ethos—"an ideological constant" against colonialism—gives way to a fascination with the then-new culture (broadcasting/radio shows), nightlife (night clubs), sports (baseball), and technology (aviation skills, medical science).[7] Kim attributes such a shift to the emergence of Korean-language scholarship on "colonial modernity" from 1999 onward, a turn toward its cultural history.[8] In contrast, in the films released in the 2010s, the impending dissolution of colonial rule and its relationship to the present plays a significant role in terms of both character relationships and spectatorship. As I discuss in the latter part of this chapter, the film cycle dealing with military sexual slavery ("comfort women" [*wianbu* in Korean; *ianfu* in Japanese])—including *Snowy Road* and *Spirits' Homecoming*—often pairs female protagonists, only one of whom survives. These films' narratives alternate between the past and the present. Looking back at the history of this time through the experience of singular survivors adds a historiographical element to be unpacked in the present, in its very process of re-writing both a post-colonial and a personal history.

In the midst of the Korean film industry's re-imagining of the colonial history, girl protagonists still remain as the victims of atrocities within the triangulation, with the two forces reconfigured as death versus survival: *girls who disappear and girls who remember*. Girls' survival and girls' memories foreground a need and desire to remember and be remembered. In this chapter, I examine girls' writing as a filmic device that asserts their limited agency, the very act of which registers the history of colonial Korea. Personal writing, in the form of diaries and letters, has offered girls a way to express their liminal desires since the 1920s and has become a persistent trope in girls' fiction and cinema.[9] The case studies examined include *The Silenced*, followed by a film cycle centered around Japanese military sexual slavery, *Snowy Road* and *Spirits' Homecoming*, focusing on the writing trope that provides the female subjects with a means to foreground their personal experience as a form of history.

Girls Who Disappear: *The Silenced* (2015)

The Silenced is set in a girls' boarding school in the 1930s, bridging the Korean contemporary girls' high school horror series (beginning with *The Whispering*

Corridor, 1998) and the military sexual slavery film cycle (2015–2016), and adopting the conventions of contemporary girls' horror (the girls' school as the principal setting, female camaraderie, and icons such as diaries, secret hiding places, and dead birds, among others).[10] Ironically, the name of the school, Gyeongseong, which is also the name given to the capital of the colony under Japanese rule, does not appear to refer to its actual locality. It is located in a remote secluded place, far from any city. Its name is metonymic, reflecting the girl protagonists' aspiration to go to the metropole; the colony's capital is displaced onto a space of girls' isolation and interiority, reinforcing the distance existing between the colony and Tokyo—a "pure exteriority" for the girls.[11] The deprival of personal writing in *The Silenced* helps to underscore the national circumstances of late colonial Korea, where girls are doubly marginalized; the future of neither themselves nor their country is assured. A Korean classical horror convention of hauntology and resentment often sees female protagonists return as ghosts to seek revenge for their own death, or to avenge or prevent the death of their beloved.[12] *The Silenced*, instead, foregrounds the exploitation and disposability of the colonial subjects. Regardless of whether one is complicit with or opposed to colonial rule, colonial subjects here are, to borrow Michele Aaron's term, "dead already."[13]

Aaron analyzes two films about suicide, *The Virgin Suicides* (Sophia Coppola, 1999) and *Paradise Now* (Hany Abu-Assad, 2005), to show how the two are governed by contrasting aesthetics. She describes Coppola's film as not just revealing but flaunting the mechanism of "necromanticism of femininity"—the West's fascination with the aestheticization of death, in particular, the suicide in "feminine" forms—by exploring the very structure of scopophilia and visual pleasure.[14] As Aaron puts it, "Film is revealed as the medium par excellence for embalming the to-be-dead woman for erotic contemplation."[15] In contrast, in *Paradise Lost*, the death of the subject is already embedded in the character's life: it is neither about "life against death" nor about "death-in-life."[16] The character's suicide mission is over-determined by both the narrative trajectory and the "imperialist economy" of the historical circumstances of the Occupied Palestinian Territories depicted; she claims, "The to-be-dead figure is the dead-already Palestinian."[17] *The Silenced* may not share the same aesthetics of *Paradise Now*—the latter's compositionally decentering the subjects filmed as well as the spectator. The framing of *The Silenced* is strikingly symmetrical and ordered—a sign that the daily routines of the girls are extremely regimented and regulated under the imperial forces, and that they should accept and occupy the role/seat allocated to each of them. Aaron's concept of "dead-already" helps to articulate the protagonists' doubly marginalized status and their compromised subjectivity within the colonial territory.

A discussion of the methodological genealogy and continuing debates on biopower, biopolitics, and necropolitics, as elucidated by Michel Foucault, Giorgio Agamben, Anchille Mbembe, and others, is beyond the scope of this chapter.[18] Yet, as Mbembe puts it, if "the ultimate expression of sovereignty largely resides in the power and capacity to dictate who is able to live and who must die," then the film's portrayal of medical experiments conducted on the girls' bodies without their knowledge or consent, both literally and figuratively foregrounds the loss of sovereignty.[19] Jin-kyung Lee elaborates on Mbembe's observations of necropolitics in her insightful discussion of Korean female sex workers engaged in domestic and military prostitution from the 1970s onward. She notes, "Extraction of [sexual] labor is related to, and premised on, the possibility of death rather than the ultimate event of death itself" and "the 'fostering' of life, already premised on an individual's death or disposability of her or his life, is limited to serving the labor needs of the state or empire and capital."[20] The films discussed in this chapter abide by such logic, both in depicting the death of a character-subject in *The Silenced* and also in the military sexual slavery film cycle. The headmistress in *The Silenced* laments that it is a "waste (*akkapne*)" that a subject, who has been medically tested and monitored, died. In *Spirits' Homecoming*, on arriving at the military base, one of the sex slaves says, "You ask where we are? We are already dead; this is a living hell"—the condition of "dead already," in Aaron's terminology.

The Silenced begins as Ju-ran (played by Park Bo-young), whose Japanese name is Shizuko, is transferred to a remote girls' boarding school. Set in 1938, a year after the outbreak of the second Sino-Japanese war, all students are expected to take medicines, do hand embroidery, and excel in sports. The reward for students' physical excellence in sports is the promise that the top two of the class will have the opportunity to travel to Tokyo. Ju-ran, who suffers from tuberculosis, gets regular injections to improve her condition. Her initial physical state and subsequent transition embody both the sickliness of the colonized subject and the promotion of the healthy body by the imperial government. Kim stresses that the sickness of male protagonists in Korean literature and film could be read as a resistance against colonization that disrupts the colonial discourse of the healthy body.[21] In her study of Japanese girls' magazines during the war, Hiromi Tsuchiya Dollase notes that the editor of *Girls' Friends* (*Shōjo no tomo*) was pressured to follow the Japanese government's censorship guidelines and standards imposed to create the image of "strong, healthy girls."[22] The stories published in the magazine became didactic, and the style of illustrations shifted from an evocation of a dreamy, unrealistic girl or girls' fantasies in the 1920s, to a "realistic" representation of a Japanese girl.[23]

The desired creation of the healthy colonial subject and her inability to write in the vernacular language (or write at all) in *The Silenced* constitute the two major threads of the film. As Ju-ran arrives, her personal belongings are taken away, including her (presumed) diary. In the name of discipline, Ju-ran's face is slapped, as she expresses her wish to keep her diary. But she later inherits from her classmate, Yeon-deok (a.s.a. Yeon-duk, played by Park So-dam), a diary whose author is named Shizuko; significantly, this is also Ju-ran's Japanese name. The pages inside the red diary are torn, preventing Ju-ran from learning any of Shizuko's personal experiences. Instead, all students, including Ju-ran, must submit a daily report, taking notes on their daily lives, including their physical changes. Later in the film, we learn that the boarding school is one of the many sites where girls have been monitored as participants in medical experiments, conducted so the Japanese government can test the effectiveness of new medicines, which would then be distributed among soldiers to improve their physical ability and increase their spirit to fight.

The girls' improving records on long jump and track and field are thus a mere testament to the effectiveness of the medical experimentation that the selected girls are undergoing; their dream of travel to Tokyo vanishes as soon as the students fulfill their purpose. While girls disappear from the school one by one, with more and more visible traces—first Shizuko (before Ju-ran's arrival), Eguchi, then Kihira—Ju-ran finds herself excelling in the sports in which she was initially timid but begins also to experience the side effects of her medication. Ju-ran's colonial subjectivity is best manifested through a white circular beam cast upon the darkened background, effectively resembling the sun disc of the Japanese flag. As the headmistress puts a headset on Ju-ran's head and asks her to face the wall, Ju-ran stares at the white circle, as if her personal dream is eclipsed with the country's imperialization, underscoring the disappearance of both into a void (figure 2.1a–b).

Ju-ran, whose father has already moved to Tokyo, is brought to school by her stepmother, who is then to follow her spouse. Ju-ran is less enthusiastic about the promised reward of Tokyo than her classmate Yeon-deok, played by Park So-dam of *The Priests* (*Geomeun sajedeul*, Jang Jae-hyun, 2015) and *Parasite* (*Gisaengchung*, Bong Joon-ho, 2019). Yet both yearn for, and place their faith in, the nearby ocean, believing Japan to lie on the other side. Escape from the pre-determined path awaiting them is shown to be impossible. Yeon-deok and Ju-ran flee and seem to finally reach the ocean. But standing on a clifftop, what they see instead is a military camp hidden in the forest, almost a mirror image of the boarding school seen in the establishing shot at the beginning of the film. The boarding school is a microcosm of the colonial state, an earlier stage for reaching the colonial subject as demanded by the imperialist

60 Forever Girls

Figure 2.1 a–b When the Headmistress asks Ju-ran to stare at the projector, what she sees is a blank sun disk (*The Silenced*, Lee Hae-young, 2015).

government. Yeon-deok and Ju-ran are destined only to be captured and brought back to school by the Japanese soldier Kenji and his subordinates.

The film is self-reflexive about writing, filled with abundant instances of writing, both personal and official (diary, daily report, bureaucratic record keeping, and even film). In one flashback, Yeon-deok tells Shizuko—the one who has disappeared prior to Ju-ran's arrival—that she will write a letter to her, and letter and diary are the same thing: two of the primary literary tropes for girls. Girls' personal writing in literature and film is always to be read and heard, a manifestation of their desire to be heard.[24] When Ju-ran and Yeon-deok sneak into the headmistress's office to search for the records of missing girls, they find not only the written reports on the aims of the medical experiments but also film reels. When Ju-ran accidentally starts the projector, the reel shows several rounds of treatments and the selected subject, Ju-ran herself: the encounter with her recorded self echoes the earlier recognition of colonial subjectivity when she stares at the blank sun disc. Ju-ran's self-recognition here could be articulated further through both colonial subjectivity and gendered difference.

In her discussion of the Hollywood gothic films of the 1940s, Mary Ann Doane notes that they replicate the representation system of the classical Hollywood mainstream cinema yet turn the female character into the subject of paranoia: "The woman's film attempts to constitute itself as the mirror image of this dominant cinema, obsessively centering and recentering a female protagonist, placing her in a position of agency. It thus offers some resistance to the narrative economy that stresses the 'to-be-looked-at-ness' of the woman."[25] Yet the apparent agency of the female protagonist ironically results in "the violent attribution of the investigating gaze to the female protagonist (who is also its victim)."[26] Doane appeals to the Freudian idea of paranoia: "The female subject does not institute a search to 'refind' the object; she becomes that object."[27] The reversibility of subject-object in women's investigation films helps to explain the narrative twist that awaits here in *The Silenced*: Ju-ran sees herself in the footage, who is smiling at the camera, and is shocked by the image and cries.

One must further pay attention to the death of the headmistress, who is "to-be-dead" yet "dead-already." She has responsibility for the school overall and also conducts the medical operation, but she is eager to produce outstanding records by accelerating the operation. Her death, however, reveals her status to parallel that of the girls. The death of the headmistress at Ju-ran's hands could be seen as a narrative punishment (as is that of the Japanese solder Kenji). But her disposability as the colonial subject is similar to that of girls, visually reinforced by the appearance of her own death; in the final shot of the headmistress, she is pinned on the wall with her body frozen, mirroring the look of the missing girls who have been kept in their individual cells in a similar condition. The entire laboratory becomes another cell, only bigger in its size, within which the colonial subject is made to disappear.

"Let's go home" is the last line uttered by Ju-ran prior to the film's final coda. The line is quite ironic: as Yeon-deok confesses earlier, she is an orphan, dreaming of social upward mobility based on her personal achievement; while Ju-ran is made unwelcome by her family with her father and stepmother already residing in Tokyo. The homelessness of the girls in fact points to the homelessness of colonial subjects in general; a sense of not belonging, with no vernacular language (e.g., diary) to express themselves. Shizuko's diary, although inherited by Ju-ran and Yeon-deok, is not filled with Shizuko's subjective experience but rather contains the hysterical outcry of Yeon-deok after Ju-ran's arrival, as Yeon-doek observes the striking similarities between Shizuko and Ju-ran.

The Silenced, examined above, is especially intriguing when it is compared, as a companion piece, to the more commercially successful *A Werewolf Boy* (*Neukdaesonyeon*, Jo Sung-hee, 2012)—a strange mélange of coming-of-age romance, sci-fi thriller, and supernatural fantasy—that was released earlier.[28] Like Ju-ran, "wolf boy" Cheol-su has been subject to medical experimentation, in this case during the Korean War (1950–1953). Cheol-su develops a romantic relationship with Sun-i (a.s.a. Sun-yi), played also by Park. Sun-i, like Ju-ran, suffers from ill health and moves to the country with her mother and younger sister, Sun-ja. Sun-i's girlhood is depicted in flashback when she visits her old cottage. Park plays both Sun-i as a teenager in the flashback, and her granddaughter, Eun-ju, in the present.

Although the exact year is unspecified, Sun-i's taming of and romance with the werewolf boy Cheol-su is set against the aftermath of the Korean War, with South Korea having entered the era of post-war industrialization and military dictatorship; on the wall of the police station hangs a portrait of Park Chung-hee (whose rule lasted from 1961 to 1979). Sun-i's family becomes a foster family for Cheol-su, and his assimilation into Sun-i's family is manifested through their mutual changes; Sun-i becomes healthier through her interaction with Cheol-su, while Cheol-su, who has been abandoned and grown up in the wild, learns to interact with human beings.

Ju-ran in *The Silenced* looks as if she has inherited the character traits of both Cheol-su and Sun-i from *A Werewolf Boy*: girl attributes from Sun-i and an extraordinary physical agility from Cheol-su. Sun-i's appearance resembles that of an effeminate girl protagonist in girl comic books. In one scene when Sun-i plays a guitar, she is framed with excessive backlight like a female star in silent cinema, being presented both to Cheol-su and the viewer as the epitome of a pensive girl; she is shown in profile with the camera slightly tilting downward, which seems to be an aesthetic rather than a narrative decision and yields the image of Sun-i as a *sonyeo* girl imaginary. When she writes, the sound of the pen is exaggerated to underscore her interiority as the writing subject. Honda Masuko pays special attention to the significance of sound in shōjo culture, as a symbol of girlhood. What she calls "hirahira" refers to "the movement of objects, such as ribbons, frills, or even lyrical word chains, which flutter in the breeze."[29] Honda pays attention to the sound of words rather than the sound of physical writing, but nonetheless the sound of Sun-i's writing nicely foregrounds the duality of girls' sensibility. For Honda, the sound of "movement" of objects associated with girls is a sign of their interiority and exteriority. She states, "The girl may try to avoid contact with the outside world when in her self-contained, inwardly converging state; nevertheless, her constant swaying and fluttering provokes and attracts the gaze of others."[30] Sun-i's act of writing is private, yet it is also an outcry to be heard by "others," like Shizuko/Yeon-deok's in *The Silenced*. The cover of her diary bears the title "Sorrow of (or under) the Moonlight," along with a warning: "stay away." This cover is already in communication with "others" or potential readers. A close-up of her diary is followed by a shot that indicates Cheol-su's presence outside: Sun-i is seen through the window from outside, with the camera placed outside the house and looking in.

Writing again becomes a salient motif in the film, as in *The Silenced*, with the agent gradually shifting from Sun-i's personal writing of a diary to Cheol-su's recording of a hidden history of the war. Sun-i teaches Cheol-su how to write, but he has already become the active subject of writing prior to her teaching. After Cheol-su has been found at Sun-i's, a policeman visits to investigate the case. But as the policeman takes notes on the case, he drops his pencil. Although the policeman mentions in passing that the Korean War created 60,000 orphans, Cheol-su's story is absent or erased in the official history of the war, as signaled by the policeman dropping the pencil. In the police station sequence that follows, we see Cheol-su holding onto a pencil. He scribbles, in subsequent scenes, on the chair or floor in the house, or on the ground while he watches the children play baseball on the hill, as if expressing a desire to record his story into the "official" history. As the narrative unfolds, we learn that Cheol-su is an outcome of a wartime experiment to create soldiers who could exceed human strength and agility—the consequences of atrocity and war.

At the film's climax, Cheol-su is framed by another male character, Ji-tae, who desires Sun-i, that Cheol-su reputedly harmed the neighbors' stock and even Sun-i. Cheol-su is "to-be-dead"—perhaps a sign of the "mortal economies" and spectacle, but more important, signaling the termination of Sun-i's own girlhood. A romance between Cheol-su and Sun-i is liminal, clearly leveled against Ji-tae's potential sexual threat to her. Ji-tae presents himself as a patriarchal figure in the absence of Sun-i's father and demands marriage to Sun-i in exchange for his financial support of her family. Her desire to escape from both the moral and the financial burden in fact infantilizes both Cheol-su and herself. In one sequence, Sun-i dresses Cheol-su in Korean traditional costume, *hanbok*, and plays a face-painting game. This gesture toward their infantilization not only underscores Sun-i's wish to remain a girl but further facilitates the gender reversal between the two. As I have argued elsewhere, a romantic relationship in shōjo anime and culture turns the two into a pair rather than a couple—especially more so here, when Cheol-su is dressed in a female costume.

A Werewolf Boy is framed as a flashback attributed to Sun-i, and the film's ending renders her girlhood, as well as her romance, frozen in the past. In a fantasy sequence, Sun-i re-encounters Choel-su, who has been faithfully waiting for Sun-i's return. Choel-su hands over to Sun-i the folded note that she had left for Choel-su in the cell as her family was moving out of the cottage. The note reads "Wait for me. I will return." The past and girlhood could be relived only in imagination or fantasy, as the present and the past are visually and temporally divided. Cheol-su reads to Sun-i the story of *The Snowman*—the book Sun-i asked Cheol-su to read to her after he learned how to write and read properly: he moves here from the writing to the speaking subject, a point that I take up in the next section. Regardless of whether the sequence is reality or Sun-i's dream, her decision to leave Cheol-su behind signals her acknowledgment of the adolescent romance and leaves it in the past.

Girls Who Remember: *Snowy Road* (2015) and *Spirits' Homecoming* (2016)

In the depiction of military sexual slaves, the present exists for the past; or the present is another form of prolonging the past trauma. From *Snowy Road* and *Spirits' Homecoming*, a pair of films that are often compared and contrasted by Korean feminist scholars, to *I Can Speak* (*Ai kaen seupikeu*, Kim Hyun-seok, 2017) and *Herstory* (*Heoseutori*, Min Kyu-dong, 2018), all four films bring back to the present the protagonists' memories of imperial military sexual slavery, when Korea was under Japanese colonial rule. Through either constant temporal juxtaposition between the present and past or a brief glimpse into the past, these films show how the present of survivors is shaped or haunted by their past traumas. Yet they further showcase how the mode of representation of historical trauma has been diversifying in the Korean film industry; the focus on survival has shifted from girls' traumatic past and victimhood, to their present, everyday struggle to overcome their trauma and sense of guilt.

The issue of Korean military sexual slaves began to attract public attention in 1990 when Yun Chung-ok published a report on the "comfort women" in *Hangyore*, the Korean newspaper. Korean women indeed constituted the largest portion of military sexual slaves during World War II with an estimated figure of 100,000 to 200,000 victims, yet their experiences have been silenced for decades.[31] Various women's organizations supported the survivors' demand from the Japanese government: a public apology along with compensation and adequate public education to raise awareness of the past in Japan.[32] In 1991, against the Japanese government's denial of direct involvement with the coerced recruitment of wartime sexual slaves, Kim Hak-sun came forward with her own testimony.[33] The landmark documentary trilogy on the subject—*The Murmuring* (*Nateun sumsori*, 1995), *Habitual Sadness* (*Nateun sumsori 2*, 1997), and *My Own Breathing* (*Sumgyeol, Nateun Sumsori 3*, 1999)—was shot during this period when the public was becoming increasingly aware of the issues, and director Byun Young-joo captured some of the movements and protests of various political organizations, including the Korean Council for the Women Drafted for Military Sexual Slavery by Japan (*Jeongdaehyeop*). The shooting of the films, more importantly, helped the survivors open up and share their own past experiences in front of the camera. In 1996, the United Nations concluded that the "comfort women" were forced to work as sexual slaves and that the Japanese government should acknowledge its legal responsibilities for causing this.[34] In the remainder of this chapter, except in the places where the original term needs to be identified, I use the terms "survivors" or "military sexual slaves," the latter of which is the official term acknowledged by the UN Human Rights Committee, instead of "comfort women," which is contradictory as well as pejorative. It should be noted, however, that neither term—military sexual slaves or "comfort women"—is appreciated by survivors for its connotations and implications.[35]

Since the early 1990s, there has been a collective effort to listen to, support, and legally compensate the survivors of military sexual slavery under Japanese colonial rule. In 2015, the issue resurfaced as the Korean and the Japanese government signed an agreement that Japan would pay $8.3 million as compensation and make an apology. Further, the two countries announced that this agreement would be a "final and irreversible resolution" to the matter.[36] The agreement was immediately criticized as inadequate by both the survivors themselves and the opposition Democratic Party; the government signed the agreement without consulting the victims who were directly involved, overriding individual positions and wishes. Recently, the survivor and activist Lee Yong-soo further criticized the exploitation of survivors by the supporting organization that has led public rallies every Wednesday since 1992, showing the complexity and variety of perspectives among survivors.[37]

Along with the public debate, the release of *Snowy Road* (2015) and *Spirits' Homecoming* (2016) further ignited a question on the adequate mode of representation of wartime atrocity and survivors: how to address the trauma of victims, some of whom were very young girls coerced to offer, and exploited for, their sexual labor, without further violating and/or fetishizing bodies incarcerated and battered by Japanese imperial armies and the managers of the wartime "comfort stations [*wianso*]." In this section, I first consider the idea of the unrepresentable and the incomprehensible in the post-colonial holocaust study, and the ongoing feminist criticism of the "victimology" of girlhood, leveled against the contemporary film cycle's rendering of former sexual slaves as girls. I will then focus on the girls' sensibility manifested through personal writing in *Snowy Road*.

The scope of scholarship on holocaust is vast, yet the ongoing dialogue between various psychoanalytic versus post-colonial approaches to trauma, in particular, revolves around the extent to which the experience of trauma can be shared. In "Art/Trauma/Representation," Griselda Pollock defines trauma as ultimately inaccessible: "Trauma is the radical and irreducible other of representation, and the other side of the subject, and as Thing, cannot thus become something."[38] For Pollock, a trauma is an "originary event" that is "an absence and a hole in the subject." It is without form and shape, yet exercises its force only in "borrowed clothes in secondary occasions."[39] In other words, trauma itself is a lack, or the void that could not directly be accessible by the subject—"Thing"—but affects the subject; trauma, in order to be detectable, needs to be redirected and channeled into something other than itself.

The originary structure of trauma proposed in psychoanalytic terms here faces a difficulty with explaining the transmission of trauma. As Pollock admits, "Trauma is transmitted: trans-subjective transport."[40] She acknowledges another level of trauma, a specificity of trauma, where "an event in life and history" exceeds the subject's capacity to process and overcome.[41] Focusing on Bracha Ettinger's conceptualization of the aesthetic encounter with trauma as trans-subjective, Pollock delineates a way in which trauma could be shared: "Transubjective futurity is an opening occasioned by encounter with its remnants or traces—the only form of others' potential sensing of it as trauma rather than it as this or that story."[42] The idea of remnants and traces recalls, although in a different context, Walter Benjamin's idea of messianic time, where the chronology and linearity of time can be reconfigured outside of the chronological framework.

Even with the distinction proposed between structural and historical trauma, Pollock notes that the latter is always an activation of the former.[43] The suggested distinction or stage here, however, fails to properly explain the experience of trauma and pain inflicted in a specific time and space under colonial rule, where the past is, as David Lloyd observes, "not a relation to one's own past but to a social history and material and institutional effects and in no simple way a matter of internal psychic dynamics."[44] Trauma of the post-colonial subject is, and needs to be, communicable to both perpetrators and members of one's community.

Cultural nationalism has been, and still is, one of the dominant ways in which collective trauma is addressed in the post-colonial context. Lloyd notes that its aim is "to produce the imagination and emergence of a national culture that can provide for its subjects paradoxical safety of public acknowledgement."[45] In constituting a new cultural subject, according to Lloyd, the process often involves a re-invention of tradition, replicating a dynamic of colonialism; the state often reproduces the effects of colonial modernity by selectively promoting the elements of culture that can be re-appropriated to serve a present purpose.[46] The state takes up the authority, exercising its "censorship," so to speak, in order to pigeonhole the national psyche into something palatable to the ideology of a new nation-state. Arif Dirlik critically examines the contradictions of post-colonial efforts involved in the building of a nation-state.[47] Dirlik concurs with the observation of Partha Chatterjee and Ania Loomba that anti-colonial nationalists replicated the same kinds of assumptions of colonial perspective that they aimed to critique, and they perpetuated colonial perspectives and practices, especially in gender relations.[48]

In post-colonial South Korea, the state and patriarchal culture had continuously silenced the experience of survivors. The 1965 normalization treaty between Japan and Korean under Park Chung-hee's dictatorship foreclosed the possibility of compensation for the labor and hardship of heavy-industry workers such as coal miners and former sexual slaves drafted during the colonial era. The "comfort women issue" was not even listed as part of the negotiation.[49] Sociology scholar Chunghee Sarah Soh attributes the perpetual neglect of military sexual slaves, by both the state and survivors' own families, to the state-led modernization as well as the patriarchy: women who returned to their hometowns after having worked as sexual slaves during the war found themselves driven out by shame or forced to lead their lives while hiding their past.[50] Even as late as the 1990s, on the request of feminist and human rights organizations to interrogate the matter, a government official dismissed it as "unimportant" since it occurred primarily to women of poor, rural families.[51]

Like the survivors of wartime atrocity, films dealing with military sexual slavery have long been absent from the public eye. Prior to the 1990s, there was a paucity of fiction films revolving around wartime sexual slaves. Even when they are present, they remain in the periphery, and their sexuality is emphasized. *Sunset on the Sarbin River* (*Sareubingange noeul jida*, Chung Chang-hwa, 1965), for instance, shows the arrival of adult women at a military base in Burma, the night before the imperial army heads to the battlefield. One of these sexual slaves, assigned to the room of the Korean male lieutenant—the protagonist Su-nam (or his Japanese name, Matsumoto)—makes fun of his naïve faith in the imperial rhetoric and ideology, and his belief that a colonial subject could be leveled up and treated the same as legitimate Japanese citizens by volunteering to serve the empire.[52] In her study of pre-1990s representations of wartime sexual slavery, Kim Chung-kang claims that it is not until films of the 1980s and 1990s that young girls in Korean traditional costumes are portrayed as being conscripted by force for sexual slavery to work at military base.[53]

Set in 1991, the year when Kim Hak-sun first gave media testimony of her experience, *Spirits' Homecoming* pairs two sets of relationships: Yeong-ok (a.s.a. Yong-ok) and Eun-gyeong in the present day, and Yeong-hui (a.s.a. Yong-hui) and Jeong-min in the past—in this case, 1943, nearing the end of the colonial era. In the present, Yeong-ok is in her sixties, working as a seamstress who specializes in Korean traditional costumes. Eun-gyeong is a young girl who has been sexually violated by an ex-convict who broke into her house. Eun-gyeong becomes a young shaman under the guidance of *manshin* Su-ryeon, whose costumes Yeong-ok has been providing. In the film's other timeline, Yeong-ok is a teenager during the Second World War; for unspecified reasons, the character's name in these sequences is Yeong-hui. Yeong-hui is forced into military sexual slavery at fifteen. She befriends Jeong-min, another teenage girl at the station. Jeong-min is killed as the two attempt to escape. In the film's climax, Eun-gyeong, the young shaman, performs a Korean shamanistic ritual *gut*, embodying the spirit of Jeong-min through which Yeong-ok can come to terms with her past and overcome her survivor's guilt over Jeong-min's death.

In *Snowy Road*, Yeong-ae (a.s.a. Yong-ae, played by Kin Sae-ron), from a rich family, and Jong-bun (played by Kim Hyang-gi), a daughter of a poor seamstress mother, are sent to Manchuria to work as sexual slaves. The girls are sent for different reasons: Yeong-ae, as political retaliation by the imperial army against her father who has been involved with the independence movement against the colonial government, while Jong-bun is forced to join by local men in her mother's absence. Both Yeong-ae and Jong-bun having worked at a military station, only Jong-bun survives the war; she lives in the present with meager subsidies and incomes by working as a seamstress, while developing a guardian relationship with a girl next door, Eun-su (a.s.a. Eun-soo), who has been abandoned by her mother and is exploited by her peers as she lives by herself.

In his study of African trauma narratives, Robert Eaglestone identifies several devices common to post-colonial literature: "the use of discourse seen as historical, diverse and complex framing devices, moments of epiphany, and confused time schemes."[54] Both *Spirits' Homecoming* and *Snowy Road* share these characteristics. The colonial history enters the narrative through an allusion to actual historical events or, in a more self-reflexive manner, by breaking from the narrative to insert the historical moments in question. *Spirits' Homecoming*, released in 2016, is set in 1991—the year Kim Hak-sun went public about her wartime experience. The film begins in fact with the voice of Kim, whose story is being aired on television. Later in the film, we also see Yeong-ok, a survivor, visit the local council office to declare herself as a victim of sexual slavery, in line with the Korean government's initiative to gather information on wartime victims. Several temporal markers are embedded and narrativized in *Snowy Road* as well. Most important, toward the end of the film a photograph shows Jong-bun sitting next to the girl statue (*sonyeosang*), which was created in 2011; it is a sign of her embracement of her past and identity and her active participation in the weekly protests held by survivors.

It is worth noting how, in diverging ways, the non-linear narrative employed in both films yields a temporal interruption or disorder. Eaglestone claims that the juxtaposition of different temporalities can reveal narrative information that may be beyond the range of characters' knowledge within the diegesis. Both films alternate between the past and the present, with flashbacks increasingly becoming longer as the films reach their ending. The epiphany, or as Eaglestone puts it, "the what," is underscored in *Spirits' Homecoming* via the shamanistic ritual, which is signaled even in the pre-credit sequence with a shot of Eun-gyeong performing a ritual, following the initial appearance of Jeong-min in her hometown.[55]

Korean-language feminist critiques of *Spirits' Homecoming* echo Lloyd's and Dirlik's reservations about cultural nationalism. Many appreciate the fact that the film was produced and released with the help of crowdsourced funding (the ending credit acknowledges all who participated by listing the names of contributors), further reigniting the public interest in, and discourse around, the matter. *Spirits' Homecoming* nonetheless does not escape the lure of "tradition" as a device to reconcile the past and present. Korean feminist scholars Joo Youshin and Sohn Hee Jeong both criticize the film's recourse to the shamanistic ritual; it is an aesthetic cliché that merges two different temporalities, gesturing toward the unrepresentable nature of the trauma of former sexual slaves, which cannot be accessed except through the traditional form of shamanistic ritual.[56] While the public reception of shamanism itself has fluctuated, subject to diverging political agendas that alternately accept or reject it, shamanism as the shared tradition here is a device that attempts to homogenize as well as alienate the spectator.[57]

Since 1992, on every Wednesday, public protests have been held against the Japanese government's refusal to compensate the military sexual slaves. In 2011, on the Wednesday marking the 1,000th protest, a statue of a girl (*sonyeosang*) was erected across from the Japanese embassy in Seoul, funded by private donations.[58] The statue is a reminder that many women were drafted and forced to work as sexual slaves when they were teens (sometimes even as young as twelve).[59] Joo and Sohn agree on the common association between girls and victimhood, including that portrayed in the films mentioned here, which map the lost sovereignty of Korea onto the body of young girls. In both films, the imagery of the adolescent girl is used to allegorize the equation often postulated between mother-land and mother-nature.[60] The two films offer an imaginary closure that re-configures the past and present through an imaginary return to the past—to the protagonists' hometowns. As in the ending of *Spirits' Homecoming*, where Jeong-min has a warm meal with her parents, in the coda of *Snowy Road*, Jong-bun sees her younger self reuniting with her mother. The girls' aspiration to return home functions as a narrative device to idealize the homeland or the national through the erasure of oppression and patriarchy from within.

The question of how to represent the wartime atrocities concerns feminist scholars. Sohn criticizes the repeated display of girls' battered bodies and sexual violations in *Spirits' Homecoming*, as it invites a voyeuristic perspective and attributes further shame to the victims shown on screen: their bodies being the site to embody the guilt of the national (male) subjectivity.[61] Joo pays further attention to the film's style, arguing that the lateral or overhead shots of incarcerated girls further inscribes a voyeuristic position in addition to, or despite, the psychological and physical abuses depicted.[62] The lateral tracking shots sometimes pass through the walls of an individual cell, while the overhead view of the entire space shows multiple cells simultaneously: each cell is occupied by a girl being physically and sexually violated (figure 2.2).

In the testimony of many survivors/victims, sexual violation marks the most vivid moment in their memories.[63] The question here is neither merely *showing* versus *not showing* nor a matter of the gender of directors (*Snowy Road* by a woman director, and *Spirits' Homecoming* by a man). It is how a mode of address may close off diverse perspectives on and receptions of the matter. Such moments in *Spirits' Homecoming* may be of much shorter duration and less voyeuristic than those in a previously released film, *Mommy's Name Was Josenpi* (*Emi ireumeun josenpiyeotda*, Ji Yong-ho, 1991), one third of which repeatedly shows the violation of female victims. In the latter, the naked, vulnerable female bodies (during and before their work) are scanned through tracking or panning shots.[64] In both films, female victims are

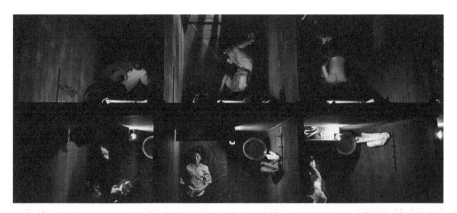

Figure 2.2 An overhead shot of the station (*Spirits' Homecoming*, Cho Jung-rae, 2016).

humiliated by being stripped naked when they violate the regulations by, for instance, attempting to escape: depicting these punishments on-screen may constitute further humiliation of the subjects by making them the objects of display. This manner of rendering sexual crimes risks audiences merely, as Kim puts it, "seeing and looking" instead of "recognizing, identifying, knowing, acknowledging and accepting."[65]

Even if the scenes examined are not framed as voyeuristic through the male gaze, some scenes are more directly aligned with a male perspective. In the medical examination sequence after Jeong-min has her first period, the Japanese doctor stares at her bottom, framed between her wide-open legs. The rendition of atrocity certainly becomes a spectacle, as in the sequence in which Japanese soldiers take several of the girls and women to be murdered; they are unable to work at the station due to sexually transmitted diseases or deteriorating health. They are executed from behind and pushed into a large hole atop a pile of other females, already dead. A Japanese official throws, *in slow motion*, a cigarette butt to ignite the corpses; the shot of bodies in the flames is held rather too long.

Aaron's distinction is relevant here: the question concerns how to avoid the "dead-already-ness" of victims being absorbed into the "to-be-dead" narrative strategy. If "dead-already" underscores both historical and individual conditions, while the "to-be-dead" refers to the prevailing narrative logic and aesthetics in the Korean film industry as well as in Hollywood, the Korean film cycle about late colonial subjectivity shows contrasting ways to delineate their relationship. In *Snowy Road*, although the physical wounds left on the face and battered body allude to the severe conditions of coerced sexual labor, the actual act is signaled indirectly through the allocation of rooms to the soldiers queued and the accumulation of paper stamps left in exchange for sex.

The consequences and ordeals that the girls/women endure are manifested only through their various daily routines—taking medications to avoid pregnancy, cleaning rooms, and washing prophylactics—and their symptoms, the visual signs of sexually transmitted diseases.[66] In *Snowy Road*, the ethics of not showing replaces the aesthetics of possible revelation of colonial subjectivities in *Spirits' Homecoming*.

Interestingly, however, *Snowy Road* unsettles the spectator by setting up a false climax/epiphany, with an opening dream sequence that shows Jong-bun and Yeong-ae on a frozen lake. Starting with first the sound, then the sight, of Jong-bun running through the snowy forests, the camera then cuts to show Yeong-ae walking on, then falling into, the icy lake—a mise-en-scène frequently used in Korean cinema to signal a female character's will to end her life. The frontal camera captures the blank stare of Yeong-ae, presents her as a character with a tragic end ("to-be-dead"), and addresses the spectator. The spectator's expectation is violated, however, when the film later returns to that very site: the apparent "to-be-dead" moment in the beginning of the film is not merely a revelation of the "what" but underscores the unending state of "dead-already" under colonial rule—Yeong-ae's attempted suicide as she has found herself to be pregnant and forced to abort. When the sequence is repeated the second time halfway through the film, a moment omitted in the opening sequence is restored: Yeong-ae breaks the ice on the lake. The camera follows both of the girls, then pans to locate Yeong-ae on the lake. A flashy camera movement around where Yeong-ae stands renders her more conventional. This is in keeping with the cinematic aestheticization of female suicide, with characters often taking their lives by drowning, as in the suicide sequence in *Untold Scandal* (*Joseonnamnyeosangyeoljisa*, Lee Je-yong [a.k.a. E-J Yong], 2003); the Lady Jeong drowns herself after having learned that her lover, Jo-won, has not indeed betrayed her despite his nonchalant declaration that he no longer loves her. Yeong-ae's action of throwing a rock to break the ice is repeated. Only the first time when the act is shown, Yeong-ae is seen picking up the rock; in subsequent attempts, her picking it up is omitted. Her desire to end her life is foregrounded rather than her subsequent actions required to break the ice or the consequences with which she or others would have to live afterward. When Yeong-ae lifts a rock and throws it over her head into the lake a final time to break the ice, the camera circles around her. The rock falls and the cracking of the ice is aestheticized *in slow motion*, aestheticizing her tragedy for the spectator. Once Jong-bun arrives on the lake, the scene repeats the end of the opening sequence, also adding what was first left off: Jong-bun's rescue of Yeong-ae and their subsequent capture by Japanese soldiers.

Both films diverge in their portrayal of how the survivors' trauma is transmitted. In *Snowy Road*, Jong-bun, in the present, interacts with the apparition of young Yeong-ae as a sign of her ongoing suffering and guilt of traumatic past; while Jong-bun's relationship with the neighborhood girl Eun-su marks a process of slow recovery and camaraderie that she needs. In contrast, Eun-gyeong's character in *Spirits' Homecoming* is purely instrumental for transmitting the past trauma of Yeong-ok/nation, while her own trauma is silenced. After Jeong-min has collapsed in the process of being beaten and abused by the Japanese official on her arrival, slow motion is used to show her being carried along a corridor, slung on the shoulder of a soldier. This may indicate Jeong-min's half-conscious state, but after a cut back to the present-day timeline, Jeong-min's state is embodied by Eun-gyeong. Wearing a Korean traditional costume, *hanbok*, Eun-gyeong finds herself walking down the same corridor; when she opens the door of an empty cell, the shot is followed by several cutaways of girls, now alone, presumably, after soldiers have left the cells. The relay between Jeong-min and Eun-gyeong, or the latter's reliving of the former's experience throughout the film, can be seen as erasing the specificities of their traumas; they are victims of different types of sexual violence.

If a glimpse into, or recovery from, trauma at the individual or national level can be achieved (as the psychoanalytic approach assumes) only through the encounter with the Other (the unrepresentable) via traces and remnants, or (as the cultural nationalists delineate) by inventing a national psyche that will secure its own collectivity, the historicity of trauma is either permanently absent or reduced to a handful of visible traces and devices at the expense of historical complexity and subject positionality. The observation of Katherine Isobel Baxter applies to both psychoanalytic and culturalist approaches: "[Psychoanalysis and European trauma literature's] prescription potentially closes off other modes of presenting trauma, a limitation which can be as problematic as the limited assumptions . . . about how trauma manifests itself."[67] Complex historical conditions and relations would be bracketed and buried; also to be curtailed is the nationalistic ideology that discourages or favors particular types of representation and resolution of trauma, foreclosing a range of diverse ways to address and overcome individual traumas. Lloyd also underscores the need to focus on "living on rather than recovery" that should guide critiques of colonial modernity and ground the aesthetic and political commitment of post-colonial work.[68]

My analysis of *Snowy Road* in the remaining pages of this chapter is very much in conversation with the feminist scholarship on cinematic girls, but I wish now to shift my focus to the girl as the "writing subject"—a trope that

I have employed in analyzing *The Silenced* earlier in the chapter. I turn therefore to examine Jong-bun, one of the two girl protagonists in *Snowy Road*, as the writing subject, initially illiterate but able to write by the film's closing. This offers an alternative way of analyzing the trope/image of girl, beyond merely one whose figure embodies the national trauma and damaged consciousness.

As interviews with Korean wartime survivors indicate, various forms of post-traumatic distress and disorder haunt them long after the end of the war. In her study of survivors, Yang emphasizes that the damage to social relationships is as important as the physical and psychological wounds that remain.[69] According to a 2001 survey, over 50 percent of wartime sexual slaves had been married after their wartime experience, while 34 percent remained unmarried.[70] But a marriage could easily be terminated after the wartime experience was revealed to a spouse or spouse's family. Pregnancy was often impossible or complicated as many had suffered from sexually transmitted diseases in the past.[71] Silence or pauses in their testimonies, Yang claims, are signs of trauma, often accompanied with their inability to adequately articulate the experience.

Jong-bun is a survivor, whose present environment visually recalls the past. Her small flat looks like the cell in which she had to work as a sexual slave. The iron frames of the security grill on her window separate her space from the outside, and the sunlight does not easily enter her semi-basement apartment. Early on in the film, Jong-bun is presented as a "writing" subject, marking a lineage with *The Silenced*, *A Werewolf Boy*, and to *Snowy Road* (and later, *I Can Speak*). After the initial flashback to the lake, which is framed as Jong-bun's dream, Jong-bun visits the local council to complete a form. She is nominated as a bereaved family member of a national patriot: Yeong-ae's deceased father, who passed away during the colonial period, working for the nation's independence. A close-up of Jong-bun's rugged hand shows her writing "Choe (a.s.a. Choi)" as her family name, then quickly scratching it out. She asks for a new form, but a female civil servant offers to complete the form on her behalf; identifying Jong-bun as "Gang Yeong-ae (a.s.a. Kang Yong-ae)." Her writing, although only one syllable here, reflects her inability to reveal herself, a form of silence that withholds the truth from the public. Later we learn that on her return to her hometown, after her escape from the military base, Jong-bun took on Yeong-ae's identity in order to receive government subsidies.

The class difference between Jong-bun and Yeong-ae is at first an obstacle to their friendship; Yeong-ae initially and continually distances herself from Jong-bun and disapproves of any romantic possibility between her brother and Jong-bun.[72] Yeong-ae is a daughter of a wealthy family who attends the local school, speaks Japanese, and aspires to become a teacher after completing a college degree in Japan. In contrast, Jong-bun's mother is a poor seamstress—a kind yet patriarchal mother—who claims that the family could afford to educate only Jong-bun's younger brother, as he is the male heir of the family.

The kindness of Yeong-ae's brother's—Yeong-ju—takes various forms, including giving Jong-bun a Korean translation of *A Little Princess* (Frances Hodgson Burnett, 1905).[73] As she is illiterate, Jong-bun is unable to read the title of the novel; the sequence in which she learns the title from an old man is telling, signaling the impossibility of girlhood for the working class under the patriarchy. In a long shot, Jong-bun walks toward the old man, who is holding a Korean traditional smoking pipe. His look and posture are emulated by Jong-bun, who sits next to him with her legs folded like a man (rather than kneeling, as expected of girls). The visual parallel between the two becomes more pronounced as the camera cuts to a profile shot of Jong-bun, who is holding a tree branch like a pipe. The previous scene, in which Jong-bun reluctantly accepts her mother's decision not to let her attend school, is in contrast chimes with her emulation of the old man's posture—a sign of her internalizing the patriarchy imposed. The old man glances over the book cover, which reads "sogongnyeo" in sino characters, the meaning of which Jong-bun does not understand; he repeats the title aloud, but translates it as pretty princess, "gongju." The over-the-shoulder shot of the book cover shows a girl with a pink ribbon around her hair (figure 2.3). Jong-bun's colonial aspiration toward modern girlhood remains an unattainable dream, given her class status and role under the patriarchy.

Sogongnyeo, which is also the Korean title of the film *Microhabitat* (*Sogongnyeo*, Jeon Go-woon, 2017) discussed in Chapter 4, plays another pivotal role in redefining the relationship between Jong-bun and Yeong-ae. After Yeong-ae has been forced to abort her pregnancy, she attempts to end her life on the icy lake glimpsed in the opening dream sequence as discussed previously. She fails and is brought back to the camp. As they are not allowed to talk through the wall, the two girls communicate by knocking on the wall; silenced and prevented from speaking in Korean (a language the Japanese guards don't understand), the sound of their tapping on the wall replaces their voices. Unrealistically, perhaps, Jong-bun is able to keep the copy of *A Little Princess* throughout her journey to China. She asks Yeong-ae to teach her how to read. This signals Yeong-ae's reciprocation of Jong-bun and others' compassion at the military base, who have softened the food, making it easier for Yeong-ae to chew, as her health was in poor condition due to abortion. The sequence in question follows shortly after Yeong-ae's apparition in the present, appreciating Jong-bun's sympathy in the past. The small individual cell where girls are forced to provide sexual labor turns momentarily into a private space of their

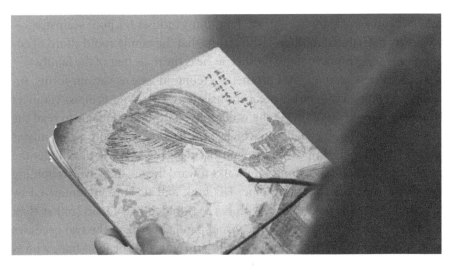

Figure 2.3 Jong-bun looks over the cover of *A Little Princess* (*Snowy Road*, Lee Na-jeong, 2015).

own, like an attic in girls' literature. The camera slowly zooms in on Yeong-ae and Jong-bun, sitting against the wall. As it passes the table on the right-hand side of the frame, the viewer sees towels, a small bottle of medicine, and a tin bucket for soldiers' receipts. In the space created, they momentarily regain their voices. Voices here are not to be publicly heard, but shared only between the two, like the unending conversation between Jong-bun and Yeong-ae's apparition in the present. Yeong-ae's reading marks the beginning of her understanding of Jong-bun's compassion, who has constantly looked after Yeong-ae and helps her regain her health after the abortion.[74]

The paring of girls is a common trope in girls' literature and drawings.[75] The shot of Yeong-ae holding the book (figure 2.4) mirrors a previous shot of Jong-bun (figure 2.3), albeit with a slightly different shot composition. To the eyes of Jong-bun, Yeong-ae still embodies the girlhood to which she aspires. Compared to the earlier shot of Jong-bun, the parallel between Yeong-ae and the figure on the book cover is more foregrounded, underscoring the girly look—an "empty, dreamy gaze." Jong-bun points out the similar facial features of Yeong-ae and her brother Yeong-ju, claiming that she likes their dreamy (*aryeonhan*) look. Yet Yeong-ae's ego has not disappeared and she still disapproves of Jong-bun's romantic longing for Yeong-ju.

The war against Japan wanes, and the military is ordered to desert the base, erasing traces of its existence. The girls are ordered to put on nurse uniforms to disguise themselves as members of the Labour Service Corp. Yeong-ae picks up her own photo (figure 2.5), an act that foreshadows her own

Figure 2.4 Over-the-shoulder shot of Yeong-ae, which mirrors that of Jong-bun earlier in the film (*Snowy Road*, 2015).

Figure 2.5 Yeong-ae, who poses as a volunteer to work in the Labor Corps, glances at herself in a photograph (*Snowy Road*, 2015).

death—a moment of what Roland Barthes calls punctum, when a photograph interrupts and disrupts one's reading of surface image.[76] She murmurs the inscription at the bottom of the photo, the "Nurse Labour Service Corp." Earlier in the film, Yeong-ae was seen marching on the street of her hometown, while leading a group of girls with the banner that reads "Women Labour Service

Corp" across their bodies, declaring that they would sacrifice and serve for the sake of Japan's victory. Similar to the moment in *The Silenced*, when Ju-ran spots herself smiling in the recorded film, Yeong-ae's disguised identity as a nurse in the photo overlaps with the colonial subjectivity: a moment of self-recognition as the colonial subject. Yeong-ae is both present and absent in that photo; she was physically present when the photo was taken, but her apparent identity as a member of "Labour Service Corp" is a disguise—a mask. The mixed temporality of her photograph signals the condition of her as a colonial subject—"dead already."

The photo is handed over to Jong-bun at the moment of Yeong-ae's death during their escape from the base. Jong-bun's relationship to this photo is not exactly what Marianne Hirsch calls "post-memory"—the memory of a generation who are removed from the actual holocaust memories of their parents, yet vicariously share in them through their deep personal connections. But this photograph fulfills the task of both visual evidence and post-memory; Jong-bun herself lived through the imperial exploitation of the military sexual slaves, of which the photograph is evidence. Yet, Jong-bun as a survivor takes up the role of both victim and one tasked with remembering, living the memory of Yeong-ae through their intertwined identities.[77] Later in the film, the same photograph is used by Jong-bun to commemorate Yeong-ae's death. Ironically, it is through Yeong-ae's death that they become "equal" friends, as it is only after having legally reported Yeong-ae's death that Jong-bun is able to regain her own self-identity, which was erased after the war.

The film finally grants Jong-bun's girlhood aspiration—a type of girlhood she was never allowed to enjoy. Jong-bun's continuous effort to locate Yeong-ju, the brother of Yeong-ae, receives an answer; she learns that he has been living in Japan since the end of the war. Jong-bun writes him a letter for the first time and includes it with her gift—a handknitted sweater she made. She addresses him as "brother (*oppa*)," as if she is still a girl. Jong-bun's trajectory as the writing subject completes not with her correction of the public record regarding herself and Yeong-ae, but with her personal writing: writing of a letter, which can be seen as a gesture that acknowledges her feelings for Yeong-ju when she was a young girl. The coda of the film enables Jong-bun to be able to finally reciprocate his kindness with her own warmth and compassion.

Coda: *I Can Speak*

The depiction of girls' subjectivities under colonial rule ("dead-already") discussed in this chapter hardly escapes the cinematic logic of "to-be-dead" and necromanticism—many scenes of girls' deaths are disproportionately displayed and aestheticized at times. Death and its historical and cinematic remembering, however, should neither choose nor yield any particular aesthetics; they are very much constructed, made for the public, to be engaged in complex ways. The girls examined in this chapter as colonial subjects are acutely aware of the limitations imposed on themselves—their bodies, their sense of belonging, and even their longings. In the cycle of films dealing with military sexual slavery, the wartime atrocity informs both their past and present. But if, as Lloyd reminds us, what is at stake in post-colonial aesthetics is "living on rather than recovery," the films discussed in the chapter offer different outlooks on both the past and the present, and on the extent to which the colonial subjects' "dead-already-ness" continues to control their present. The acts of remembering and writing not only grant them a limited agency but also invoke a desire to further express and speak.

In *I Can Speak*, the female protagonist Ok-bun (played by Na Moon-hee, *Miss Granny*, discussed in chapter 4) is initially represented as a cranky old lady, who frequently visits the local town office to file endless complaints about the problems in her neighborhood. She becomes acquainted with a civil servant, Min-jae, and begins to learn English. But her reason for learning to speak in English is revealed two-thirds of the way through the film: in front of a number of US senators, she testifies in English on behalf of her dear friend from the war period, who had been an activist around the issue of military sexual slavery but is now suffering from dementia. Ok-bun (a.s.a. Ok-boon) desires to speak, a desire that is finally answered. An opportunity to speak is not automatically granted but is earned through overcoming not only her trauma but also a long silencing by her family and the state. In one scene, Ok-bun visits the site where her parents were buried and laments how she could have opened herself to the public in the past, when her very family rejected her upon her return. From her compilation of the apparently trivial and unnoticed violations of laws in her neighborhood, to the historical atrocity about which she ultimately testifies, her incessant desire to record, and finally to speak, is a process of overcoming the "dead already-ness" and embracing the urge to "live on," with the national becoming part of her every day, not the other way around.

3
Death of a Girl

Necro-cinematics and Bong Joon Ho's Girl Trilogy

In the Korean crime film, *The Gangster, the Cop, the Devil* (*Akinjeon*, Lee Won-tae, 2019; *The Gangster* hereafter), one of the major premises regarding the villain K, a serial killer, is that his victims tend to be mostly men, physically stronger than he is. To catch K, the cop Jeong Tae-seok (also spelled as a.s.a. Jung, played by Kim Moo-yeol) teams up with a crime boss, Jang Dong-su (a.s.a. Dong-soo, played by Ma Dong-seok, also known as Don Lee). Jang, who was stabbed earlier in the film by the serial killer, is the only victim to have survived an attack by K; and he is also the only witness who can identify the serial killer. K constantly outwits both Jang and the cop Jeong, taunting them by leaving evidence to show that he has been in their vicinity but escaped. K further provokes Jang by killing a schoolgirl with whom Jang has recently become acquainted; Jang gives the girl his own umbrella when the two meet at a bus stop in the pouring rain. The earlier postulation about K's victimology is violated to advance the film narrative, bringing about its climax by requiring Jang to seek revenge both for his own injuries and for the subsequent death of his loyal subordinate O-seong [a.s.a. Oh-sung].

Death of a girl has been depicted as a form of resistance, as in the novella *Death of a Girl* (*Eoneu sonyeoui sa*, 1920) by woman writer-turned-monk, Kim Il-yeop, and the image of the girl is constantly subject to the depiction and remembrance of national development and post-colonial traumas—from the 1970s girls examined in Chapter 1 to the girl victims of sexual coercion during World War II as discussed in Chapter 2. The victimhood further extends to the political trauma, like the unnamed girl in *A Petal* (*Kkotnip*, Jang Sun-woo, 1996), which is one of the first cinematic depictions of the 1980 Gwangju democratic movement; and to the social "memory" of the Hwaseong serial killing (1986–1991), cinematically rendered in *Memories of Murder* (*Salinui chueok*, Bong Joon-ho, 2003). The girl's death in *The Gangster*, in contrast, is tangential to the main character, Jang, and barely serves a narrative purpose other than gesturing toward the protagonist's relative moral position (compared to

Forever Girls. Jinhee Choi, Oxford University Press. © Oxford University Press 2025.
DOI: 10.1093/9780197685822.003.0004

the main villain K, he is the lesser evil) and reinforcing the actor Ma's star persona.[1]

In this chapter, I examine the image of death associated with girl victims of sexual violence and crimes: to what extent their deaths have become a prevalent trope and are merely instrumental in advancing the narrative in contemporary Korean cinema. Necro-cinematics is required here to understand how death functions in its narrative and aesthetic construction. In this chapter, in addition to the afore-mentioned scene from *The Gangster*, I consider Bong's *Memories of Murder* and *Mother* (*Madeo*, Bong Joon-ho, 2009) and his unofficial "girl trilogy"—The *Host* (*Goemul*, 2006), *Snowpiercer* (2013), and *Okja* (2017)—as major case studies. Does Bong allow girls' agency only with the implication of sexual violence inflicted or motherhood assumed? I end the chapter with a discussion of *Poetry* (*Si*, Lee Chang-dong, 2010) and *Han Gong-ju* (Lee Su-jin, 2014) in order to seek an alternative aesthetic strategy: how a pairing of girl or "girly" protagonists (a narrative principle discussed in Chapter 2) and the spectator's sharing of a girl's sensibility could offer a glimpse—even vicariously—of their subjectivity.

Necro-cinematics

Films often begin with a girl's death or end with its revelation, in commercial as well as art-house or auteur cinema: to name a few, *Old Boy* (*Oldeu boi*, Park Chan-wook, 2003); *Mother, Poetry, The Neighbours* (*Iutsaram*, Kim Hwi, 2012); *After My Death* (*Joe manheun sonyeo*, Kim Ui-seok, 2017); *Second Life* (*Seon-huiwa Seul-gi*, Park Young-ju, 2018); and *Next Sohee* (*Daeum So-hui*, July Jung, 2023). The death or revenge of male characters in Korean crime and art cinema has been discussed in depth and even philosophized, yet the function of female victims has hardly been at the center of close analysis in the English-language scholarship on contemporary Korean cinema. The dominant reading strategy has been that of nationalizing and excusing male anxiety and incompetence, subsuming them under the South Korean history and specificity: a sign of national or post-colonial impasse.[2] Michele Aaron critiques the Western preoccupation with the imagery of death, in particular, female suicide. Under what she names "necromanticism," she focuses on the politics of death: how death functions within the "mortal economies" of commercial cinema.[3] In the context of South Korean cinema, necromanticism as gender ideology and necropolitics as the dictating socio-political conditions cannot neatly be mapped onto a divide between the aestheticized death versus the death registered in the post-colonial situations depicted. Necromanticism hovers over and above various modes of filmmaking: commercial, post-colonial, art, or independent cinema. As analyzed in Chapter 2, Yeong-ae's attempted suicide in *Snowy Road* (*Nungil*, Lee Na-jeong, 2015), with which the film begins and to which it returns, underscores her attempt to end with her death the coerced sexual labor during World War II. Yet the camera work aestheticizes her act, filming it similar to the Confucian custom of a virtuous woman's suicide after sexual violation. With the appearance of Jong-bun at the scene, halfway into the film, Yeong-ae's escape from the camp is viewed in a different light. Through the analysis of the bus stop scene in *The Gangster*, with which I started this chapter, and of a comparable scene from *Memories of Murder*, I will advance the necro-cinematics as a persistent narrative logic and an aesthetic strategy of contemporary Korean cinema: consistent with what Aaron characterizes as the mortal economies and their "capacity to dictate who may live and who must die."[4]

The bus stop scene in *The Gangster* strangely recalls or alludes to Bong's *Memories of Murder*, released more than fifteen years earlier. It condenses and displaces several motifs and tweaks the character relationship of *Memories of Murder*: the death of a girl; the killer (or suspect); and the rain and umbrella. After Jang lends his umbrella to the girl and she climbs into the bus, an attentive spectator would glimpse K already seated in its back row. The significance of the girl's death in *The Gangster* is minor compared to that in *Memories of Murder* and is even contradictory, given the established criminal patterns of K up to that point. When Jang learns of the girl's death through a television bulletin, the camerawork within the news footage zooms in to show the chequered umbrella that he lent her. Such an insert and camera work could be self-referential, as the scene is tied to the beginning of the entangled relationship between Jang and K; earlier in the film, K has attacked and attempted to kill Jang under an umbrella. The girl's acceptance of Jang's umbrella and her subsequent death are purely instrumental to stage a male rivalry that reaches its peak shortly after Jang's close subordinate, O-seong, is killed by K, when the two split to chase K in narrow alleys.

Bong's *Memories of Murder* follows the investigation of the Hwaseong serial killing that took place between 1986 and 1991. The last death of a girl depicted in the diegesis leads to a significant moral turning point for Detective Seo. Seo is from the capital, Seoul, and he volunteered to assist in the investigation of the serial killing in a provincial town, Hwaseong. His encounter and gradual acquaintance with two schoolgirls during the investigation lead to a crucial clue. Seo visits the girls' school to check a rumor circulated about the serial killer—that the killer appears in the outdoor toilet in the backyard. With the help of a school nurse, a survivor is found in the vicinity of the girls' school. The survivor's testimony helps to locate the third and last suspect in the film—Hyeon-gyu (a.s.a. Hyun-gyu), a factory worker. Seo falls asleep in his car while tailing Hyeon-gyu, who is on the bus and slides out of Seo's sight. In the penultimate crime scene, the killer's gaze oscillates between two possible targets as his next victim: the schoolgirl, who is heading back home, and the local detective Bak's (a.s.a. Park's) partner, Gwak (a.s.a. Kwok, played by late Jeon Mi-seon), who is on her way to visit a patient. The girl is killed while Seo is desperately searching for Hyeon-gyu.

In the film's climax (or as Joseph Jeon notes, "an anti-climax par excellence"), Seo transforms from a firm believer of rational scientific investigation relying on objective, material evidence to the emotionally deranged figure who confronts the suspect, Hyeon-gyu.[5] Such a change is indexed on the death of the schoolgirl, which was inspired by the real life incidence of the female victims of the Hwaseong serial killing, victims aged between thirteen and seventy-one.[6] But the chronology of the actual crime is re-ordered to anchor the climax around the death of the girl. The film's investigation of the murders ends in 1987, which, Jeon claims, coincides with the end of Chun Doo-hwan's military dictatorship.[7] Yet the real teenage victim, after whom the film's girl character must have been modeled, was murdered in 1990 after the film's investigation plot has come to a close; similar to the film's depiction, her body was damaged by the killer with her own stationery items and belongings.[8]

Throughout the film, the spectator has been denied a view of the killer's sexual violation of his victims, only seeing them either before or after. As the film nears its climax, the crucial verbal testimony by the female survivor, who has been hiding in a shabby house behind the girls' school, is accompanied by a brief flashback; her face is covered with her own underwear, which is identified as the repeated pattern the killer uses. She also recalls that the killer's hands were soft. With the girl victim, however, Bong shows the actual crime scene: the killer carries on his shoulder the girl, dressed only in her underwear, with her hands and feet tied together in the back like a hunted animal. The camera focuses on the killer taking out her personal belongings, followed by a rack focus shot of his hand placing them on the ground one by one—a pencil knife, a pen, and a fork. The focus shifts from the girl's belongings lined up in the foreground to the girl's face in the mid-ground. After a few cut-away shots to show Seo, still searching for Hyeon-gyu during the town's night fire drill, the camera returns to the murder scene: the girl's fear is even more palpable with the killer's flashlight pointing at her face. When she looks up to see the killer's face, the film cuts to show Seo instead from a low angle, replacing the perpetrator with the failed detective. The girl's death becomes even more disturbing when another shot is added; as the killer pushes the girl's head to the ground, her bound legs shake a little, indicating her losing consciousness or death, reminiscent of the helpless rabbit that shakes its body when it is shot to death during the hunting scene of *The Rules of the Game* (*La regle du jeu*, Jean Renoir, 1939). If not to the extent that *The Gangster* makes the girl's death perfunctory, Bong nonetheless instrumentalizes the girl's death to stage the final, male confrontation.

The "suspenseful" depiction of the girl's death is in sharp contrast to the accidental death of the first suspect/witness, Gwang-ho (a.s.a. Kwang-ho), who is the mentally challenged son of a restaurant owner. If the torture of male suspects has been detailed in the film's social criticism, repeatedly presenting them as victims of incompetent police investigation (and the false signs of masculinity fostered under several decades of military dictatorships between 1961 and 1987), Gwang-ho's death is immediate, excusing male deaths as victims of "an encroaching modernity."[9] Realizing that Gwang-ho's earlier testimony must have been as a witness, local detective Bak (played by Song Kang-ho) follows him in order to have him testify and possibly identify the killer. But Gwang-ho is hit by a moving train and killed immediately. The use of the train as a sign of modernity, a cliché, is repeated in the final confrontation between Seo and Hyeon-gyu; the darkened tunnel into which Hyeon-gyu escapes functions as a sign of unknowability. The moral deliberation quickly dissipates; Seo's hope to arrest Hyeon-gyu as the killer is shattered with the arrival of the DNA test result that disproves his identification. The failure of the investigation is quickly replaced with, and deemed as, the "epistemological uncertainty" of Korean modernity—as Hyeon-gyu escapes into the dark tunnel with no evidence to be convicted—substituting individual victimhood for national tragedy.[10] It is interesting to note that the 2019 capture of the real killer, Lee Chun-jae, happened by accident, while the police were searching for a DNA match to a different crime.[11] Lee had already been serving a sentence since 2014 for different crimes he committed after the Hwaseong killing. He finally acknowledged and admitted his past crime. When asked why he killed the thirteen-year-old girl, he answered that he "didn't have a reason" and said that it "was an impulsive act."[12]

Memories of Murder has been praised for its gesture toward filmmaking as a historiographic endeavor and its self-reflexivity onto its own genre: a cinematic re-telling of the serial killing as a form of historiography and its unsatisfactory closure to the investigation that initially begins the film. Nonetheless, discussion of gender is rarely part of the existing English language scholarship on Bong. Among Bong's oeuvre, *Mother* is one of the few films where the question of gender is foregrounded, yet motherhood is again contextualized as a gender trait within a larger social issue in Korea. Ji-yoon An approaches Bong's *Mother* as exemplary of the recent trend of "mother thrillers," while Nam Lee considers the film through the lens of Bong's authorship, but both see the depiction of motherhood as indicative of larger societal gender inequalities and absurdities. Lee notes that the film "questions the traditional virtue of sacrificial motherhood in the context of the twenty-first century social conditions."[13] The mother's excessively protective behavior toward her mentally challenged son is contradictory and even hysterical, yet it is portrayed as "understandable."[14] Neither author, however, notes the death of the girl, A-jeong (a.s.a. Ah-jeong), that anchors the narrative.

As a supporting character in the film, Jin-tae remarks that the girl's dead body was on "display for the townspeople to see" as if it were on a "clothesline" (figure 3.1). A-jeong's dead body may not be a spectacle, but the crime itself is. When the crime scene is re-enacted by the mentally challenged son, Do-jun (a.s.a. Do-joon, played by Won Bin), with a dummy, neighbors gather to fill the alleyways. It is an ironic visual allusion to the dialectic montage of *Battleship Potempkin* (*Bronenosets Potemkin*, Sergei Eisenstein, 1925) when townspeople gather to the shore to greet the arrival of the ship; in *Mother*, the scene accentuates the villagers' complicity rather than their foreseeable victimhood as in Eisenstein's film. During the re-enactment, the dummy's head falls repeatedly like a heavy rock—a rock that we later learn was thrown by Do-jun and instantly killed the girl.

Throughout the film, the crime scene is glimpsed bit by bit both to mirror Do-jun's fragmented memory and to provide cues that help the mother to arrive at the truth. The entire crime scene is shown through the perspective of a witness—the old man, who owns a junkyard. He waits for A-jeong to turn

Figure 3.1 A-jeong's dead body is on display (*Mother*, Bong Joon-ho, 2009).

up in an abandoned house for sex, in exchange for a bag of rice. The camera is located inside the house, to signal the perspective of the witness; Do-jun and A-jeong are framed through two apertures, divided by the rectangular window frame. As A-jeong cries out that she is sick of men and calls Do-jun an "idiot," he picks up the huge rock to throw back at her—the very rock which she initially used to intimidate and prevent Do-jun from following her. It hits her head and she collapses. Her immediate death shocks the spectator and momentarily suspends their sympathy for her.

In the crime scene, male perpetrators are either absent or obscured. Once the perspective is established as that of the old man, he remains off-screen. Do-jun's face is shown through an aperture—the dusty broken glass—while A-jeong is presented more clearly through another aperture on the right. Both Do-jun's manslaughter and his subsequent dragging of A-jeong's feet as he moves her body to the rooftop, is shown through the window, with the camera located inside the house. The perpetrator here is not unknowable, like the serial killer in *Memories of Murder*, but in this case is the town's complicity, which exploits A-jeong and drives her to death. She can find no safety either inside, where the old man awaits her, or outside, where she is stalked, killed, and then "displayed" for the town to witness.

The film, as the authors above suggest, points to the survival and protection of the marginal *at the expense of* the even more vulnerable; a similar rhetoric is found in Bong's other works, including *Parasite* (*Gisaengchung*, 2019).[15] Yet, as An notes, the mother has been portrayed empathetically.[16] In this role, Bong has cast Kim Hye-ja, one of Korea's most beloved actresses, who has played the role of mother in numerous television series. The spectator's sympathy for the mother is premised on, as An observes, the film's "condemning depiction of a society that is repeatedly represented as masculine."[17] Initially, the familial relationship of the mother and son replicates the exclusivity of the patriarchal legal system, from which the weaker are excluded—such as A-jeong and another mentally challenged boy, Jong-pal, who at the film's end is imprisoned instead of Do-jun. Maternal or familial protection is constantly signaled by the use of doorframes. When Do-jun returns home after he is released from the police station for his vandalism of a Mercedes, the mother and son are framed inside the door frame of her herbal shop, as if she could provide him with a modicum of protection, even if only temporarily. The mother's protection of her son is not foolproof, however, but feeble and constantly susceptible to the external; the sounds from the outside (wind and rain) repeatedly infiltrate the interior space of the mother's shop or of Jin-tae's little hut, where she searches for evidence to save her son. The door, although within the sub-genre of Hollywood paranoia films, claims Mary Ann Doane, "is yet another surface which separates one space from another, activating the dialectic of concealing and revealing."[18]

The film's irony is that it leaves the actions of both the mother and Do-jun excused, if not justified. As in the Hollywood melodrama, the paranoiac investigation of *Mother*'s female lead is only directed at herself.[19] The mother, in disarray, dances in the open field after her murder of the old man in the junk yard, connecting the beginning and ending of the film in full circle to reframe and redirect the film's trajectory as that of the mother's own murder to save her son. A-jeong's grandmother, who suffers from dementia, acts like an abusive father, drunk and selfish, as seen in many Korean gangster films and melodramas. A-jeong's death is displaced onto the overly protective yet self-regarding mother, who in the end replicates, if not reinforces, the patriarchy by "extremising its very same principles."[20]

The two accidental deaths, that of A-jeong by Do-jun and that of the old man by the mother, remove the moral deliberations of either Do-jun or the mother, with no proper mourning of A-jeong's death or that of the old man. In an earlier scene at the funeral of A-jeong, the mother confronts the girl's family, declaring that Do-jun is innocent. Even after realizing that Do-jun is responsible for the girl's death, the mother visits Jong-pal instead. The mother and Jong-pal are framed through endless apertures and seated in the far background, further removed from the front room where we have, in several earlier scenes, seen Do-jun talking to his mother. The shared victimhood of Do-jun and Jong-pal is in focus over the victimhood of A-jeong. Judith Butler underscores the lack of grieving as a marker of the underprivileged: "As we think about the prevailing and differential ways that populations are valued and disvalued, protected and abandoned, we come up against forms of power that establish the unequal worth of lives by establishing their unequal grievability."[21] The death of A-jeong would dissipate between the mother's "forgetting and amnesia"—the mother's effort to "physically erase [her] own wrongdoing" in her trance-like dance.[22]

Necro-cinematics here may intersect with both Aaron's characterization of necromanticism—"the erotic allure of the to-be-dead girl"—and of the necropolitical conditions that determine the narrative outcomes of characters—"dead-already-ness" under occupied territories.[23] I have foregrounded necro-cinematics as one of the prominent cinematic governing principles of South Korean cinema, under which death becomes increasingly instrumental. In her examination of neo-liberal governance, Wendy Brown defines governance as a mode: "a domain of strategies, techniques, and procedures through which different forces and groups attempt to render their program *operable*" (my italics).[24] Brown notes, "Governance focuses on tools

88 Forever Girls

and instruments for achieving ends, rather than preoccupation with specific agencies or programs through which purposes are pursued."[25] If her observation on governance is deemed to be transferrable to cinematic strategies, with which this chapter is concerned, the question should be reoriented to what is achieved *at the expense of* cinematic death and amnesia in the South Korean context: a patriarchal hierarchy destabilized momentarily, excused, and reinstated through the sacrifice imposed on the even more vulnerable; in particular, girls at the bottom of the tier. They function as a means to level the male moral agency otherwise latent up to that point.

Bong's Girl Trilogy

Bong's authorship has been repeatedly contextualized within the nexus of global and local: Bong adopts Hollywood generic conventions to register and explore the specificity of Korea as a nation-state, and his meticulous mise-en-scéne as a director is underscored by his nickname, Bong-tail (as in de-tail).[26] Recent scholarship shifts its attention to the ecological and social significance of his work—the anthropocene or neoliberalism manifest in Bong's *Snowpiercer* and *Parasite*, respectively. The celebratory mood surrounding Bong's Palme d'Or win at the Cannes Film Festival; his Oscar win with *Parasite*; and the state of Korean cinema in general, prevents English-language authors from offering any in-depth interrogation of gender representation. As a personal anecdote, while watching *Parasite*, I was curious about the fate of the daughter Gi-jeong (a.s.a. Ki-jung, played by Park So-dam, *The Silenced*) in Gi-taek's family (a.s.a. Ki-taek, played by Song Kang-ho). As I expected, she faces a shocking, undeserved death.

The Korean-language scholarship on Bong's oeuvre, in contrast, pays closer attention to Bong's gender representation. Such authors as Chin Eun-kyung and Ann Sang-won approach the film *Okja* through the lens of eco-feminism; several journal articles touch upon motherhood in his films, including *The Host* and *Mother*.[27] My aim here is to bridge the two, opening up a conversation between the existing scholarship in and outside Korea, through the figure of the girl. I further raise the necro-cinematic mode as problematic through the analysis of the girl figure in Bong's (unofficial) girl trilogy—*The Host*, *Snowpiercer*, and *Okja*. Girls figure in each film as part of an ensemble cast or as the protagonist: Hyeon-seo, Yona (both characters played by Ko Asung), and Mi-ja (played by Ahn Seo-hyun) must voluntarily or involuntarily embrace the protective, "maternal" role throughout the film (*The Host* and *Okja*) or at the film's closure (*Snowpiercer*) for their companions—boys or

Death of a Girl   89

a fellow creature—in the absence of the mother. The sisterhood that concludes his fiction debut, *Barking Dogs Never Bite* (*Peurandaseuui gae*, 2000) has disappeared; only sexualized girlhood or desexualized womanhood remain.

One of the readings of Bong's *Snowpiercer* ingeniously approaches the narrative trajectory through the lens of Fanon or Virno's "exodus."[28] The irony prevails; authoritarian rule over the survivors on the last train on earth, designed and controlled by Wilford (played by Ed Harris), cannot be subverted through class struggle, unless one escapes the entire social system of the train. Although I shy away from such an allegorical reading of Bong's apocalyptical depiction of social stratification, this reading briefly mentions the stereotypical rendering of gender and ethnicity: "Tanya's black female body more inherently combat-ready than Yona's Asian female body"; the "film deploys familiar tropes about men protecting women and children."[29]

Yona's role in *Snowpiercer* is functional and tangential to the main plot. As a clairvoyant, she could warn and help the revolting crowd, led by Curtis (played by Chris Evans), in their progression toward the front section of the train where its "sacred" engine is located. Yet Yona's image constantly oscillates between that of a seventeen-year-old girl, and that of a child ("train baby," those who were born on the train and never led a life outside), eventually becoming a prospective maternal figure. A secret note hidden in a protein bar suggests that Curtis approach Namgoong (played by Song Kang-ho), a train engineer. Namgoong is locked in the prison section and can help the crowd move forward as he can close and open the gates that firmly divide the sections (classes) of the train. When he is taken out of a morgue-like cell in the prison section, he also informs the crowd that he would take his daughter Yona with him, both of whom are imprisoned due to their addiction to the substance called kronole. When Yona's cell is opened, she looks like an adolescent with her shaggy hair reaching her revealing shoulder. But soon she tugs her hair inside the black hood and is shortly introduced as a train-baby. Such an introduction immediately desexualizes her through a fetus-like image.

Yona joins the rebellion as a fellow traveler and "ironic observer" with her father.[30] On their way forward, she tries to attack the brutal and unbeatable bodyguard Franco the Elder (played by Vlad Ivanov) in the service section; she repeats her attack in the final shootout. In the first instance, Namgoong, her father, prevents her from fighting against Franco the Elder. When the guards are searching for them, Namgoong and Yona hide in an individual sauna cell, behind a woman who is enjoying the steam bath. As Namgoong struggles on top of, and against, Franco the Elder, Yona grabs the knife that Tanya has dropped—a material link between the two female characters and their roles. But Namgoong prevents her attack by holding and twisting her hand, forcing her to drop the knife. This conventional narrative of parental protection, however, is to stage male confrontation: Curtis picks up the knife and stabs Franco the Elder. Prior to this combat, when the train makes a sharp curvy turn, Franco the Elder fires an automatic machine gun at the rebellious crowd from afar. Yona dodges the bullets, but the subsequent shot-reverse shot between Franco the Elder and Curtis frames her as a bystander of the two parties: the ruling and the revolting, as well as the two representatives of Cold War ideology—a Russian bodyguard of the authoritarian, Wilford, against the Captain America (the Marvel Comics hero with whom Evans is associated) figure for the masses. Yona must step aside in order not to interfere with the male confrontation, while Curtis continues the mission to lead the revolt and to earn personal redemption. In the film's climax, shortly before Curtis is invited to meet Wilford, Curtis shares with Namgoong a long lamentation over a cigarette; during this, Yona is high on kronole and passes out. She literally stays out of the frame until Franco the Elder reappears. While Wilford tries to convince Curtis to take over his role to control and preserve the ecological balance as well as "humanity," Yona fires at Franco the Elder, disobeying her father's order not to; she defiantly says "no" this time. But she must soon follow her father's command to install the bomb against the gate to explode it, while leaving the final duel between the two male characters—Franco the Elder and Namgoong.

Curtis's cooperation with Namgoong's escape plan hinges on Yona's revelation of Tim, Tanya's little boy who has been taken away earlier in the film. Her clairvoyance leads them to the floor under which Tim manually replaces a broken part, working as part of the train engine. Yet her clairvoyant insight is as flimsy as her agency, working only intermittently; an addict as well as a daughter. Yona's knowledge serves to help Curtis's sacrifice and redemption; her obedience to Namgoong gives him a chance to save his daughter, which Gang-du (a.s.a. Gang-doo, also played by Song) failed to do in *The Host*. In both *The Host* and *Snowpiercer*, a daughter must die or sidestep to stage the ideological division and the final dual as a male rivalry.

There are striking similarities between *The Host* and *Okja*, not only through the prominence of girl characters and their relationship to non-human creatures (a monster and a super pig), but also through the exploration of urban space. The Mirando headquarter sequence in the latter film recalls the navigation of Uncle Nam-il (played by Park Hae-il) in the former when he sneaks into the telecommunication company where his college friend works and then successfully escapes when chased by the police; the Myeongdong arcade sequence in *Okja* resembles the scenes set in the underground sewage of *The Host*, in that both the female protagonist and the creature navigate (or are kept in) the underground. In both films, the use of vertical space around the bridge over the Han River visually counterbalances the horizontally organized chases in the sequences already mentioned. All these visual parallels and gender reversals deserve in-depth discussion, but I will focus on the girl protagonists' relationship with the non-human species, and the violation inflicted on the "gendered" body.

The antagonistic relationship between Hyeon-seo and the monster in *The Host* is reversed in *Okja*. The long opening sequence establishes the reciprocal relationship forged between Ok-ja (as a name in contrast to the film's title and to be consistent with how character names are spelled in the book) and Mi-ja. Their relationship could be seen as caring for each other rather than nurturing or protecting; as shown in the photo toward the end of the film, they grew up together like siblings. This kind of caring, reciprocal relationship is in contrast with the antagonistic relationship between Hyeon-seo and the monster (*geomul*) in *The Host*; Hyeon-seo must make a continuous effort to escape being devoured by the monster. Meera Lee observes that the monster in *The Host* is not merely a threat but in fact embodies both monstrosity and humanity—a creature that is an outcome of both external forces (the US army pouring toxins into the river, or neoliberalism more broadly) and a sign of the marginal (or underclass) that needs to steal (*seori*) in order to sustain itself (an act comparable to stealing of bus fares by bus conductors to compensate their low salary, discussed in Chapter 1).[31] Although the value and signification of both the monster and the urban space are foregrounded in Lee's analysis, gender representation is omitted in the process of discussing the family unit. According to Lee, Nam-ju (played by Bae Doona), who is Hyeon-seo's aunt, does not register the socio-political reality of the post-International Monetary Fund (post-IMF) South Korea as acutely as the male characters: Gang-du, Hyeon-seo's dad, is an inadequate son and father, while Nam-il, her uncle, represents the student activist generation that is disillusioned by the gap existing between their political ideals and neoliberal forces.[32] Regarding the only adult female character in the family, Nam-ju, Lee notes: "[Her] characteristics run counter to the rhythms of urban life through her slowness and hesitancy, which is quite ironic in light of her occupation as a professional athlete."[33] The female character is viewed here as obscure and subsidiary in both characterizing the family as a unit and the role she serves within it. Lee further notes, "*The Host* is particularly interesting in how it purposely excludes those once-emblematic female roles to embody the contemporary, postdemocratization and post-IMF subjectivities of Korean males and females in the metropolitan space of Seoul."[34]

I concur with Lee's observations on the ambiguity of the monster in the film, yet her exploration of gender dynamics within the family is undeveloped. Hyeon-seo voluntarily takes up a maternal role, protecting the little boy, Se-ju. As Lee Hee-seung notes, it is the grandfather, Hui-bong (a.s.a. Hee-bong, played by late Byun Hee-bong), and Hyeon-seo who manifest "maternal" traits.[35] Employing Julia Kristeva's notion of motherhood, Lee construes the motherhood manifest in *The Host* as a gender trait that is inclusive, embracing rather than rejecting the other. Lee further argues that in the ending of *The Host*, Gang-du inherits the maternal role from both Hui-bong and Hyeon-seo; Gang-du is transformed from the initial inadequate father to finally become the embracing mother figure.[36] Although I disagree with the significance of the final scene at the kiosk (to which I will return), the inclusive conception of motherhood regarding the self and other is still associated with the traditional, sacrificial Korean motherhood (or girlhood); both Hui-bong and Hyeon-seo are the characters that are sacrificed to protect the family during the chase of the monster (Hui-bong) and a boy from the monster's attack (Hyeon-seo). The two male characters (Gang-du and Se-ju), who benefited from the sacrifice of these two motherly characters, form a new family. In fact, Gang-du is responsible for the death of, and has risked the life of, Hui-bong and Hyeon-seo; it is Gang-du who exchanged his gun with his father's with the belief that his father's gun still had one bullet left (when in fact it was empty); and it is Gang-du who held the hand of another girl, instead of Hyeon-seo's, when they initially fled the monster's attack. The shot composition both of Hui-bong and of Hyeon-seo, whose safety was most severely affected by Gang-du's actions, are parallel at the moment of risking their lives, with Gang-du shown in shock.

Okja ends with a newly formed family eating around the table back in their mountain home, much as we have seen Gang-du and Se-ju inside the kiosk in *The Host*. Nonetheless, the spatial connotations seem to differ. In addition to Ok-ja, whom Mi-ja has rescued from the slaughterhouse, there is a super piglet, which they took on their way out. If Mi-ja has to this point performed a parental role in Ok-ja's rescue, now the two jointly accept the newly adopted role of mother figure to the piglet. A close analysis of the two endings helps to tease out the similarities and differences between the two scenes. Mi-ja is now wearing a light-colored costume (white shirt and beige skirt), in contrast to the purple athletic uniforms that she has worn throughout the film. Her once childish smile is now more subdued, although she is still smiling at Ok-ja's whisper; her childish liveliness and energy are replaced by her calm demeanor.

In an interview for the release of *Okja*, Bong claims that he envisions Mi-ja as a female counterpart of Conan, from the Japanese anime *Future Boy*

Conan (aired in Japan on NHK1978; in Korea on KBS 1982).[37] Yet the agency attributed to Mi-ja as a girl leaves her body battered, and Ok-ja can be rescued only through monetary exchange; the "adulthood" of both Mi-ja and Ok-ja is reached after their bodies are (sexually or otherwise) violated. As Kelly Oliver argues, even if "tough hunting girls prove themselves to be equal-opportunity killers, they continue to be beaten, battered, and assaulted" and rape is often part of the story of a girl's coming-of-age.[38] Although the film *Okja*'s opening sequence narrativizes the mating of pigs (as Lucy Mirando claims that the super pigs are the products of unforced, natural mating), in the meat industry artificial insemination is widely practiced. The forced mating between Ok-ja and the alpha male pig, Alfonzo, mostly takes place off-screen but is glimpsed through a small computer monitor that the Animal Liberation Front (ALF) members are watching. It is followed by a shot of Ok-ja with her body curled up, against which drunken Johnny Wilcox (played by Jake Gyllenhaal) leans— an all too familiar image of girls who are abused or even sold by an alcoholic father for sexual labor. As she tries to walk away from Johnny to find a place in the opposite side of the room, she falls. Ok-ja's body is repeatedly violated, first sexually and then as a commodity, when Johnny extracts meat samples out of Ok-ja's body.

In her analysis of *The Hunger Games* (2012), Oliver notes, "Like Hanna [in *Hanna*], Katniss is a virgin who has never been kissed. For both, the transition from the forest into the high-tech world parallels their violent transition from girlhood to womanhood."[39] Ok-ja's treatment in the lab and then the slaughterhouse is no exception, and the violence is occasioned by the male characters and their lies: first the grandfather, who misinforms Mi-ja that the family has bought Ok-ja from the company, and then by the ALF member K, who mistranslates Mi-ja's wish to go back to the mountain instead of heading to New York. When the ALF members unplug the computer monitor at the sight of Ok-ja's mistreatment, it is ironic that K's finger bleeds from the prick of torn wires. Oliver offers the reading of contemporary Hollywood cinema with active girl protagonists as the continuation of the rape theme in the tale of *Sleeping Beauty*. Girl characters in *The Hunger Games* (2012) or *Divergent* (2014) who are "self-sufficient" and "can take care of themselves" constantly face actual or near rapes.[40] I would not go so far as to read *Sleeping Beauty* as rape, but the fairy tale is evoked both by K's bleeding finger—the prick of a spindle—and the mocking reference to Mi-ja as "princess" when Mi-ja is eager to speak over the phone to Ok-ja in the lab. The film places multiple characters, Ok-ja, K, and Mi-ja, in an odd permutation and gender reversal of victim versus rescuer: the association of bleeding as the loss of virginity, is embodied by both K and Mi-ja. Entering adulthood may be inevitable, but

94 Forever Girls

the acceptance of motherhood seems unnecessary and forced; there is no in-between state between girlhood and motherhood. Not only is the transition from girlhood to womanhood a violent one in *Okja*, but girls' sexuality and reproductive capability are clearly presented as commodities that can be exchanged and purchased, as in *Mother* when a girl prostitutes herself in exchange for a bag of rice. Mi-ja can take Ok-ja back only through an exchange with Nancy (played by Tilda Swinton), the former CEO of the Mirando Company, trading her a pig-shaped gold figure that was given to Mi-ja by her grandfather, informing her that he saved it as a form of dowry.

Women, animal, and nature are conventional tropes that are often contrasted to civilization and its deplorable consequences; yet such an association is merely reinforced by imposing stereotypical gender constraints on girl characters. In his debut feature, *Barking Dogs Never Bite* (*Barking Dogs* hereafter), the exchangeability or association between animal and women characters has already been set up. The male lead Yun-je (played by Lee Sung-jae) kidnaps and kills a dog by dropping it from the rooftop: this is soon followed by the death of an old woman, who is its human companion. Yun-je's wife, Eun-sil, is advised to quit her job due to her pregnancy and the subsequent need for childcare, so she acquires her own puppy, which then goes missing. Finding it is a condition that Yun-je must meet, in exchange for which he may use his wife's compensation pay to bribe his way into a full-time college professorship.

The film *Okja*, unlike in *Barking Dogs* or *Snowpiercer*, does not end with the image of open space or nature; two leads, Ok-ja and Mi-ja, return to the forest but to the domestic space. Unlike in *Parasite*, where the patriarchy is re-established or at least fantasized by the male lead, the promise of domestic(ated) life that awaits both Mi-ja and Ok-ja is unclear. The "girls" are more tamed or mature than before, with Ok-ja excluded from the family, spatially, seen outside the house through the aperture of the window. *Okja* is certainly self-reflexive in the employment of a girl character and presentation of her agency. Bong emphasizes the merit of reversing the gender role.[41] As Lucy in the New York headquarters notes, the sentimental reunion between Ok-ja and Mi-ja at Times Square would attract and move the public (in the film) and the audience (outside the film): girlhood codified as innocent and nurturing self, functions as a commodity within the film's narrative. In fact, Bong's film itself packages girlhood as such. Chin and Ahn define the feminine traits manifest in *Okja* as "reproductivity, caring, tenderness, life and healing."[42] Nonetheless, the apparent reversal of gender norms seems to limit rather than de-limit character traits. Mentioned traits are attributed to the motherly as if girl characters should eventually embody them; otherwise, one becomes ruthless and unforgiving, like Lucy/Nancy—girly or bitchy.

Cinematic Mourning: Sharing of Girls' Sensibility

If the death of Hyeon-seo and the sedated state of Yona in Bong's Trilogy is to awaken and to enact the fatherhood, the death of a girl in *Poetry* brings two socially marginal characters together through their shared sensibility: the junior high school student Hui-jin [a.s.a. Hee-jin], and the elderly Mi-ja (played by late Yoon Jeong-hee). The narrative begins with some young children's discovery of a girl's dead body floating in the river, face down, and ends with partial repose for her soul through the recitation of a poem dedicated to her by the protagonist, Mi-ja. However, the death of the girl, Hui-jin, is less of a narrative kernel that advances the story than a structuring absence that triggers different reactions from the characters, including Mi-ja. Mi-ja's grandson, who is staying with her after his parents' divorce, is one of the six male students who have been involved in the sexual assault and rape of Hui-jin over the previous six months. The crime is not visualized but only referred to (and in fact too neatly summarized) by the parents of the male students, with Hui-jin's own experience very much tangential to both the students' and parents' unethical, crude reactions to her death. Only Mi-ja, who is struggling both financially and mentally (she is experiencing early symptoms of Alzheimer's disease), sympathizes with the dead girl. Unbeknownst to her, Mi-ja runs into Hui-jin's mother outside a hospital; the mother is distraught and desperate after having learned that her daughter has committed suicide. On her way home after enrolling in a poetry class, Mi-ja further stumbles upon a Mass at a Catholic church, dedicated to the death of Hui-jin. The mirroring of Mi-ja and Hui-jin is established as Mi-ja holds up the framed photograph of Hui-jin and puts it into her purse. Mi-ja still embodies a girly sensibility to a certain extent; as Mi-ja puts it, "I do like flowers and say odd things," and the disabled man, Mr. Gang (a.s.a. Kang), for whom Mi-ja is a paid carer, describes her as "chirpy (*jongaldaeda*)"—a similar wording "chirpy (*jaejaldaeda*)" employed by Ha Gil-jong to describe the female lead Baek-hwa (played by Moon Sook, *A Woman Like the Sun* [1974]) in Lee Man-hui's *The Road to Sampo* (1975).[43] Mi-ja embarks on pursuing her girlhood dream of becoming a poet. Hui-jin's paths are partially retrieved by Mi-ja, as she visits the science room, where the rape reportedly took place, and stops by the bridge, where Hui-jin is presumed to have jumped to end her life.

Mi-ja's reactions to the death of Hui-jin, due to her dementia, oscillate between naïve sentimentalism and deep sympathy. She finds poetic inspirations in the flowers outside a restaurant—inside, the parents of the other five boys discuss an out-of-court settlement—and yet sometimes cries uncontrollably at the thought of the girl's plight. The fact that Mi-ja agrees to do a sexual favor for Mr. Gang, who wishes "to be a man one last time before he dies," further establishes a parallel between Mi-ja and Hui-jin; Mi-ja, who is sixty-six, is yet still exposed to inappropriate sexual advances by a male. Ed Gonzales, writing for *Slant Magazine*, describes the act as "the sex, a rape of sorts," which places Mi-ja even closer to Hui-jin.[44]

"*Agnes' Song*," a poem that is dedicated by Mi-ja to Hui-jin at the end of the film, is a poetic conversation between Mi-ja and Hui-jin. It is Mi-ja's farewell to the dead girl whose spirit may be still hovering over the site of her death, and possibly a recognition of Mi-ja's own precarious, unstable life ahead. Nonetheless, the girl's subjectivity has never been accessible to anyone throughout the film, even to Mi-ja as a surrogate figure. As Mi-ja leans against the bridge to look down at the water underneath, her white hat flies off into the air then lands on the river—the lightness of a hat in contrast to the weighty dead body found on the river. Mi-ja is seen sitting by the riverside for poetic inspiration; she tries to take notes but is unable to write; only raindrops fill up the empty page. The poem can be seen as a cinematic atonement, offered by the filmmaker for both Mi-ja and Hui-jin, then from Mi-ja to Hui-jin, a clear leap or transcendence from Mi-ja's naïve sentimentalism, witnessed earlier in the film, to an aesthetic accomplishment. It is certainly a different aesthetic strategy from that found in *Mother* in relation to the victim, A-jeong; here we encounter a cinematic mourning of Hui-jin's death.

If *Poetry* spatially traces Hui-jin through the surrogate character Mi-ja, the film *Han Gong-ju* sonically registers the post-traumatic stress disorder (PTSD) of protagonist Gong-ju (played by Chun Woo-hee, *Sunny* [2011]) after she has become the victim of sexual violence. The film constantly juxtaposes the past with the present, initially thwarting but eventually leading to the revelation of a sexual crime inflicted on Gong-ju and her friend, Hwa-ok (played by Kim So-young). Jay Weissburg, in his review for *Variety*, finds such a narrative construction frustrating: "alternations between present and past, each transition providing only a modicum of information before the film jumps back again."[45] The constant juxtaposition of the present and the past indeed delays the full picture of the crime until the end of the film, yet to me it signals the inseparable entanglement of the two; how the present is experienced by Gong-ju as both the continuation of, as well as a possible rupture from, her traumatic past. The film's usage of sonic device as a key transition from the present to past subtly registers Gong-ju's fits and startles.

There is a certain similarity between *Poetry* and *Hang Gong-ju*, in the way that the girl victim is paired with a female adult character; in the latter, Ms. Jo (a.s.a. Cho), with whom Gong-ju stays after she is transferred to Incheon. Both Ms. Jo and Gong-ju are cast as outsiders: Ms. Jo had an affair with the police chief of a small branch in town, and Gong-ju had to be transferred as a result of the sexual assaults. Unlike in *Poetry*, the bonding (or tenuous solidarity) between Ms. Jo and Gong-ju is neither based on a girl's sensibility embodied by another character, such as Mi-ja in *Poetry*, nor extended to grief over Gong-ju's possible death. While their social circumstances bring the two closer (and in part Gong-ju's free labor offered at Ms. Jo's shop), it is Gong-ju's (and the film's) own sensibility that aids the filmic construction of the past. The film opens with Gong-ju's voice-over that whispers:

> If I draw out a tune in my mind . . . everything before me turns into notes. Then, the song begins. The sound of breathing, footsteps, the wind . . . even scratching metal sounds saying, "It's okay . . ." Then, for a moment, I forget the loneliness or sadness, [and fear].

The mode of her speech is rather ambiguous here, although it sounds as if she's talking to her peer rather than to a superior; there is another voice, the identity of which is never clearly identified in the film—possibly it is that of Eun-hui (a.s.a. Eun-hee, played by Jung In-sun, a little girl that Bak sees at the murder site in the last scene of *Memories of Murder*), a cheerful girl that she meets later when she is transferred to a new school. This voice answers, "Then, singing is like a religion to you, Gong-ju." As the film unfolds, Gong-ju's reaction to sound, however, betrays this initial confession; various sounds startle rather than console her; interestingly the subtitle of this opening dialog omits "fear."

In the sequence where Gong-ju follows her former homeroom teacher and visits schools to seek a possible transfer, subjective and objective sounds are juxtaposed, taking her in and out of her environment. After her transfer to a new school in Seoul has been denied, she travels to another school in Incheon. The prospect of acceptance appears to be promising with the principal's big laughs heard outside the office, with Gong-ju's gaze first glancing in the direction of the principal and the teacher, but then slowly moving to the trophies displayed in a glass cabinet. A clock's clicking noise is added to the soundtrack, as if Gong-ju builds layers of sound, swelling to a melody. But this moment of hope and tranquility is shattered when the noise of staple guns wakes Gong-ju out of her reverie. I am interested less in identifying the source and authenticity of sound used in this sequence—whether the music and the sound of the clock ticking and staple gun, are diegetic or non-diegetic sound, or subjective or objective—than in exploring how the film's aesthetic strategy emulates Gong-ju's musical sensibility (or more broadly her sensitivity to sound). More important, such use of a sound bridge underscores the weight of her past trauma that crushes her present and her temporary inner sanctuary. The staple sound is a reminder of her friend Dong-yun's being bullied by his peers; he would later, although involuntarily, become one of the perpetrators who sexually violate her.

Throughout the film, sound bridges often provide transition between cuts. These not only cue the spectator to the beginning of a flashback but further embody Gong-ju's PTSD. Once she is moved to Incheon, Gong-ju begins to learn to swim, for the reason that is later revealed in the film—she does not want to drown like her friend, Hwa-ok, but to float. One day she receives in the locker room a phone call from the father of Dong-yun. Startled, Gong-ju accidently traps her finger with a cabinet door, being dismayed and distraught, as she had not shared her new phone number with anyone other than her former teacher and her father. The film cuts to a similar accident in the past, where Gong-ju's finger had again been caught in a closing cabinet door. Gong-ju's finger being caught, shown in the present and past, underscores both a different sense of pain and a promise that was never fulfilled—that Dong-yun would like to see her performance in the future. When the film cuts back to the present, Gong-ju is in yet another space, gazing instead at the instruments in a music room at her school. She then performs alone with a guitar. Gong-ju's singing is appreciated not by Dong-yun but by her new peers at the school. Sound cues are repeatedly employed to mark the flashbacks to the sexual violation of Gong-ju in the past. Later in the film, the former homeroom teacher's voice asking Gong-ju, "How's your life in the new school?" slightly overlaps with the sound of the wind chime in Gong-ju's room in the past, where she was sexually violated.

In contrast, Gong-ju's imaginary interaction with her friend Hwa-ok often defies clear temporality of present or past, as in the way Hwa-ok is first introduced in the film after Gong-ju unpacks at the house of Ms. Jo and goes to the bathroom, or later in the classroom, as if they are facing each other. Such seamless editing and staging enable apparent interactions between Hwa-ok and Gong-ju across the past and present, merging different temporalities and emotions—a sign of both haunting and guilt. Both Hwa-ok and Gong-ju are victims of the same sexual crime, and yet they are unable to help each other. When Gong-ju was violated in her room, by Dong-yun and his cohorts, one after another, Hwa-ok was forced to witness and unable to help her; for her part, Gong-ju confesses to Ms Jo that she ignored Hwa-ok's pregnancy afterward, which led Hwa-ok to commit suicide.

I am somewhat reluctant to accept Brian Masumi's distinction between affect and emotion and their corresponding correlation to intensity and qualification, but Masumi certainly sheds insight on the possibility for affect to forge "a different connectivity, a different difference, in parallel."[46] I take it to mean that unlike emotion, where the physiological register of affective states is labeled and identified by their objects, affect is "unqualified" in the sense that it is "purely autonomic."[47] A similar distinction is embraced by cognitivists, who claim that "affect" narrowly construed is cognitively impenetrable (insular), in that affect can occur independently of its formal object—prior to the forming of propositional attitudes (such as beliefs or imagination) toward an object of emotion.[48] Startle response and affective/motor mimicry are often cited by cognitivists as examples of such affects.[49]

My digression to Masumi's and the cognitivists' typology of affect and emotion here is to tease out the implications of the narrative and aesthetic strategies employed in *Han Gong-ju*. Sonic texture (sonic memories, pains, and traumas), rendered through the repeated linking of the sound from present to past, should not be seen as a mere transition device to a flashback to a narrative event in the past. Rather, such recurrent cues indeed help the spectator to form a different level of connectivity between Gong-ju's present and past experiences, in addition to the forming of the story of the horrific rape and the building up to the final revelation of its nature. As Masumi notes, the forging of a parallel connectivity at the affective level may resonate and/or interfere with the narrative linearity. Unlike the review cited earlier, such sonic or affective connectivity emerging from the discontinuity of narrative construction in fact underscores Gong-ju's struggle in terms of coping with her surroundings, both past and present.

Sonic rupture, from past to present or vice versa, begins to suggest that Gong-ju perhaps may be able to finally get on with her new life and friends. From the helpless face of Gong-ju, unable to stop a boy's verbal and physical bullying of Dong-yun, the film cuts to the screaming of Eun-hui and the other girls at the news that Gong-ju has passed an informal singing audition. Such a change is cued not only through the visual contrast forged by the position of mobile phones (in the flashback, Gong-ju's phone is taken away as she calls the police; in the present Eun-hui enters the frame with a mobile phone in hand, as if she is bringing Gong-ju's phone back from the past). It is also through the sonic contrast of the two scenes (from a girl being silenced to girls' screaming) that suggests Eun-hui is willing to help Gong-ju to gain agency and experience happiness in her new life.

100 Forever Girls

Gong-ju's attempt to "restart" her life fails, however, due to both the publicity of the sexual crime in the media (her rape was summed up in an internet news article) and her friends' learning of Gong-ju being the victim of that crime. The ambiguity of the final scene, the question of whether Gong-ju survives after jumping into the river, could be interpreted in one way, given the analysis of sonic cues that I have traced in this chapter. The opening sequence, mentioned earlier, is accompanied by the sound of Gong-ju humming, while the ending scene of Gong-ju swimming under water toward the foreground of the frame is accompanied by a cappella singing, practiced by Eun-hui's group at the new school seen earlier in the film. Gong-ju's swimming away under water can be interpreted symbolically—as an indicator that she has failed to lead the new life she had hoped for but perhaps can begin again only below the public radar. Regardless of whether the film *Han Gong-ju* ends with a positive or skeptical note on the prospect of Gong-ju's survival, the film provides another way to depict and convey victimhood. The film's sonic texture that operates at multiple levels (as a cue, as a rupture, or as a theme) in fact enables the spectator to share the sensibility of Gong-ju as a girl with a determination to start again, underscored by her eagerness to master swimming, which is yet repeatedly thwarted by various parties—her parents, clueless friends, the police, and the legal system. I do not see such an aesthetic strategy as something specific to art cinema or post-colonial cinema or indie film, the convention of which departs from that of Hollywood, as E. Ann Kaplan suggests.[50] Affective connectivity either parallel to (reinforcing) or independent of (undercutting) the narrative development and linearity is not specific to one or other mode of film practice. What is intriguing about *Han Gong-ju*, however, is the way the film resonates with Gong-ju's auditory sensibility, which further invites the spectator to share some of Gong-ju's memory, trauma, and even possibly some hope. While Gong-ju is hiding in a Korean spa/sauna (*jjimjilbang*), in fear of the parents of the perpetrators finding her whereabouts, she checks news articles on the internet. What escapes the journalistic summary of the crime is, of course, Gong-ju's subjectivity, which the film partially reconstructs and complements.

Johnathan Flatley, in his book *Affective Mapping*, notes, "Since value for Heidegger . . . is a question of affective attachment, this is another way of saying that it is only possible to be affected when things have been set in advance by a certain mode of attunement."[51] Flatley further cites Heidegger's own example: "Only something which is in the state of mind of fearing (or fearlessness) can discover what is environmentally ready-to-hand is threatening. Dasien's openness to the world is constituted existentially by the attunement of a state-of-mind."[52] The film *Hang Gong-ju*, through its repeated sonic connectivity between present and past, helps the spectator to foster a sensibility akin to Gong-ju's, to be in that "state-of-mind," fearful of every sound in her environment, which is seen as readily (or potentially) threatening.

Conclusion

After a class on Korean cinema, one of my students asked, "Why, in all the Korean films that I have seen, do the characters always die?" I answered that there are many Korean films in which none of the characters die. When I have introduced a film at the British Film Institute or other festival venues in London, I have received similar questions; for example, I am asked to make a connection between Korean films and the increasing suicide rate of the country (South Korean having the highest rate among OECD countries).[53] Death is prevalent in many Korean films across, some of which I have discussed so far within the context of South Korean modernity (chapter 1; colonial conditions and post-colonial traumas (chapter 2); and narrative development and aesthetics (chapter 3). Regardless of whether a film's purpose is to reveal, expose, or critique the nationalistic ethos and modernity, colonial brutality and legacy, lingering patriarchy and South Korean's collective complicity, one should examine whether it could not be achieved without the expense of girls' deaths or sexual violation in the film. What would be a cinematic strategy to reconfigure the relationships without recourse to their cinematic death? What would be a way to grant girl characters a sense of integrity, agency, freedom, and even idleness?

In the independent film, *Jamsil* (*Nuechideon bang*, Lee Wanmin, 2016), the death of Seong-suk's (a.s.a. Sung-sook, played by Hong Seung-yi) best friend from her high school days is strangely revived and embodied by a stranger, Mi-hui (a.s.a. Mihee, played by Lee Sanghee), who turns up at the door of Seong-suk's home. The intricate yet perplexing narrative development reveals the past, the present, and even the haunting future, where individuality is reconfigured to free the two from their past traumas and disappointments; as a *Variety* review puts it, "Somehow buried underneath *Jamsil* is a thoughtful, resonant, all-too-rare exploration of female friendship. The bond between the unconventional two women in a country that devalues them is the beating heart of the narrative."[54] In the last two chapters of this book, I will explore ways to grant such friendship, through the idea of "shelter writing" and "idleness." I will discuss the female support manifest in such films *A Girl at My Door* (*Do-huiya* [a.s.a. *Dohee-ya*], July Jung, 2014) and *The House of Us* (*Urijip*,

Yoon Ga-eun, 2019) to re-examine and overcome the dichotomy, present in many of the films discussed so far, between modernity/capitalism/neoliberalism and nature, the latter of which is often associated with or attributed to women/girls, and the extent to which the caring or nurturing role associated with motherhood and/or girlhood could be re- and de-gendered.

4
Directing Girls

Korean Indie Women Directors and Girlhood

The number of women directors in the South Korean film industry is on the rise. In 2020, that number was slightly over 20 percent within the commercial sector, more than double the number just a few years before: in 2017, it was less than 10 percent.[1] Nonetheless, given the gender ratio in film-related departments of higher education institutions, where women consist of almost half the enrollment, it is the indie scene that better reflects those demographics. As an example, 47 percent of the independent films shown at the Seoul Independent Film Festival in 2017 were made by women.[2]

The Korean popular film magazine *Cine 21* marked 2009 as a turning point for a burgeoning Korean indie scene, with indie films such as *Breathless* (*Ttongpari*, Yang Ik-jun, 2009), the first indie film to sell more than 100,000 tickets. (This is 1/100 of the industry threshold, which is 10 million for megahit status in Korean commercial cinema.)[3] Since the mid-2010s, independent filmmaking has become more vibrant and diverse; works by women directors have premiered both in and outside of Korea, receiving critical acclaim. These included films by Shin Su-won (*Madonna*, 2015), Yoon Ga-eun (*The World of Us* [*Urideul*], 2015; *The House of Us* [*Urijip*], 2019), Jeon Go-woon (*Microhabitat* [*Sogongnyeo*], 2018), Yi Ok-seop (*Maggie* [*Megi*], 2018), and Kim Bora (*House of Hummingbird* [*Beolsae*], 2018).

The focus of this chapter, however, is not the history of Korean indie cinema. Rather, I hope to trace some of the continuities and transformations present in the films of women directors, working under the rubric of independent cinema, that feature girl protagonists and a preoccupation with adolescence. The subject matter of these films varies and so do the female characters' desires or frustrations, but girlhood is a persistent theme. In terms of film outputs, a peak was reached in 2018: *Miss Baek* (*Misseu baek*, Lee Ji-won, 2018); *Second Life* (*Seon-huiwa Seul-gi*, Park Young-ju, 2018); *House of Hummingbird*; *Adulthood* (*Eoreundogam*, Kim In-seon, 2018); *Young-ju* (*Yeong-ju*, Cha Seong-deok, 2018); and *Ghost Walk* (*Bamui muni yeolinda*, Yu Eun-jeong, 2018) joined earlier examples including *Snowy Road* (Lee Na Jeong, 2015;

Forever Girls. Jinhee Choi, Oxford University Press. © Oxford University Press 2025.
DOI: 10.1093/9780197685822.003.0005

104 Forever Girls

examined in chapter 2); *Jamsil* (Lee Wan-min, 2016); *The World of Us* (Yoon Ga-eun, 2015); *A Girl at My Door* (July Jung, 2014); and *Crush and Blush* (*Misseu Hongdangmu*, Lee Kyoung-mi, 2008). However, girl protagonists or girlhood are not tropes exclusive to the films of women directors. They also inspire male directors working in both independent and commercial cinema. Examples are *Another Child* (*Miseongnyeon*, Kim Yoon-sik, 2018); *The Witch Part I, II* (*Manyeo 1, 2*, Park Hoon-jung, 2018, 2022); *Omok Girl* (*Omok sonyeo*, Baek Seung-hwa, 2018); *The Villainess* (*Aknyeo*, Jung Byung-gil, 2017); *Yongsoon* (Shin Joon, 2016); *Queen of Walking* (*Geotgiwang*, Baek Seung-hwa, 2016); *The Silenced* (*Gyeonseonghakgyo; sarajin sonyeodeul*, Lee Hae-young, 2015) discussed in chapter 2; *Coinlocker Girl* (*Chainataun*, Han Jun-hee, 2014); the two films previously discussed in chapter 3, *Han Gong-ju* (Lee Su-jin, 2013) and *A Werewolf Boy* (*Neukdaesonyeon*, Cho Sung-hee, 2012); and *Sunny* (*Sseoni*, Kang Hyeong-cheol, 2011), which will be discussed in chapter 5.

The abundance of girl protagonists in the last decade both mirrors and challenges the profusion of films centered around male adolescents that dominated the Korean film industry in the 2000s: teen pictures or gangster films entirely or partially set in boys' high schools. With the success of *Friend* (*Chingu*, Kwak Kyeong-taek, 2001), which the director claims to be semi-autobiographical, high school has become a site for longing and nostalgia; male friendship has developed yet is unable to be sustained in the near future, once the boys cross the threshold of adulthood. Women directors Byun Young-joo and Jeong Jae-eun, who debuted in the 1990s and early 2000s, also briefly took part in this production trend of male coming-of-age stories, although their focus shifted away from the generic violence of the dominant cycles. Both Byun and Jeong initially explored films with women subjects: Byun's documentary series, *Murmuring* (*Nateunmoksori*, also spelled as [a.s.a.] *Najeun moksori*, 1995–1999) was concerned with the survivors of military sexual slavery during the late colonial era, and Jeong's debut feature, *Take Care of My Cat* (*Goyangireul butakhae*, 2001) dealt with five high school girls who face various challenges after graduation. Yet their subsequent fiction films, *Flying Boys* (*Ballegyoseupso*, Byun, 2004) and *The Aggressives* (*Taepungtaeyang*, Jeong, 2005), focus on male protagonists who form alternative families through their extracurricular activities and hobbies—ballet for Byun and skateboarding for Jeong—both of which films I discussed in *The South Korean Film Renaissance.*[4]

There is no neat way of mapping out films with girl protagonists, in terms of either genre or gender of filmmakers. My examination of cisgender women directors in this chapter thus avoids essentialist assumptions about gender and gender representation. Yim Soon-rye, a pioneering woman director who began working in the industry in the 1990s, featured male protagonists in her early work: *Three Friends* (*Sechingu*, 1996) and *Wikiki Brothers* (*Waikiki Beuradeoseu*, 2001). She claims, "I was often asked why I'm not telling women's stories as a woman director. After having studied in France, I found Korean society violent and lacking diversity, and wanted to discuss that through my films; although my films are less centered on women, [the] women characters are rebellious, confident and strong."[5] I focus on the thematic of girlhood as a site of subjectivity and value, moving away from seeing girl characters instrumentally, as a mere narrative trope of victimhood or a vehicle to trigger a moral dilemma for male character: in Michele Aaron's term, "to-be-dead."

This chapter is structured around the ideas of "shelter," domesticity and girlhood. In her book *Extreme Domesticity: A View from the Margins*, Susan Fraiman examines literature, television programs, and even television celebrities such as Martha Stewart, in the light of "shelter writing."[6] Fraiman dissociates everyday domesticity and its practices from the bourgeois ideology and values associated with femininity; considering "shelter writing" in both a literal and a metaphorical sense, she refers to detailed descriptions of homemaking and her key example is, interestingly, *Robinson Crusoe* (Daniel Defoe, 1916).[7] Crusoe's furniture building is seen as a form of homemaking, a way to create security: in Defoe's words, finding "some order within doors."[8] Domesticity in such texts, Fraiman claims, is a sign of "safety, sanity and self-expression: *survival* in the most basic sense" (italics are mine).[9] Homemaking could be seen as a means of self-assertion and defiance as well as self-sufficiency. If the gothic house "imprisons" women, the domestic practices and personal places in the works Fraiman examines, conversely, "shelter" women.[10]

The search for shelter or home, literally and metaphorically, has been a frequent subject of contemporary Korean films with girl protagonists: to name a few, *A Brand New Life* (*Yeohaengja*, Ounie Lecomte, 2009); *Wild Flowers* (*Deulkkot*, Park Seok-yeong 2014); *Steel Flower* (*Seutil peulawo*, Park Seok-yeong, 2015); *Miss Baek, Ghost Walk*, and *Fighter* (*Paiteo*, Yun Jero, 2020). These films have minor or adult protagonists who are abandoned or in need of shelter from sexual or physical violence and even death. Further, indie films have increasingly featured homeless adolescents who have formed their own "fam" (family, *paem*) in which their survival often relies on illegal means or even sexual exploitation—as in *Jane* (*Kkumui Jein*, Cho Hyeon-hoon, 2016) and *Park Hwa-young* (*Bak Hwa-yeong*, Lee Hwan, 2017). The films analyzed in this chapter are neither cinematic renditions of "shelter writing" in

106 Forever Girls

the strict sense, nor comparable to feminist experimental films such as *Jeanne Dielman* (Chantal Akerman, 1975), which details the titular character's meticulous domestic practices of cooking and cleaning as well as her domestic space. Perhaps *This Charming Girl* (*Yeoja Jeong-hye*, Lee Yoon-ki, 2004), which is directed by a man, is a closer example of the aesthetics of shelter writing: the viewer closely observes the protagonist Jeong-hye's daily routines and domestic labor, only to later learn her painful childhood trauma of sexual violence. Nevertheless, shelter "searching" or "dreaming," if not the "writing" advanced by Fraiman, enable us to better locate the narrative and aesthetic continuity of the films discussed here, despite their differences in tone and narrative outcome.

Fraiman provides two opposite poles of shelter writing: one represented by a homemaking guru like Martha Stewart, and the other by the socially marginal or outcast, "scarred by domestic trauma, shunned by the mainstream as queer/poor/alien, in some cases lacking even enough to eat or a regular place to sleep."[11] This latter conception of shelter in crisis helps to trace a common journey among the protagonists of the films I will examine here. In *The House of Us*, on the brink of her parents' divorce, Ha-na makes frequent visits to the house of two younger girls, Yu-mi and Yu-jin, who are worried that they may lose their rented home while their parents have temporarily been relocated to a sea town to make a living. Do-hui (played by Kim Sae-ron) in *A Girl at My Door*, who has been both physically and verbally abused by her family in a small village, finds a temporary shelter in the flat of a police officer (played Bae Doona), who has newly been transferred, due to her queer sexual orientation. In *Microhabitat*, Mi-so (a.s.a. Miso, played by Esom), a homeless person (although in her late twenties or early thirties and thus not a girl in a demographic sense), pays visits to the homes of her five friends from her college days, seeking a temporary place to stay. Although the individual circumstances of these characters vary (and some, like Mi-so, could be seen as a "girl" only in an extended sense), their narrative journeys share a search for "shelter," an outcome that remains tenuous or ambiguous at best. In these three films, the traditional home is unable to offer any security or stability. In contrast to the girl protagonists examined in chapter 2, who retreat inward from national or personal traumas, foregrounding their interiority, these girls move outward, "searching for" emotional as well as physical shelter. Before these films are examined more closely, a brief history of women's experimental and independent filmmaking in South Korea is in order, with a focus on the connotations of "indie" within the industrial, political, and aesthetic contexts.

The Indie Scene

Women's independent and experimental filmmaking in South Korea can be traced back to the 1970s, with the founding of the Kaidu Club in 1974. The Club lasted for five years, until one of its founding members left the country.[12] Although the 1970s is the decade in which Korean society saw the formation of labor unions and their collective actions, the films produced by the Kaidu Club were not closely tied to the labor movement at the time. Founding members of the club, such as Han Ok-hui, Kim Jeom-seon, Lee Jeong-hui, and Han Sun-ae, were all graduates from Ehwa Woman's University, a prestigious private university with a long history in the country. No Cheol Park says of the filmmakers that "neither mainstream society nor working class accorded them a legitimate membership . . . in the 1970s, marginalized female intellectuals strove to affirm their gender identity through cultural activities."[13] They screened their films at the first and second Experimental Film Festival in 1974–1975.[14] Their work could be considered "independent" in a broad sense in that they actively and consciously distanced themselves from Chungmooro ("off-Chungmooro"), the business district for the Korean Film Industry at that time, yet their activities were more experimental than contemporary "independent" cinema. Park finds it difficult to locate within the works of the Kaidu Club members any consistent aesthetic thread, except perhaps "self-expression" broadly construed.[15] With some of the members leaving the country to study or reside abroad, the club came to a natural end.

Film activism dominated the 1980s and '90s; some of the prominent film societies and clubs were initially based in universities but moved out of the academic base to be heavily involved with labor movements. Yallasheong (founded in 1980 and based in Seoul National University); the Seoul Film Collective (Seoul Yeonghwajibdan, 1982–1986); Jangsangotmae (1988); and the Research Center for National Film (Minjokyeonghwa yeonguso, 1988–1991) all formed in the 1980s. This period also saw the making and sharing of the documentary *Sanggyedong Olympics* (*Sanggyedong olimpik*, Kim Dong-won, 1988), which captures the residents' struggles to find alternate places to settle after having been evicted from the Sanggyedong area due to its redevelopment to host the Seoul Olympics. Activist films, both non-fiction and fiction, were "ritualistically" consumed and typically exhibited outside the commercial theater circuits; *The Night Before Strike* (*Paeopjeonya*), a fiction film produced by Jangsangotmae in 1990, for instance, was never theatrically released until its twentieth anniversary in 2019.[16]

With the emergence and visibility of the *minjung* movement in the 1980s, and up until the early '90s, women filmmakers also turned toward more acute social issues, including women's labor. This is when Kim Soyoung and Byun Young-joo, both of whom are still active in documentary and fiction filmmaking, were introduced to the scene. Kim's career path interestingly embodies the development of film culture and government initiatives in filmmaking education within Korea. Kim received her film education as a member of the first cohort of the Korean Academy of Film Arts (KAFA), which was founded in 1984 with Korean government subsidies. Following in the footsteps of Han a decade before, she continued the legacy of the film club by forming Nue (Silkworm) in 1985, and organized the women's independent film collective Bariteo in 1989.[17] Kim further contributed to the dissemination of feminist film criticism in South Korea after having studied in the United States; she has also taught at the Korean National University of Arts (often referred to as Hanyejong as an abbreviation in Korean, and as K-Arts hereafter), which was established in 1991. After she made several shorts with Nue in the 1980s, Kim's first film with Barieto, *Even Little Grass Has Its Own Name* (16mm, 1990), concerns the casualized labor of, and gender discrimination against, women workers. Byun, who worked as a cinematographer on the film, began making her own films shortly after, beginning with her documentary *Women Being in Asia* (*Asiaeseo yeoseongeuro sandaneun geoteun*, 1993).

The antagonistic relationship between the state and the film activism that had dominated the indie scene since the 1980s began to transform due to the changing political climate during the post-authoritarian era. Contemporary independent cinema increasingly distanced itself from the ideological function and discursive strategy of film activism in the earlier period. In her discussion of contemporary Korean independent documentary filmmaking, Maeng Su-jin claims that the *minjung* rhetoric gave way, to be replaced by the "progressive (*jinbo*)," a term that is applied beyond the political sphere to encompass the culture, collective unconsciousness, and everyday realities that were sidestepped or ignored due to the focus on the national and class struggles.[18]

The independent film scene, however, had initially been heavily gendered, revolving around male leadership and communal filmmaking. Some of the film activist groups, were "extremely hierarchical and . . . ultimately elitist."[19] As Young-a Park notes, "The moral authority of those who participated in the 1980s social movement began to emerge as an important form of symbolic capital, especially in cultural institutions."[20] Some women directors, who had previously worked with prominent male film activists and had been involved with independent filmmaking, expressed their disillusionment about the exclusivity of male leadership:

> The new cultural institutions, networks, and apertures which emerged in the context of a symbiosis between the post authoritarian Korean state and KIFA [Korean Independent Film Association], opened up space for female independent filmmakers to contradict or even to challenge the communal activist subculture. This communal activist culture had been based on male leadership drawing on moral authority and exclusive social networks founded on this moral privilege.[21]

With the establishment of democratic governments, the 1990s saw film festivals of diverse scales emerge, notably, the Busan (a.s.a. Pusan) International Film Festival (1996, BIFF), followed by the Seoul International Women's Film Festival (SIWFF) in 1997 and the Korean Independent and Short Film Festival in 1999. In 1998, the Korean Independent Films and Video Association (KIFVA) was founded, headed by Kim Dong-won, a prominent documentary filmmaker. This indie scene created a new space for both filmmakers and audiences, especially for those who did not have to undergo the Korean industry's apprentice system. As Park notes, recognition at film festivals helps a director to skip the period of apprenticeship or accelerate their directorial debut.[22] As mentioned, in the fiction filmmaking, Yim, similar to male directors who debuted around the same time such as Hong Sang-soo (debuted in 1995), skipped the long period of apprenticeship. Other directors who debuted slightly later than Yim, such as Jeong Jae-Eun (*Take Care of My Cat*, 2001) and Yoon Jae-yeon (*Wishing Stairs*, 2003) also first showcased their shorts at film festivals; Jeong's *Secret Code* (*Dohyeong ilgi*, 1997) and Yoon's *Psychodrama* (*Ssaikodeurama*, 2000) were shown as part of closing galas at SIWFF, in 1999 and 2001, respectively.[23]

By the early 2000s, the independent film scene and film festivals had become active content-seekers as well as providers of funding for newcomers, creating alternate venues for many film graduates, including women directors. Mun Hak-san notes that three principal groups constitute the independent short film scene in Korea: first, film school graduates (including KAFA, K-Arts, and other film schools); second, those who were trained in the independent film sector; and last, those who studied abroad.[24] Many women directors were educated at K-Arts; some began their filmmaking career after a break, having re-enrolled in film school after earning their undergraduate degrees in other disciplines—for instance, directors Shin Su-won and Lee Kyeong-mi. Not only the film festivals but also corporate sponsorship contributed to the growing number of women directors' feature films; beginning in 2010, as part of the Butterfly project, the industry/higher education collaboration (*Sanhakhyeopryeok*) between conglomerates (such as CJ E&M and

K-Arts) provided funding, although limited, for some women directors, including Yoon Ga-eun (*The World of Us*, 2016).[25]

The history of women's independent filmmaking has underscored the relationship between the personal and the political, which has been continued by contemporary women directors. The subjects taken up by early independent women filmmakers, such as patriarchy and gender inequality, casualization of women's labor, or the jeopardy to women's careers due to motherhood and childcare—the thematic concerns of *Even Little Grass Has Its Own Name*. Some of the recent short films that were well received at film festivals deal with similar gender issues to those explored by earlier independent women directors: *The Monologue* (*Jayuyeongi*, Kim Bo-young, 2018) features an actress whose career has been interrupted by a child for whom she is the primary caretaker; *Testimony* (*Jeungeon*, Woo Kyung-hee, 2018) touches on sexual harassment and the lack of women's solidarity in a work space; and *My Turn* (*Naecharyae*, Kim Na-kyung, 2017) examines the pressure on nurses to take turns to have a child, or otherwise abort a child to accommodate the needs of the hospital where they work, as the shortage of nurses is so acute.

As in Hollywood, where the referent and connotations of "independent film" have varied throughout history, the Korean industry terms are insufficient for a clear demarcation of independent cinema.[26] The "indie" is primarily and initially characterized through both aesthetic and ethical aims: "films that encourage the audience to see the world in a new way, to dream of a better self and believe in a better society."[27] However, the Korean Film Council (KOFIC), a semi-independent government body, sets out very specific requirements for a film to be "classified" and "recognized" as an independent film. In terms of artistic aims and function, independent films do not diverge greatly from art cinema; in fact, both independent and art cinema fell under the category of "diversity films" until 2015; in 2016, the name of the category changed to "independent-art film." KOFIC's industry reports noted that many applications overlapped the two categories of independent and art cinema, and over 80 percent of 2016 independent films were also officially recognized as art cinema.[28] Independent films must satisfy a set of very specific technical criteria; a film is "automatically" recognized as an independent film if it has received financial support from KOFIC or from a regional government or film committee.[29] It must also not have a major distributor or utilize the saturated booking system.[30] Such broad and mixed criteria, in fact, produce eclectic rankings among independent and art cinema, both domestic and imported. In 2018, for instance, a Korean independent documentary film, *Intention*, which deals with the sinking of the Sewol ferry, was ranked second, while foreign art films such as *Call Me by Your Name* (Luca Guadignino, 2017) and

Shoplifters (*Manbiki kazoku*, Kore-eda Hirokazu, 2018) landed on the top 10 chart of both domestic and foreign films combined. Although it did not make it to this top 10, *Microhabitat*, discussed later in this chapter, was ranked second among Korean independent/art cinema releases that year. But an interview with director Jeon gave me a more precise answer than government funding: independent film budgets often do not exceed 300 million KRW and are now often picked up by independent distributors, such as At9 and exhibition venues.[31]

The trope of girlhood has played a significant role across both genre cinema and independent films, although not necessarily dictated by gender of director, as sketched in the introduction of this book. In the remainder of this chapter, I will focus on three independent films—*The House of Us*, *A Girl at My Door*, and *Microhabitat*—that depict girlhood as something untenable within Korean society. To what extent do these films depart from the earlier generation of women directors' films that focused on adolescents, or from the previous representations of girlhood—such as the 1970s reference girl—in terms of their sensibility and agency? My attempt here is diagnostic, focusing on the idea of "shelter" while tracing the continuities and transformations among women directors' works. The films are not discussed in chronological order but by the degree to which the girls have been granted agency in their search for shelter, metaphorical and literal.

Shelter Making: *The House of Us* (2019)

Yoon, a K-Arts graduate, has been praised for the sophisticated depiction of young girls' psychology in her feature debut, *The World of Us*. Yoon's aesthetics of "apparent" naturalism conveyed through the performance of child actors, is an outcome of careful planning at all stages. Yoon's directing in fact combines all three types of spontaneous acting methods developed by J. L. Moreno: the spontaneous, the planned, and the rehearsed.[32] Children were given plenty of time to get to know each other before shooting. Yoon had rehearsed with the actors for a long period of time (two to three months) prior to shooting, helping them become familiar with filmic situations rather than having them memorize exact lines.[33] Yoon's working relationship with child actors helped to foster an environment where a sense of spontaneity could be better conveyed.[34] Dialogues were revised to reflect the actors' own words or expressions. At the time of shooting, they could improvise their lines as long as they fit the overall aim of particular scenes or situations.[35] Despite the apparent naturalness of performance, however, the film's shooting and editing were painstakingly coordinated; some scenes required many extensive takes, and in an interview that accompanies the film's DVD release, the editor, Park Se-young, claims that she had to work with multiple sound tracks to select the best bit of each word, for which she earned the nickname of "nano-editor." She cut and edited dialogue even at the level of word suffixes to create the best lines and more nuanced delivery from her actors.

Yoon's protagonists are pre-adolescents, younger than those in the works of most Korean directors in the commercial sector or the indie scene. Yoon moves her protagonists out of the usual high school setting found in the horror film series, *Whispering Corridor*, or contemporary indie films such as *Second Life*, *Another Child*, and *After My Death* (*Joe manheun sonyeo*, Kim Ui-seok, 2017). Her characters are in primary school, spending most of their time at home or a friend's home during their summer vacations. In contrast to other women directors' films such as *A Girl at My Door*, *House of Hummingbird*, and *Miss Baek*, which consider the formation of a guardian relationship beyond the extended family, Yoon's films portray children who begin to forge a meaningful relationship outside the family in their friendships or sisterhood. In *The World of Us*, Ji-a is transferred to a new school; Seon is another student who has been ostracized by her class. The two quickly bond over the summer break but as school is about to resume, their relationship becomes stranded; Ji-a gets closer to Bo-ra, the popular girl in school, leaving Seon by herself again. In *The House of Us*, fifth-grader Ha-na is eager for her family to stay together and believes that a summer trip together would help to mend her parents' strained relationship. Ha-na begins to visit her neighbors, Yu-mi and Yu-jin, two little girls who spend most of their time by themselves, their parents having temporarily been relocated for work. Yearning for continuity at home, the two girls welcome the visits of Ha-na. The three girls have fun by themselves, while also sabotaging the landlady's attempt to look for a new tenant. Although Yoon's two features deserve close analysis, I will focus on the depiction of domesticity and "shelter" manifest in Yoon's sophomore film, *The House of Us*, and discuss how the protagonist Ha-na seeks a "shelter" outside her own home through "little actions": both cooking and dollhouse making.[36]

The narrative of *The House of Us* revolves around Ha-na's overall change from reaction to action through her "shelter writing" within her family as well as outside her home. Just as *The World of Us* begins and ends with scenes of the schoolchildren playing dodge ball, *The House of Us* has a cyclical structure, bookended by sequences in which Ha-na asks her family to eat together. In the pre-credit sequence, Ha-na's request for her family to have breakfast together is ignored. In the final sequence of the film, Ha-na returns home and sets the table: she has disappeared for a day out of frustration and disappointment with her parents' separation. After a few concerned looks from her family, they all sit down at the table. Ha-na serves each a bowl of rice with an egg on top; it is Ha-na's turn, this time, to politely ignore her family's questions and reactions. The camera zooms slightly to frame Ha-na alone in one shot, as she says "Let's all eat and get ready for a trip." Although her action will not change the course of her parents' divorce, the camera places her at the visual center, with her family finally attentive to her actions: "restoring order" now at her disposal.[37] As Fraiman characterizes it, shelter writing is "a mode that may center on anyone whose smallest domestic endeavors have become urgent and precious in the wake of dislocation whether as the result of migration, divorce, poverty or a stigmatized sexuality."[38] Both Ha-na and the two neighbor sisters—Yu-mi and Yu-jin—feel anxious about Ha-na's parents' upcoming divorce and their possible relocation. Like Ha-na's cooking, the girls' dollhouse building can be seen as shelter writing, however limited their agency may be.

The opening scenes of the two films—*The World of Us* and *The House of Us*—share a similar style, showing the protagonist being ignored at school and at home, respectively. With the protagonist standing static in the center, other characters enter and leave the frame in front of or behind her. In the pre-credit sequence of *The World of Us*, the camera focuses only on Seon, while leaving her classmates mostly off-screen. She remains passive, with her changing facial expressions subtly registering her disappointment when her classmates choose her last as a teammate. In a review of the film, Lee Ju-hyeon notes that the girls world represented in the film is the world of words (*mal*); "girls world is a world of words rather than actions. And the film constantly carries the presence of girls through the sound of their chatting off screen: like in the first scene where the invisible words uttered during students' dividing the two teams to play a dodge ball."[39]

The pre-credit sequence of *The House of Us* also consists of the parents' interaction on- and off-screen, while the camera focuses on Ha-na's attempts to initiate on-screen action or conversation, which is ignored by both parents. Ha-na's expression is even more obscure than Seon's—it is ambiguous whether she is frustrated or fearful witnessing the increasing tension between her parents; hers is a dismissal by her family, instead of an ostracization by peers. The sequence recalls the scene in which Antoine converses with a psychiatrist in *The 400 Blows* (*Les quatre cents coups*, Francois Truffaut, 1959), albeit less disciplinary in nature. Just as the camera fixes on Antoine's reactions, answering and at times feeling embarrassed, Ha-na's reaction is foregrounded, with the voice of Ha-na's mother representing the authority of the house and disapproving of Ha-na's efforts at domestic chores.

114 Forever Girls

Unlike the opening and ending scenes of *The World of Us*, which leave the prospective relationship between the two girls—Seon and Ji-a—ambiguous, in *The House of Us*, the decision on the divorce of Ha-na's parents is final. Her parents agree to go on the family trip for which Ha-na has been begging, but this is merely a concession to their children before they separate. Throughout the film, Ha-na's actions, or those of her friends, are at best "mildly disruptive"; neither hiding the mobile phone of Ha-na's father nor spilling milk on the laptop computer of Ha-na's mother deter the parents' actions or trigger any angry response. Likewise, the efforts of the two sisters to keep their own house do not discourage the landlady from finding a new tenant. The futility of their efforts to keep the family or house culminates with their destruction of the dollhouse that they built together; the value of her "action" is not "shelter" writing but shelter "writing" with a focus on their activity—a form of self-expression.

Unlike *The Silenced* (examined in chapter 2) or the other girls' high school horror films that preceded it, where girls create their own hidden secret space within the public space of school, Yoon's protagonists move between both private and public spaces, filling gaps between home and school and trying to find a way to preoccupy themselves as their family members are frequently absent due to divorce or work. Although her parents are on good terms, Seon in *The World of Us* is raised in a working-class family, where both of her parents are often not present, leaving Seon to be responsible for looking after her younger brother Yun. A similar responsibility is allotted to Yu-mi in *The House of Us*, who is looking after her younger sister, Yu-jin. In the film, we never get to see their parents except, possibly, early in the film when Ha-na passes by a family consisting of two young girls and three adults, who are walking down the hill with their backs to the camera; they appear to be the family of Yu-mi and Yu-jin (including their uncle, who is also mentioned but otherwise not shown in the film).

Ha-na's shelter writing, as performed through her recipe diary and cooking, finds an outlet in her repeated visits to Yu-mi and Yu-jin's house. After having helped Yu-jin recover from indigestion, during her initial visit, Ha-na looks around the house, while Yu-mi, the elder sister, answers a telephone call from her mother. The house, although small and cluttered, is brightly lit and exudes a warm tone. As Ha-na's gaze lands on various objects in the house, she touches them one by one: a bag of collected seashells, leftover wallpaper, little accumulated boxes, tiny socks hanging by the window as well as notes on the wall with lists of "do's" and "don'ts." In her characterization of "shelter writing," Fraiman emphasizes the significance of objects in the house, their "smallness," and their being "responsive to our touch."[40] The two sisters' house becomes

Directing Girls **115**

instantly tactile and intimate, and Ha-na's desire to keep her family intact is displaced onto the sisters' home—a place of warmth.

With Ha-na's visits, the guidelines set out by the parents of the two girls are violated. These restrictions include "don't invite a stranger"; "don't tell people that parents are away"; "don't use the gas stove." The first two are violated instantly with Ha-na's initial visit; the last, when Ha-na cooks for the two sisters on her subsequent visit. After having enjoyed the first dish together—egg omelet in the Korean style—the three go up to the rooftop of the house. Again, Ha-na circles the rooftop space while touching the objects she finds: a box of wallpaper rolls, which belong to the parents, who make their living through home decorating and improvement; the hula-hoops, and finally a small fallen tomato in the family planter. The exclusivity of family is extended to include Ha-na, as Yu-jin allows Ha-na to touch the plant; a sense of home is activated by Ha-na's little actions: touching, cooking, playing, and decorating.

The motif of the box is constantly present throughout the film: Ha-na's secret box; a smiley face hidden in a tiny box that Yu-mi gives Ha-na to cheer her up; and finally, the dollhouse built out of small boxes that Yu-mi has been saving and decorating. If the bracelets shared between Seon and Ji-a in *The World of Us* signify Seon's wish to connect and be connected—her longing for a friendship—boxes in *The House of Us* become both metaphorical and metonymic. Upon her first visit, Ha-na asks Yu-mi to keep her secret box, in which she has hidden her father's mobile phone, thinking that her father may be having an inappropriate relationship with his subordinate at work. As the three girls become closer, she unseals her own box and agrees to use it for the dollhouse. She empties the box of her belongings as well as her father's phone; her "interiority reaches the outside."[41] Fraiman insightfully describes how the interior in shelter writing is intimately bound with an exterior. Shelter consists of both "what we enclose" and "what encloses us."[42]

Each box is a unit, member, and part of a whole—be it a house or a family—whose boundaries can be easily crossed and which is hard to keep intact, with or without the presence of adults. What passes through the wall of Ha-na's room is the sound of tension and parental conflict, while in the two sisters' place, it is the unwanted visits by the landlady who hopes to increase the security deposit by renting their home to a new tenant. Unwanted visits drive the girls to go outside and out of town, endangering the security or sisterhood they have formed (a similar pattern is present in *A Girl at My Door*, as I will discuss later in this chapter). Fraiman also emphasizes that doors both "exclude and admit."[43] Both the movement of characters and their contrasting desires cross the divide of inside and outside home (even abroad), or shelter and expedition.

The inside/outside divide also plays out in the framing of the girls on- and off-screen. The bonding of the three girls is constantly reinforced throughout the film via framing both inside and outside domestic space. Their attachment is manifest through the *additive* shot composition, in contrast to the opening sequence where Ha-na's family ignore her by entering and leaving the shot. Kore-eda often employs similar framing to show the unity of family or sisterhood in such films as *Our Little Sister* (*Umimachi Diary*, 2015), although Yoon's framing is tighter, with the camera closer to her characters. In the rooftop sequence mentioned above, Ha-na touches various household items and sits in front of a cherry tomato tree—picking up a tiny, dropped tomato. The youngest girl, Yu-jin, enters the shot and sits next to her; a single shot becomes a two shot. When Yu-mi calls them, from off-screen, the two leave the shot; the camera lingers on the plant in the foreground, as if considering what constitutes a "family." Next the girls re-enter the frame, this time in a three shot, running past behind the plant.

A similar kind of framing and composition is found in a scene on the beach; on their way to find Yu-mi and Yu-jin's parents, the girls' frustration reaches a climax. Not only are they lost, but they also have no means by which to reach anyone for help as Ha-na has lost her mobile phone and the battery of Yu-mi's phone has died. Their frustration escalates, each accusing one another for the futility of their trip, and they crush the dollhouse they have built together; Yu-mi enters the one shot of Ha-na, who sits and starts to cry. The camera cuts for a slight reframing to capture all three girls crying together in one shot (figure 4.1a–c). Like the way they built the dollhouse by gluing boxes together one by one, a shot of one character attracts another to form unity with each one sequentially entering the shot. Glue, sweat, and tears all bring the girls closer, sticking them together rather than tearing them apart: an island—or isolation—of their own, but collective rather than individual. This is further reinforced by a visual echo between the shot compositions of the girls and the contours of an island in the far background (figure 4.2).

In her examination of the images of water and ocean in Kore-eda's oeuvre, Linda Ehrlich points out that the function of the ocean is not to solve or resolve but to be "an indicator of change, a metaphor for psychological transformation."[44] The trip to the beach in *The House of Us* could be seen as "a reminder of fragile balances."[45] The children's independence and courage are not enough to face an unexpected challenge, yet they make an effort to protect their newly formed sisterhood. Lost and frustrated, Ha-na kicks the dollhouse they built. Yu-mi joins her and steps on the house, acknowledging the futility of their project instead of getting angry at Ha-na for destroying it. What shelter writing stages, Fraiman says, are "feelings born of a sense of physical

Figure 4.1 a–c After a heated debate, Ha-na is about to cry, feeling frustrated. When Ha-na begins to cry, Yu-mi enters the shot to sit next to her. The camera then cuts for a slight reframing to show Yu-jin joining the two, with all three girls crying together (*The House of Us*, Yoon Ga-eun, 2019).

118 Forever Girls

Figure 4.2 A shot composition of the three girls resembles the shape of an island in the far background (*The House of Us*, 2019).

and social precariousness.... [T]he comfort they represent is usually too temporary."[46] Fraiman advances her framework of shelter writing through consideration of two primary texts: *Robinson Crusoe* and Leslie Feinberg's novel, *Stone Butch Blues* (1993). As Fraiman notes, the homes of both Crusoe and Jess, the protagonist of Stone Butch Blues, are damaged by earthquake and fire, respectively.[47] Home is always "vulnerable and provisional."[48] And that is why shelter writing constantly involves "both dreaming and desire."[49] While the three lost girls aimlessly walk on the beach, they see a couple leave in a hurry for the pregnant wife's imminent delivery, deserting their tent and belongings. The three girls spend the night together in the tent, as in a fairytale, wishing it to be their own home. They list the food that Ha-na could possibly cook (or rather, what they want to eat): pizza, chicken. They will or should resume their daily lives with or without each other, yet they make efforts to stay together.

It is hard to avoid comparing the portrayal of children in Yoon's work with portrayals of the two Japanese directors, Ozu Yasujiro and Kore-ea, known for family drama in the region and whose work Yoon herself acknowledges as endearing.[50] Among the three directors, Kore-eda links different generations of characters through more intriguing moral dilemmas. In Yoon's works, the actions of children least affect the adults in the narrative, as mentioned above. In Ozu's work, a parallel between children and adults is constructed visually and narratively, to be both undermined and reinforced, especially when young children play a relatively significant role in advancing the narrative, as in *I Was*

Born But . . . (Otona no miru ehon - Umarete wa mita keredo, 1932) or *Ohayo* (1959). For instance, in *I Was Born But . . .* , the boredom of work and school is established as similar or familiar through a tracking shot that links the boys' school to the office where their father works. But later in the film, when child characters become aware of (and await) a set of social norms and hierarchy by which their parents should abide, the boys and the father mutually accept this difference. The parallel established between children and adults in *Ohayo* is rather superficial—indicative of which is the "fart" gag shared between generations—and is not enough to close the gaps in their understanding of social customs and language, as when the aunt wittily mistranslates what the boys say when they are on a silence strike, or when her small talk with the boys' English teacher remains unchanged at the end of the film.

In Kore-eda's films, the inter-generational conflicts between adults and child protagonists are more acute than in Ozu's or in Yoon's.[51] In such films as *Like Father, Like Son (Shoshite chichi ni naru*, 2013) and *Shoplifters*, despite the growing attachment among the members of an "unusual" family, adult characters face and resolve both moral dilemmas and legal conflicts. In *Like Father Like Son*, two boys have been switched at birth, causing each to be raised by a family with no blood tie. The parents of both families are compelled to set straight the family genealogy, and both parents and children resume their lives, with enormous challenges ahead. In *Shoplifters*, an alternate, extended family is formed, with members of both kin and non-kin, and the family breaks up again after the mother's imprisonment as the parents have no legal rights over the children. Even in *Nobody Knows (Dare mo shiranai*, 2004), Akira's dilemma results from his oscillating roles: both child and surrogate parent to his siblings.[52]

Ha-na might be comparable to Akira in *Nobody Knows*, but only to a certain extent. Yoon's children do not pose the same kind of dilemma for adults or themselves, nor does the absence of adults cause them to suffer the same degree or severity of consequences. As mentioned, Ha-na's parents will divorce despite Ha-na's wish for them to stay together. The messy flats in the two films are outcomes of a different kind: Ha-na and the two girls in *The House of Us* intentionally create domestic disorder by throwing out household objects and clothes to make it difficult to rent their home to someone else, whereas the mess in *Nobody Knows* is a result of the mother's long absence and the children's lack of everyday necessities.

The parents of the two girls in *The House of Us* are almost entirely absent; apart from the presumed appearance in the opening scene mentioned above, they do not appear on screen nor are their voices heard by the audience, even during phone conversations between Yu-mi and her mother. There are constant signs of the girls' struggles and fatigue in *The House of Us*; not only has Yu-jin fallen sick with no adult to care for her, but also the girls' foreheads are always smudged with wet hair and sweat, a sign of hot weather with poor air circulation in the house. The absence of their parents and uncle in *The House of Us* leaves the spectator to withhold their moral judgment on them, unlike Akira's mother, Keiko, or the four children's respective birth fathers in *Nobody Knows*. Keiko is not demonized, but the severity of the children's living conditions and the eventual death of the youngest, Yu-ki, make it hard not to pass moral judgment on the adults including her mother as well as the social welfare system.

Yu-mi and Yu-jin pose only two micro-level dilemmas for Ha-na. The first is that Ha-na must decide whether to stay with them during a final viewing of the flat or go on the family trip that she's so longed for. The other is whether to keep her promise to the two little girls that she would remain their "sister" even when they move away. The first dilemma is resolved quickly, once Ha-na realizes that the family trip is intended as a pre-divorce farewell rather than an opportunity for reconciliation. The girls' disastrous trip to locate Yu-mi and Yu-jin's parents is a product of Ha-na's attempts to avoid her own family issue: she is behaving more as a child herself than playing a parental role to the two girls. And their safe return home affirms neither whether the girls' family will indeed have to move out nor whether Ha-na can keep her promise to stay in touch with the girls. In both films, despite the different degrees of the children's struggles, the children become, as Ehrlich puts it in her discussion of *Nobody Knows*, "compelling individuals"—what is foregrounded is "what the children have, not what they lack."[53]

The House of Us departs from Yoon's previous work in that the climactic moment is not marked by characters' aggression or injury. In her feature *The World of Us*, the narrative climax occurs when the intimacy between Seon and Ji-a has become a threat to each of them. Their strained friendship manifests through covert, indirect aggression—gossiping about the drinking problem of Seon's father, or Ji-a's lie about her mother's whereabouts—followed by a physical fight in front of their peers.[54] In Yoon's short, *Guest* (*Sonnim*, 2011), high school student Ja-gyeong visits the house of a woman with whom her father is having an affair. She is greeted by two small children: a nine-year-old boy and a six-year-old girl. Ja-gyeong and the boy get into a physical fight, while the girl is accidentally injured off-screen, which stops the fight. The girl's injury, although not Ja-gyeong's fault, marks her changing relationship to the children. It is a wound that she recognizes both in them as well as in herself; while hiding behind the door, she spies on the father's visit—a confirmation of his affair. Regardless of whether the aggression of the girls in these films is part of the deplorable practice and rule of "girl world," the physical injuries inflicted on themselves or others not only point to the damage such aggression causes to their own relationships, but more important, to their own wounds and frailties.

The conflict between Ha-na and Yu-mi in *The House of Us*, however, is expressed face-to-face and verbally through their language and enunciation, rather than any physical violence directed at each other: during the argument on the beach, their pronunciation suddenly becomes extremely articulate, in contrast to their usual mumbling speech. Their destruction of the dollhouse at first is a channel for their anger and frustration with one another, but quickly turns to mutual acknowledgment of their futile efforts to keep their respective home and house. A sense of sisterhood eases anxiety over their respective crises of disintegration and family relocation. This sisterhood contrasts with the competition, rivalry, and jealousy among the girl characters in *The World of Us*—not only Seon and Ji-a but also Bo-ra, the popular girl—all of whom make brief appearances in *The House of Us*.

Girls are exposed to various forms and degrees of aggression and violence in the film. More severe aggression and violence feature in Yoon's short film *Guest*, as well as in *House of Hummingbird*, another indie film by a woman director, Kim Bora. In the *Hummingbird* film, the girl protagonist, Eun-hui (a.s.a. Eun-hee) endures domestic abuse by her elder brother as well as witnessing her parents' physical violence toward one other. In *The House of Us*, Ha-na witnesses her parents' physical confrontation, the sound of which disrupts her sweet dream of the afternoon with the other girls. Yu-mi and Yu-jin's house is a site of both safety and danger, as indicated by the parental list of "do's" and "don'ts," as well as their helplessness when the younger girl becomes ill. Yet Yoon's girl protagonists in *The House of Us* do not mimic or replicate what they have witnessed or experienced, unlike the elder brother of Ha-na, who at times screams at both his parents and Ha-na.

An ironic reversal is found in both *Guest* and *The House of Us*: Ja-gyeong as an intruder versus Ha-na as a surrogate elder sister. Both are strangers to the younger children; the significance of their actions could be easily exchanged. Once Ja-gyeong enters the house of her father's mistress, she looks through the woman's belongings and touches them: a sign of intrusion rather than of instant intrigue or attachment as in Ha-na's case. Yet Ja-gyeong cooks noodles for the two little children in *Guest,* an act of reconciliation she performs after realizing that the boy may suffer as much as she does. When leaving the place, she warns the children not to open the door to any strangers, including herself. Given how actions of similar types—visiting, touching, and cooking—carry contrasting significance or effect in Yoon's films, it is not Ha-na's cooking per se but her cooking as a form of "shelter writing" that provides her a sense of safety and hope. Ha-na keeps her records in a hand-drawn recipe book, with the film showing her execution of the recipes in a reverse order, from back to front page of the recipe book, and from more elaborate to simpler dishes. The last dish she serves her family is a bowl of rice with an egg on top. What she desires the most for her family is simplicity, not the complication or emotional mess that she witnesses daily. All the dishes that Ha-na cooks, like Miso in *Microhabitat*, use eggs as ingredients. While this makes sense given her age and skills, it can also be read symbolically as an indication of her need for nourishment, nurture, and protection. In the same vein, the roof of the dollhouse is made of the yellow-painted egg cartons: the girls are unprotected and vulnerable, both inside and outside their homes.

Fraiman's primary texts and examples of shelter writing are both literary and practice-based (considering real life routines of the homeless as well as television programs, such as *Martha Stewart Living* and *Queer Eye for the Straight Guy*, that encourage homemaking/shelter writing practices). And the action of writing itself, as represented by Robinson Crusoe or Jess in Feinberg's novel, can further be tied to the act of writing of the novelists themselves; "Crusoe's journalizing references Defoe's own act of narration" and Jess's painting and writing Feinberg's own artistry.[55] As Fraiman notes, "The descriptions of characters making and keeping house offer writers a store of images for their own barely waged work of conjuring and furnishing spaces for which people dwell."[56] In Yoon's film, there are no extensive scenes of Ha-na's cooking—what Fraiman calls "step-by-step" narration in the novels that she examines. Instead, this narration is replaced with, and condensed to, flipping the pages of Ha-na's cooking journal. But perhaps we could forge a different set of relationships between characters' cooking or doing, and shelter writing as a mode of narration: what we find is neither narrating nor showing of Ha-na's cooking step-by-step, but what I propose to call "cinematic sheltering." In Yoon's case, she and her crews are known to create an environment in which her actors can feel and perform comfortably. Such cinematic sheltering, the protective working relationship she builds with her child actors, is comparable to the spatial relationship shown in the mise-en-scène of a bus stop in *The House of Us*; the landscape is painted inside the wall of the bus stop, echoing the scenery in the far background. The scene shows the intricate relationship and reversibility between inside and outside, manifested through various spaces—box, house, bus stop, and tent—but the film in this way also creates an intermediate shelter to protect the children; their actions are still staged inside, signaling that they have not completely been lost yet and will find their way back in the end.

(Un)Settling: *A Girl at My Door* (2014)

The two female leads of *A Girl at My Door* are, in different ways, iconic in their stardom and embodiment of girlhood. *A Girl at My Door* features a prominent star, Bae Doona, as Yeong-nam, a local police chief. Bae starred in local, regional, and global films including *Take Care of My Cat*; *Barking Dogs Never Bite* (*Peulandaseuui gae*, Bong Joon-ho, 2000); *The Host* (*Geomul*, Bong Joon-ho, 2006); the regional schoolgirl film *Linda, Linda, Linda* (Yamashita Nobuhiro, 2005); and the Hollywood production, *Cloud Atlas* (the Wachowskis and Tom Tykwer, 2012). Kim Sae-ron plays Do-hui, the titular character of the original Korean title, *Do-huiya* (a.s.a. *Dohee-ya*). Kim was an immediate success when she debuted in *A Brand New Life* (*Yeohangja*, Ounie Lecomte, 2009); she next starred in a popular crime film *The Man from Nowhere* (*Ajeossi*, Lee Jeong-beom, 2010) and in a re-enactment in the documentary film *Manshin: Ten Thousands Spirit* (*Mansin*, Park Chan-kyong, 2013).[57] Kim's on-screen presence, however, has been in decline since she was charged for driving under the influence in 2022.[58]

Yeong-nam (a.s.a. Young-nam) is transferred to a small town by the sea due to her queer sexuality. Yeong-nam offers a temporary shelter at her own place for Do-hui (a.s.a. Do-hee), who has been abused by her stepfather and grandmother at home. Their relationship sways between that of mother/daughter, of sisters, and of girls; Bae, whose star persona developed through her performance of a girl in several coming-of-age films, constantly yields her guardian role, slipping away to land in the realm of two "girls," who need a shelter of their own. In *The House of Us*, the girls' shelter-making is partially motivated by their anxiety over the unstable living conditions arising from the parents' divorce or work demands; in *A Girl at My Door*, the action revolves around Yeong-nam's actual re-location: her arrival at and leaving a small seaside town after her short stay as a police chief there. Fraiman discusses the challenge to "remake home" after the protagonists' national dislocation in such novels as *The House on Mango Street* (1984) by Sandra Cisneros and *Lucy* (1990) by Jamaica Kincaid.[59] Although, as I will discuss, the marginality of Yeong-nam (due to her sexual orientation) and Do-hui (due to domestic abuse) are compared in the film to that of an illegal Indian immigrant, Bakim, their moves do not represent re-location on a national scale. Nonetheless, Yeong-nam's attempt to settle in her new domestic space and Do-hui's constant effort to escape abuse recall Fraiman's discussion of the immigrants in the novels mentioned above, their "incomplete domestic arrangements—deficient in dreamed-of-safety, beauty, autonomy, and belonging," and home/shelter as a site of vulnerability and heterogeneity.[60]

124 Forever Girls

The visual assimilation that takes place between Yeong-nam and Do-hui reinforces Do-hui's admiration of Yeong-nam as well as their shared girlhood and marginality; Do-hui gradually adopts the style and look of Yeong-nam (swimsuit, sunglasses, and haircut). As Deborah Shamoon observes, "sameness" was visually emphasized in homogender relationship in Japanese girl culture during the 1910–1930s; when there is an age disparity, the older often represents the "idealized self."[61] Yeong-nam acknowledges such a relationship through her dialogue: saying that Do-hui is fond of her, as she seems to have power over the ones who have been harassing Do-hui, including her stepfather and peers at school. But more important, their marginality is manifest through their posture and relationship to their respective home or space: the way each crouches against the wall in the dark. Both are withdrawn even in their own home, and a sense of safety is felt through the absence, instead of the presence, of an object or a person.

In the search for a home-shelter, patriarchy keeps both Yeong-nam and Do-hui from finding a safe place. After Yeong-nam moves into her seaside home, the irreconcilability of her public self with her private, queer self becomes immediately visible. Yeong-nam has successfully graduated from the police academy, which is considered prestigious, yet the institutional heteronormativity imposed on her deprives her of any chance for promotion or any real opportunity to find happiness. After a small chat with the neighbors, Yeong-nam enters her new place. She first irons her police uniform and hangs it on the wall. She leans on the wall and starts drinking a big glass of *soju*, Korean hard liquor, which she has disguised as water, while the uniform hovers over her like the symbolic order that suffocates her. Bae's unfocused gaze, a sign of both intoxication and resignation, differs from the empty look associated with her star persona; Bae's blank stare has been a sign of empowerment in other films despite the fact that she has no clearly set goals for her future. In *Take Care of My Cat* or even *Barking Dogs Never Bite*, her strength and tenacity do not stem from her intellectual sharpness but rather her ability to defy (or at least disregard) the social and gender norms expected of her; her agency is not in her performing but in her un-performing or even idleness, as will be discussed in chapter 5. In this scene, however, her look is a sign not of liminality and defiance but of impasse and acceptance.

The aim of Yeong-nam's relocation or the process of her settling is not to look for a "shelter" in the sense defined by Fraiman. Her new place is not exactly a home; sparsely decorated and with no furniture of her own, it does not operate as one for long. The green lampshade, hanging above the dining table, replaces and condenses the conventional ambient green tone or hue of an old-fashioned interrogation room. And the conversations that take place between

Yeong-nam and Do-hui at the dining table with the green shade above often recall those of a police station, such as when Yeong-nam questions Do-hui about her stepfather's physical violence.

Although Yeong-nam is the chief at the local police station, her agency is still limited by the patriarchy and racism of the town (and by extension the entire country). She is increasingly decentered even at her work. In one scene, the grandmother, who is complicit in her son's abuse of Do-hui, chases her on her scooter in order to beat Do-hui and take her home. These actions—Do-hui being chased by the grandmother and Yeong-nam running after both—clearly show that Yeong-nam is unable to escape from the social hierarchy or order based on gender and age. Shortly after, the abusive grandmother is found dead by the sea. In the police station, Yong-ha (the stepfather) and Do-hui are asked to sign the autopsy report on the grandmother; the staging (even if it is narratively motivated) further presents Yeong-nam as literally placed in the back seat. The scene visually revolves around the senior male police officer, who mediates Yong-ha/Do-hui and Yeong-nam. In the foreground, the local policeman reads the report and asks Yong-ha to sign it, while Do-hui sits in the far background. Yeong-nam is completely off-screen until the senior male officer turns around to ask Yeong-nam whether they need Do-hui's signature as well; the camera then cuts to reveal Yeong-nam, her own desk set back behind the front desk, spatially reinforcing her role as a mere bureaucrat, disempowered and unable to issue orders.

Yong-ha's practice of hiring illegal immigrants from South and Southeast Asia also ties the town's sexism to racism. The townspeople praise Yong-ha as one of the few who stayed to run several businesses in town. There is not much difference in his mistreatment of both low-wage migrant workers and women. When Yeong-nam is (wrongly) accused of sexual molestation of a minor (Do-hui) and put behind bars, Bakim, from India, is in another cell, with the two visually mirroring each other. Women (and ethnic minorities) are often excluded as proper subjects from the national developmental ethos (even as girls emblematically embody the nation's victimhood of colonial history). As Jin-kyung Lee notes, the mistreatment of migrant workers in contemporary South Korea is a parallel to the forced migration of Korean workers during the colonial era to Manchuria, Japan, and other places; the migrant workers' "ghostly presence in South Korea, both indelible as well as fleeting, brings us back to the former era that has not yet gone by."[62] The violent colonial history is replicated internally and echoed by shifting victimhood from the self to others.

When Yeong-nam is with Do-hui, she is relatively free from the patriarchy. But there is no shelter for either "girl" at Yeong-nam's place or in this small town. Do-hui's abusive family often drives her out of the home. When Yeong-nam first meets Do-hui on the street near the girl's house, Do-hui runs away from the screen foreground, vanishing to the field in the far background. Her existence is at best ghostly, both in public and private space. Do-hui begins to visit Yeong-nam's place and later is allowed to stay with Yeong-nam during her summer vacation. As Fraiman notes, however, "households of more than one person are heterogeneous . . . and almost always structured by inequality."[63] Yeong-nam initially feels unease, startled by the presence and actions of Do-hui, who stares at Yeong-nam from above while she is asleep or enters the bathroom when Yeong-nam takes a bath. Yeong-nam's place becomes disorderly; an increasingly insecure Do-hui fears being abandoned by Yeong-nam; and Do-hui's companionship slowly takes away even Yeong-nam's limited agency. Shortly after Do-hui escapes from her home to stay with Yeong-nam, both Do-hui and Yeong-nam are seen in their uniforms: school and police uniforms, respectively. Do-hui tries on Yeong-nam's hat, foreshadowing their role reversal later in the film. No privacy is permitted, with more visitors arriving at Yeong-nam's door—Do-hiu's stepfather Yong-ha and the police officers who come to arrest her. Like the landlady's visits in *The House of Us* that move the girls out of their home, however temporarily, Yeong-nam is eventually "evicted" when Do-hui manipulates situations to suit herself so that Yeong-nam is imprisoned for the false charge of child molestation.

The death of the "institutional" mother (the grandmother) is only the beginning of Do-hui's punishment of the town's complicity. Adults are eliminated and excluded, one by one, from her ghostly world. When Do-hui further manipulates events to have her stepfather Yong-ha apprehended for his sexual abuse, the divide between patriarchs (stepfather, state) and the socially marginalized (women, ethnic minorities) is temporarily transferred to that between girlhood and adulthood. As Yong-ha gets increasingly drunk, Do-hui undresses herself and lies next to him; she exploits her sexuality by putting her identity aside (literally undressing from her tight student uniform, which she has outgrown) in order to disrupt the power hierarchy. Having dialed the number of a local policeman, she creates an apparent crime scene, taking advantage of her stepfather's drunkenness setting the scene to ensure his capture. Do-hui's premature entry into "adulthood" and exploitation of her own sexuality momentarily exclude both Yong-ha and Yeong-nam from her own world of girlhood. Do-hui temporarily stops all the adults in town from exercising any control over her; first the grandmother, then Yeong-nam and finally, her stepfather.

For girls, Fiona Handyside observes, home "is a suffocating, oppressive space, which they seek to escape. . . . [T]he home is frequently figured as similar to a prison or a tomb, anticipating the narrative fate of characters who finish the films either dead or in prison."[64] In a visual parallel to an earlier image of Yeong-nam in her own place, Do-hui is shown crouched against the wall in the dark room of her house, with her skinny legs exposed. Kim has played a range of characters as a girl, from an orphan eager to be adopted (*A Brand New Life*, 2009), to a cute innocent girl to be protected by a former agent-turned-pawnshop owner (*The Man from Nowhere*, 2010), to a military sexual slave (*Snowy Road*, 2015), as discussed in chapter 2. Her physique and mannerisms may sometimes embody the idealized girlhood, as fantasized in girls' comic books; but Do-hui's actions in this film undercut such an image, oscillating between girlish frailty and monstrosity (as a young local policeman puts it), making girlhood inscrutable.

The insularity of girlhood could easily be transformed into either exclusivity or singularity to leave a girl deserted or alone. Do-hui's actions seem different, subject to whether she is by herself or with the company of others. A sense of relief, if not freedom, is achieved through the absence, rather than the presence, of adults; constantly seeking their acceptance, she otherwise rejects them instantly. The visual motif of "seen by" or "seen through" is repeated, underscoring Do-hui's performance of girlhood in front of adults (and for the spectator). Unlike some of the later indie films, such as *House of Hummingbird*, that do not show the domestic abuse of girls on-screen but leave it to be heard off screen or mentioned among characters, Do-hui's battered body is constantly shown and witnessed by adults. Consider Do-hui's similar types of actions, which differ in their performance, aim, and significance. When she dances alone by the pier, her posture is open, with her arms stretched and body feeling the air, in contrast to her contrived movements when emulating the cute dance choreography of the girls' idol band on Yeong-nam's television screen. Contrast the way she drinks a glass of milk with her meal at Yeong-nam's (figure 4.3), with the behavior seen through the glass window of the investigation room later in the film. She picks up the glass, drinks the milk, put the empty glass down, and slides it to the side slightly, emulating the way Yeong-nam slid the glass of liquor when Do-hui entered the bathroom earlier in the film. Then Do-hui looks at the partition, clearly aware of the presence of Yeong-nam looking through the one-way glass (figure 4.4a–b). The pairing of Do-hui's victimhood and the strength associated with Kim's star persona is unsettling, as if she questions the mortal economy of pity taken on her battered body, not only in this film but in other roles that she has performed, by turning the spectator's gaze and reaction back to themselves.

Yeong-nam visits Do-hui's place twice after she has been released from the prison: the first time to inform and the second to invite. Yeong-nam

Figure 4.3 Do-hui drinks milk with a meal at Yeong-nam's (*A Girl at My Door*, July Jung, 2014).

assures Do-hui that her stepfather would no longer be near her and questions whether Do-hui has framed him, making her partially responsible for the grandmother's death. In tears, Do-hui does not deny it. When Yeong-nam returns to Do-hui's place the second time, she (re)traces Do-hui's movements, seen when Do-hui hoped to trap her stepfather for sexual abuse. Yeong-nam opens the door of the same room to look for Do-hui, but finds the room empty. Instead, she sees Do-hui by the sea, on the pier where Yeong-nam has seen her dancing earlier in the film. Yeong-nam asks if Do-hui wants to come with her, an "invitation" to leave the town with Yeong-nam, even though they both know Do-hui's involvement with a crime: an act, which is in contrast to Yeong-nam's actions of "answering" the door at Do-hui's knocking on the door of her flat throughout the film. Yeong-nam drives the same road seen in the beginning of the film. When she arrived in town on this road, her car tires splashed water over Do-hui, but now Do-hui is comfortably asleep inside. Their co-existence is possible only within the space outside the town's patriarchy, spaces in-between or in transit.

The doubling of the two female characters in *A Girl at My Door* is reminiscent of similar pairings in other films, such as *Poetry* (*Si*, Lee Chang-dong, 2010—Lee was one of the producers of *A Girl at My Door*), and *House of Hummingbird*. The pairings in these films are also grounded in the marginality and vulnerability of female characters: in *Poetry* the pairing is established between Mi-ja, who suffers from Alzheimer's disease, and a girl, Hui-jin, who has committed suicide after being sexually abused by local boys (including

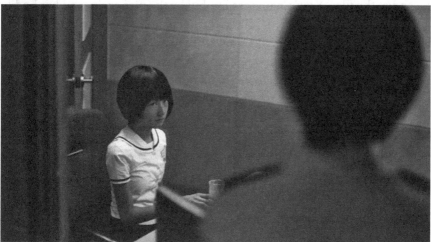

Figure 4.4 a–b Do-hui drinks milk defiantly in the investigation room in contrast to an earlier shot of her drinking milk at Yeong-nam's. As she slides the glass slightly, she looks in Yeong-nam's direction (*A Girl at My Door*, 2014).

Mi-ja's own grandson). In *House of Hummingbird*, Eun-hui (who is about the same age as Do-hui) becomes increasingly attached to her female tutor Yeong-ji at a learning center where she studies Sino-Korean characters (*hanmun*). Both Eun-hui and Yeong-ji cannot fit comfortably in their respective environments, trying to find their own place in the world. *A Girl at My Door* is further reminiscent of, but also departs from, Jung's earlier work, *11* (2008). In this short film, a woman police chief, Yu-jin, assists a woman, Myeong-suk, who has been found distraught and collapsed on the street. Yu-jin offers Myeong-suk a place to rest within the station. Myeong-suk says that she has been abused by her own mother since she was eleven years old (hence the title of the film). The film suggests a parallel between the two women who both suffer from aspects of the patriarchy, both at home and at work. Yu-jin has no option but to have Myeong-suk arrested once her crime turns out to be a homicide: the murder of her own mother. The mother in *11* and the grandmother in *A Girl at My Door* are played by the same actor, Kim Jin-gu, and their murder and death, respectively, represent a narrative punishment for those who endorse the patriarchy that persists at home—and the outcry of the victimized girls. Perhaps, realizing that leaving Do-hui alone may yield a similar outcome to that seen in *11*, Yeong-nam's invitation is an acknowledgment of the further support needed for the battered and abused girl, Do-hui.

Bae's star persona, which is caring and sympathetic but not necessarily nurturing, complicates the female relationship posited in *A Girl at My Door*. At the end of the film, Yeong-nam sees Do-hui by the pier again, and her bodily gestures have minutely shifted from the earlier jogging sequence, set soon after her arrival in town; although distraught, she retains a blank facial expression, recalling her performances in other films. After Do-hui accepts Yeong-nam's invitation to come with her, Yeong-nam embraces her and strokes Do-hui's back—an awkward gesture toward nurturing, as if their relationship is not quite identified; it shows the uncertainty of their relationship rather than their shared liminality.

From Trail to Trace: *Microhabitat* (2018)

In her discussion of Sofia Coppola's work, which she characterizes as "a cinema of girlhood," Handyside observes that many of Coppola's female leads are essentially girls, despite their ages: Charlotte in *Lost in Translation* (2003) as the "lost girl" and Marie Antoinette in the film of the same title (2006) as the "shattered self."[65] Instead of the girlhood valorized in the light of liminal freedom, girlhood can also yield an insecure sense of self, further shaken by the protagonist's relationship to home. Handyside argues that Coppola's girl-focused, post-feminist work renders home "abandoned, destroyed, invaded, vulnerable."[66] Girlhood dissociated from its demographic sense certainly applies to Mi-so in the Korean indie film, *Microhabitat*. Probably in her late twenties or early thirties, Mi-so is well beyond the age limits of girl in a demographic sense, but the original Korean title of the film, *Sogongnyeo*, and her character traits provide an interesting intertextuality and intersection with the girlhood examined in this book. The English title, *Microhabitat*, plays on the double meaning of Mi-so (played by Esom)'s name, which could mean both "smile" and "micro"; while *Sogongnyeo* is a term rarely used in common speech and mostly associated with the Korean translation and adaptations of the novel *A Little Princess* (Frances Hodgson Burnett, 1887–1888, 1905). The Korean title is a translation of the novel's Japanese edition, which began circulating during the colonial era and which became an important motif associated with colonial girl culture, as we saw in chapter 2; this is the model of girlhood to which Jong-bun in *Snowy Road* aspired. Both Mi-so's *soneyo*-like (*shōjo*, girlish) visuality (her long hair and physique) and her efforts to prolong the fading friendships and liminal freedom of her college days further place girlhood in the past tense—something to look back on but which cannot be sustained in the present.

Faced with rising rent and her dwindling income as a house cleaner, Mi-so decides to move out of the single room she has been renting; she hopes to save up a deposit and find a new place with a lower monthly payment. Mi-so's oversized orange suitcase, decorated with many labels, carries most of her belongings while she hops between the homes of her friends and customers. Her favorite habits are smoking and visiting a whiskey bar. She is in a relationship with Han-sol (played by Ahn Jae-hong), an aspiring cartoonist yet to find commercial success. The film follows Mi-so's visits to five friends from her college days, former bandmates: Mun-yeong (bass), Hyeon-jeong (keyboard), Dae-yeong (drums), Rok-i (singer a.s.a. Rok-yi), and Jeong-mi (guitarist). Each member not only displays a different relationship with Mi-so, but also conveys a different sense of, as well as space for, home.

Mi-so's economic status and profession reference both the present and the past: the "n-po" generation and the major trope of the 1970s girl—housemaid or domestic helper (*gasadoumi*), both exploited for their labor and sexuality. Critical discourses in Korea have underlined how *Microhabitat* appeals to the sensibility of the "n-po" generation, an abbreviation that refers to the number ("n") of basic needs that this generation should give up (*pogi* in Korean)—dating, marriage, having children—with this number ("n") seemingly increasing.[67] The term began to circulate as the unemployment rate of youth aged fifteen to twenty-nine rose rapidly and disproportionately: in 2016, for instance, this rate was 8.4 percent in contrast to the average overall unemployment rate of 3.2 percent.[68] Some of the characters in the film, Mi-so in particular, register this generation's frustrations—the lack of job prospects, the concept of the "house-poor," and the fixed gender expectations. I intend here, however, to shift the focus slightly toward Mi-so's "homeless domesticity," a term that Fraiman defines as the daily domestic needs, practices, and desires that are "imperiled and reinvented as an effect of homelessness."[69] I explore the "fragmented manifestation" of homeless domesticity in relation to Mi-so's

132   Forever Girls

decreasing privacy and the intimacy that she hopes to sustain through her relationships and friendships.[70]

Mi-so's attitude toward her profession is manifest in the opening sequence; she cleans a toilet with a Bosch drill, with a brush attached instead of its regular head. But her wages and the few clients she maintains are certainly insufficient for her to keep up with the rising costs of housing, and Mi-so is unable to afford a space of her own in the city. After having cleaned her friend/client's home, Mi-so asks for some rice in addition to the payment she has received. She carries the rice in a black plastic bag, unaware that it is spilling through a hole, and the whole bag is empty when she reaches home—a sign of her profession being inadequate to meet her daily needs. The film does not depict Mi-so as a character like the 1970s girls—sexually exploited, tragic heroines—yet she becomes increasingly decentered both in the city and in her favorite places. The film strings together Mi-so's visits to her friends' homes and downplays the risk of sexual violence inflicted on girls and women on the street. Although there is an implication that she has to stay overnight in public spaces, such as a coffee shop, no sexual threat is depicted other than a casual marriage proposal from one of her friends. The family home may be a site of violence for many battered women, runaway teens, and the elderly, but according to Jesook Song, the street is the last resort for homeless women due to the prevalence of sexual harassment and violence there.[71] Song's field research, conducted with homeless women during the economic downturn in the late 1990s and early 2000s after the country's International Monetary Fund (IMF) crisis, further found that homeless women were against the idea of staying at government-sponsored shelters due to the "strict" regulations, including the banning of smoking, which is one of Mi-so's favorite activities.[72] Mi-so, although homeless, is neither forced to resort to her sexuality to make ends meet nor compelled to stay in a public shelter.

Along with Mi-so's work as a cleaner, her leisure routines—smoking, drinking, and cooking—are interspersed with her visits to friends' homes. Mi-so and her friends associate smoking and drinking with their past, and some longingly reminisce about these activities. Mi-so, however, is one of the few who still smokes, an indication of their different priorities and ambitions and social positions. In the absence of her own home, Mi-so navigates both public and private spaces in the film, yet neither can provide a proper sense of privacy for either Mi-so or her friends. Fraiman observes that for the homeless "privacy" no longer means ownership but rather conditions for them to "wash up, change clothes, . . . get a good night's sleep and [be] shielded from the gaze, interference, and moralizing of others," conditions that Mi-so asks from her friends.[73] Early on, even before Mi-so gives up her room, it is too cold for her to have sex with her boyfriend, Han-sol. Hyeon-jeong, the first friend to allow Mi-so to stay, lives with her in-laws, and has neither privacy nor ownership of her own home. Hyeon-jeong's unpaid labor is taken for granted by her in-laws and husband, and Mi-so has to queue in order to use the bathroom, as one would to use a public toilet.

As the film critiques social expectations by reversing the priority between basic needs and leisure, it further invites the spectator to reconsider the value of unpaid domestic labor, often feminized and devalued, and which the housed have taken for granted. In contrast, the unpaid domestic labor offered by Mi-so is a form of safety as well as intimacy. Through cooking, Mi-so can temporarily exercise her agency—making this a form of shelter writing. Intimacy for the homeless, Fraiman claims, consists both of kinship-like relationships to others, and of closeness to objects.[74] Throughout the film it is repeatedly mentioned that Mi-so does not have any immediate family, as her parents have both passed away. Friendship for Mi-so is a form of kinship—an "affiliation based on choice supplementing or replacing" biological kinship— and cooking is something that allows her to show intimacy with her friends.[75]

She brings two dozen eggs to her friends' homes, as an expression of her gratitude for being allowed to stay overnight. In an interview, director Jeon explains Mi-so's choice of eggs, stating that eggs are practical and filling.[76] Like Ha-na in *The House of Us*, most of the dishes Mi-so makes for her friends or customer are egg- (or chicken-) based. Cooking seems to be an activity that further marks differing degrees of her relationship or intimacy with others. Among the five friends, she cooks only for two: Hyeon-jeong and Dae-yong. Mi-so makes some side dishes for Hyeon-jeong, who has fallen asleep, being exhausted from the domestic labor she provides daily and does not enjoy. While making eggs brewed in soy sauce, Mi-so peels and eats one egg herself in a form of delayed sharing with Hyeon-jeong, who she hopes will enjoy it later. Hyeon-jeong is the friend with whom Mi-so shares the most intimacy; the night before, the two slept side-by-side together on the floor. Both Hyeon-jeong and Mi-so offer unpaid labor, the former to her family and the latter for her friend, but with different motivations: Hyeon-jeong out of obligation as a daughter-in-law, Mi-so out of affection.

In addition to cleaning the mess that Dae-yeong has created in his own flat after his wife has moved out, Mi-so prepares, and shares with him, a nice breakfast. Toward the end of the film, Mi-so's young customer, Min-ji, a sex worker, has found herself pregnant. Although Min-ji can no longer afford to pay Mi-so, Mi-so cooks chicken stew (*samgyetang*), which the two share. In her brief discussion of the US television show *Queer Eye for the Straight Guy*, Fraiman posits that the five queer hosts' capability to revamp the homes of straight men resides in "their heightened understanding of the need we all share for shelter, in their privileged relation to the shelter writing as a discursive effect of the unsheltered life."[77] Likewise, Mi-so, who is unsheltered herself, is able to provide a sense of home or even order to those who are vulnerable.

Microhabitat critiques the gendered expectations around domesticity by showing and appreciating different motivations and types of domesticity. Still, all the male characters—her friends Dae-yeong and Rok-i, Jeong-mi's husband and Mi-so's boyfriend, Han-sol—partially or entirely abide by patriarchal values. The male characters encompass a wide spectrum of masculinity, from the conventional to the effeminate and the vulnerable. Jeong-mi's husband expresses the most conventional masculinity, taking for granted the overly attentive wife who even cuts his food at a restaurant. Dae-yeong is a typical case of house-poor; he bought an apartment as a marital home, taking on the heavy burden of a mortgage, and now he finds himself divorced. Rok-i, unmarried and still living with his parents, suggests to Mi-so that they get married so that she can alleviate his mother's domestic chores. Mi-so finds herself the next morning physically locked in Rok-i's house. In a horror-comedic flashback, the family's earlier hospitality is revealed to be a strategic plan to literally trap Mi-so and have her marry their son. Rok-i's marriage proposal is exactly in exchange for Mi-so's domesticity, similar to Jeom-sun in Choi's film *Daughter-in-Law* (1965) discussed in the Introduction, and his house is a space of both psychological and physical confinement, from which she escapes. Mi-so does not necessarily oppose the idea of marriage. When she mistakenly thought Han-sol would propose, she was delighted; only when marriage is imposed does she actively reject it.

Han-sol still wants to meet traditional gender expectations: being the breadwinner and affording a place to live together with nice things. He finds it unacceptable for Mi-so to stay with her male college friend Dae-yeong; Mi-so initially defends her relationship with him but soon accepts Han-sol's discomfort and leaves Dae-yeong's place after staying for only a few nights. None of these male characters is demonized, yet Han-sol's leaving of Mi-so is certainly sentimentalized. Mi-so is inexpressive throughout the film apart from only a few emotionally charged scenes with Han-sol: first when Han-sol informs her that he is leaving the country to work abroad and save money, and again when he leaves the factory dormitory for the airport. In both scenes, it is Han-sol who leaves and re-enters the frame, leaving Mi-so behind. In the latter scene, Han-sol's saying goodbye to Mi-so is shown in one take, and the camera stays with Mi-so until Han-sol re-enters the frame to give her a farewell kiss. Then the camera cuts to show the van driving around the corner and back to

Mi-so's reaction in close-up. Han-sol has been disillusioned about their future prospects and sees himself as inadequate. Yet he still perceives himself as a romantic and justifies his leaving of Mi-so as being practical, demanding emotional sacrifices from both Mi-so and himself. His departure completely takes away the little bit of privacy and intimacy left to Mi-so by that point; in the next shot, we see Mi-so sleeping at a laundromat. Fraiman is critical of the conventional gender divide, which places a masculine form of leaving home in opposition to a feminine domesticity, with the former often seen as "heroic" while the latter is "undervalued."[78] Han-sol's departure is not heroic, yet it is certainly self-regarding.

Although Mi-so occasionally smokes, drinks, and eats with other characters, she keeps her favorite leisure activity—drinking a glass of whiskey—solitary. Various types of food are mentioned, cooked, and consumed in the film. Although we see Mi-so and her boyfriend Han-sol doing things together—playing a hand game, donating blood to earn some spending money, and smoking—they are rarely seen properly eating together, only partaking of some street food. Kathleen McHugh insightfully discusses the divide between domesticity and leisure in the South Korean melodrama and notes generic differences between Korean and Hollywood melodrama in the representation of leisure. In Hollywood's idealization, the middle-class home is the site of leisure which domestic labor is required to maintain.[79] In contrast, all the leisure pursued in the film *Madame Freedom* (*Jayubuin*, Han Hyeong-mo, 1956) takes place outside the home, with the female lead, Seonyeong, increasingly drawn to elements of Western culture such as the dance hall. McHugh further argues that the punishment of women's agency, economic or otherwise, has more to do with their pursuit of (Western) leisure than any aspect of their professions.[80] Although there is a temporal as well as a class difference between the subjects of *Madame Freedom* and *Microhabitat*, the similarities are striking. Mi-so's friend, Jeong-mi, the last friend she visits and with whom she stays the longest, is most comparable to the Hollywood (or Korean television series) melodrama heroine; she belongs to the upper class, living in a mansion that she and her husband inherited from her in-laws, in a posh area, with a domestic helper of her own. Mi-so looks upward when she first arrives at Jeong-mi's house. When Mi-so offers to clean Jeong-mi's place in exchange for her stay, the domestic helper working for Jeong-mi is framed in the far background, visibly startled at the thought that she may lose her job. Jeong-mi turns down Mi-so's offer but Jeong-mi's dissatisfaction with her marriage is expressed by several slips of her tongue as well as through her visual isolation in her own home, as when she is shown drinking by herself later in the film.

136 Forever Girls

All three female characters are attracted to Western goods: in the case of Seon-yeong in *Madame Freedom*, it is the Western-style dance hall; for Jeong-mi, fine dining; and for Mi-so, malt whiskey and her Zippo lighter. For the housed, Seon-yeong and Jeong-mi, leisure is something to be enjoyed while their other needs are met through the assistance of their domestic helpers, while for the homeless Mi-so, leisure replaces her other needs and duties. Mi-so is not viewed as "immoral" for her decision to appreciate leisure like Seon-yeong or Jeong-mi, but she is scolded as "inadequate" by the latter. The film's ironic priority reversal of shelter and whiskey, however, does not function to portray Mi-so as vain, nor to "identify herself with the privileged," but rather frames Mi-so's pursuit of leisure as something that she "deserves."[81] Nonetheless, her desire leaves her in a similar position to Seon-yeong in *Madame Freedom*: an isolation or symbolic death, cut off from their connection to the world.

After Han-sol's departure, we only have glimpses of Mi-so on the street, at her work, and then in her favorite bar. She becomes ghostly: her hair is more gray (she has stopped taking medicine to prevent this), and she only leaves traces of herself behind, like the trail of rice that she left in the beginning of the film, or the little notes that she has left for her friends when leaving their places. She is shown walking over the bridge in slow motion, against the direction of the camera that moves from right to left showing vignettes of Seoul; it is as if her existence is out of sync with the rhythm and desire of the city. With her meager income and living circumstances, her dreams of intimacy or dignity in the city are, as some of her friends put it, "fanciful" or even "pathetic." In one final visit at Mi-so's favorite whiskey bar prior to the closing credits, she's visually decentered, with another customer having taken Mi-so's spot. When the camera moves down the bar counter to show other customers drinking and chatting, Mi-so is already leaving the place, turned away from the camera. In her previous visit, right after seeing Han-sol off, her solitude is still emphasized alongside that of her friends, who are shown in a montage with each drinking alone or playing music. Here, in contrast, Mi-so's solitude turns into isolation.

The mere presence of her traces mentioned above could even be considered her symbolic death, given the earlier funeral scene of Rok-i's father. She is the only one who is absent among her "gang," each of whom reminisces about Mi-so's visit. In her discussion of the '80s Korean novella *A Room in the Woods* (*Supsokui bang*, Kang Soek-kyeong, 1985), Jini Kim Watson associates the inability of the female lead, So-yang, to occupy space with "the unstable positioning of woman."[82] The last passage of So-yang's diary, which guides her elder sister's investigation into So-yang's eventual death, reads, "I'm an island, an island that traps me and touches me nowhere."[83] The imagery of isolation in the novella is strikingly similar to the last shot of *Microhabitat*. From Mi-so's own abandoned room, surprisingly in the middle of the city, to Mi-so's little tent framed by the dwarfing skyscrapers on the other side of the river, her world increasingly shrinks, leaving Mi-so none of the shelter or intimacy she has longed for.

Mi-so's rejection of both materialistic motivation and patriarchal values—including the marriage and gender roles expected of, and imposed on, women—leaves her no place to occupy in the city. Writing of So-yang's death in *A Room in the Woods*, Watson states, "If [a] woman cannot be self-evidently present, only the traces and tracks of her existence . . . indicate her location."[84] Mi-so is pushed from the center to the periphery, from being a person who used to offer a place and help for her friends in the past to being the only one who is absent when the band members meet at the funeral of Rok-i's father; from occupying the center of the band's college photo to becoming the homeless woman who cannot secure shelter. As the director has stated in a private interview, the city of Seoul is an integral part of the film.[85] However, Mi-so is not exactly a flaneuse or counterpart like the male flaneur protagonist Yeong-su in *Café Noir* (*Kape nuareu*, Jeong Seong-il, 2009). Lack of a sense of belonging underlies both films, but Mi-so's priority is not aimless wandering like Yeong-su's, but instead her search for homeless domesticity.

Mi-so perhaps does not consider herself a homeless person; in her conversation with Rok-i, she characterizes herself as "on a journey."[86] Mi-so belongs to a class that one of Song's homeless subjects calls "standbys, people who sojourn until they can resume their normal social life."[87] Mi-so's desire for intimacy and connection with others is highlighted, manifested through the visual motif of the window: throughout the film, she is seen constantly cleaning the windows of her friends and customers (figure 4.5). Importantly, this is a form of shelter dreaming: to have a window in her own place, as her letting agent reminds us, is a requirement for the place she hopes to rent. But with the little light coming out of her tent, her shelter dream appears more inaccessible than ever, shrinking from a room of her own, to a window and a fading streak of light (figure 4.6).

Conclusion

The female characters examined in this chapter—Ha-na and the two sisters, Yu-mi and Yu-jin, in *The House of Us*, Do-hui and Yeong-nam in *A Girl at My Door*, and Mi-so in *Microhabitat*—are in need of shelter for different

138 Forever Girls

Figure 4.5 Mi-so is seen repeatedly cleaning the window throughout the film (*Microhabitat*, Jeon Go-woon, 2018).

Figure 4.6 Mi-so's isolation as a sign of her symbolic death (*Microhabitat*, 2018).

reasons: anxiety over family breakdown, domestic abuse, relocation, and homelessness. But each film dwells on what Fraiman calls "shelter writing," moment-by-moment narration of domestic activities as part of the yearning for order, safety, and intimacy. Domesticity here is construed not as a feminized gender obligation, internalized by female characters but a means to achieve a sense of agency and earn happiness in "doing little actions"—making dollhouses with paper boxes; ironing a police uniform; cleaning, polishing, and cooking. The sense of home or shelter achieved through these activities is temporary, making both the process and outcome tenuous. The leading woman director in the Korean film industry, Yim extends the possibility of shelter writing in her film, *Little Forest* (*Liteul poreseuteu*, 2018) with the protagonist Hye-won returning home after her struggle to find a stable job in the city, in order to relive her girlhood and recreate her mother's recipes.[88] Hye-won's progress, from preparing simple dishes to drying and preserving food and fruits, and her appreciation of every step required to prepare each dish, are part of the long process of her settling, finding, and (re)creating a shelter for herself in the world.

Contemporary Korean independent films such as *Steel Flower, Queen of Walking, Omok Girl,* and *Fighter* (*Paiteo,* Yun Jero, 2020), and the documentary *Dance Sports Girls* (*Ttanppo geolseu,* Lee Seung-mun, 2017), all explore girls' leisure as an essential part of their lives that helps build a sense of belonging: dancing, race walking, go play, and boxing. They continue and redirect the thematics of women directors' earlier work such as *Flying Boys* and *The Aggressives,* locating the place of safety outside home and regular school curriculum or work.[89] Girls' leisure and a possibility of granting their idleness would be the focus of the last chapter of this book.

Women directors' previous work and collaboration with prominent male directors, however, continues to form a marketing strategy or at least guides the audience's expectations of the films' shared aesthetic sensibilities or tonal similarities, even though the master-apprentice system no longer rules the field. Yim worked as an assistant director on Yeo Kyun-dong's *Out to the World* (*Sesangbakeuro,* 1994); Park Chan-ok was assistant director to Hong Sang-soo's *Virgin Stripped Bare* (*O! Sujeong!* a.s.a. *Oh! Soo-jung!* 2000); Lee Kyoung-mi served as script supervisor for Park Chan-wook's *Sympathy for Lady Vengeance* (*Chinjeolhan guemjassi,* 2005). Both Park and Bong Joon-ho praised Lee's feature debut, *Crush and Blush* (2008) with Bong making a cameo appearance in the film. July Jung and Yoon both worked closely with Lee Chang-dong either at the pre-production stage (Yoon) or throughout (Jung). For the premiere of *Heart* (*Hateu,* 2019) by Jeong Ga-young at the London International Film Festival, the synopsis of her film read: "Fleabag meets Hong Sang-soo."[90] The frame of reference here should be re-considered and re-located to a more complex context of independent cinema as proposed in this chapter.

5
Idle Girls

Sunny (2011), *Miss Granny* (2014), and *Queen of Walking* (2015)

In *Sunday Night and Monday Morning* (*Ilyoil bamgwa yolyoil achim*, Choe In-hyeon, 1970) late Yoon Jeong-hee (also spelled as [a.s.a.] Yun Jeong-hie) was cast as the female lead, So-hui, who works at a small travel agency. She laments, with her boyfriend, Cheol, that after paying monthly bills, there is little left of their meager paychecks for simply enjoying their time together. The two decide to do some extra work so they can afford to take a short trip on the coming Sunday, but when the day arrives, Cheol is called up to cover for his boss's absence. While So-hui waits for Cheol to finish work, she wanders the city with the hope that they will shortly be able to travel as they originally planned. She visits various sites in Seoul, as does the character of Hyeon-ju in another film featuring the same actress, *Night Journey* (a.k.a. *Night Voyage*, *Yahaeng*, Kimg Soo-yong, 1977) discussed in chapter 1.

There is a stark contrast, however, between So-hui and Hyeon-ju in terms of types of leisure activities they can afford and enjoy. So-hui is denied any leisure except what the city can offer for no charge. After having learned that Cheol must work until his boss returns to the office, So-hui tries to keep herself busy: she reads in the park; she goes to the cinema but finds the movie ticket too expensive; she wants to surprise her boyfriend by treating him to a nice Chinese meal for lunch, but he must leave before they finish eating. So-hui only consumes street food and drinks by herself at the end of day, and finally embarks on a journey by herself. For a female office worker from a working-class family with a single mother and younger siblings, consumption or leisure is not granted but must be earned through extra work to secure the resources to pay for the treat. In contrast, Hyeon-ju, the female lead in *Night Journey*—who works at a bank and has more experience and income—almost indulges herself during her annual leave. She takes a leisurely walk at the park, followed by a cup of coffee; she visits a beauty salon and bowling alley. At the end of her day, she drinks by herself at a bar and spends a night with a stranger at a hotel, although the reality of the last event remains ambiguous as

Forever Girls. Jinhee Choi, Oxford University Press. © Oxford University Press 2025.
DOI: 10.1093/9780197685822.003.0006

Idle Girls **141**

to whether it actually takes place or is her sexual fantasy. Neither protagonist is a girl in demographic terms, yet the unaffordability of leisure for So-hui is quite telling, as if nothing could compensate for her girlhood missed or past.

Sunday Night and Monday Morning begins and ends with the glimpse of So-hui and Cheol's consummation of their romantic relationship. As So-hui is seen on her way to meet Cheol on Sunday morning, her girlish hairstyle of two braids falling around's her neck underscores her sexual inexperience. The film is indeed promoted as the rendering of So-hui's first sexual experience. In the upper corner of the original poster released, we see So-hui holding a man with his back to the camera—she is visually foregrounded as the star (figure 5.1). Titles in the upper part of the poster read "Time Has Usurped Love Affair (*ukcheui gantong*)"; "Work Has Usurped a Time of Intimacy."

Figure 5.1 A poster of *Sunday Night and Monday Morning* (1970).

142 Forever Girls

I have metaphorically translated the marketing phrases on the poster, which do not make clear sense even in Korean; taken literally, the wording suggests adultery (*gantong*) or rape (*ganggan*). Both the advertising and the film's framing of the narrative trajectory around the sexual relationship misrepresent the major plot: the film principally depicts So-hui's solitary wandering of the city as a flaneuse, comparable to Cleo in Agnes Varda's *Cleo from 5 to 7* (*Cleo de 5 a 7*, 1962). Other key words on the film poster, however, hint at the relationship that is at issue here: time, work, and body (*yukche*), with a heavy visual emphasis on the female body: the sino-word *gan* used in the two words mentioned (*gantong; ganggan*) consists of the sign, woman女, compiled three times in a pyramid shape. At the bottom of the poster, the bodies of the two leads are folded on top of each other with the line below reading, "the pain of first experience . . . a thrilling love serenade." While So-hui's wandering of the city points to the possibility of her idleness, the leisure she hopes to enjoy is constantly denied, as she has no resources.

As discussed in the previous chapters, the girl's liminal status in the history of Korean cinema from the 1970s is constantly controlled and subsumed by the national developmental ethos and modernity (chapter 1); colonial traumas and sexual violation (chapter 2); and perfunctory, functional death (chapter 3). The irony lies in the very gap between the labor expectations imposed on girls by family and industry and the lack of social safety nets and responsibility for their welfare, which is often symbolized through nominal or literal death. Girls have used their meager incomes to provide financial support for their families as dutiful daughters, and they have worked and contributed to make the national economy competitive internationally (especially in service and light industries), but they are granted little leisure time for themselves. In memoirs and oral labor histories, women workers repeatedly mention the value of labor unions not only for conveying their legal rights and conducting negotiations with employers but also for the leisure activities that members shared with fellow workers: excursions to the mountains or outskirts of a city; educational opportunities; and volunteer activities outside their work.[1]

Yet neither Korean society nor cinematic representation have allowed them sufficient leisure. In *The Maiden Who Went to the City* (*Dosirogan cheonyeo*, Kim Soo-yong, 1981), discussed in chapter 1, bus attendant Mun-hui spends a leisurely time at an amusement park, hoping to work better with the bus driver, who has been bullying her. In the end, though, this effort leads to a near sexual assault, from which she escapes. In the seventies "enlightenment (*gyemong*)" films, such as *Wives on Parade* (*Anaedeului haengjin*, Im Kwon-taek, 1974), women's labor is depicted as only to help the family to prosper and the village to modernize, the very theme of the New Village Movement (*Saemaeul undong*). In the film, the rocky start of a newlywed couple is smoothed over when the wife becomes the village leader who helps a village to build the infrastructure needed, and teaches her abusive husband to repent his misdeeds.

This chapter will pick up from the previous chapter: girls' leisure and idleness. As mentioned, girls' leisure provides girl protagonists a dream of leading an alternate life: singing in *Han Gong-ju* (Lee Su-jin, 2013) discussed in chapter 3; tap dancing in *Steel Flower* (*Seutil peulawo*, Park Seok-yeong, 2015); race walking in *Queen of Walking* (*Geotgiwang*, Baek Seung-hwa, 2016); dance sports in a TV documentary *Dance Sports Girls* (*Ttanppo geolseu*, Lee Seung-mun 2017); *Omok* game ("five-in-a-row") in *Omok Girl* (*Omok sonyeo*, Baek Seung-hwa, 2018); boxing for the North Korean defector protagonist in *Fighter* (*Paiteo*, Yun Jero, 2021); or "idol" dance cover in *Next Sohee* (*Daeum So-hui*, July Jung, 2023). I will examine the significance of girls' idleness—punctuation to the endless expectations on productivity and industry from both family and work—drawing on Brian O'Connor's conception of "idleness" as a form of freedom. He defends the notion of idleness against the modern philosophical treatment of it as a moral vice and sees it as an authentic form of freedom, "a knowing indifference to specific recommendations about how one ought to live."[2] This chapter examines in depth three films that feature the actress Shim Eun-kyung: *Sunny* (*Sseoni*, Kang Hyeong-chul, 2011); *Missy Granny* (*Susanghan geunyeo*, Hwang Dong-hyuk, 2014); and *Queen of Walking* (*Geotgiwang*, Baek Seung-hwa, 2016). They show the extent to which idle play, leisure, or idleness in each film could be seen to contribute to a positive form of freedom, questioning the progress ethos that has long governed the South Korean society, and challenging the patriarchal, developmental context.

Coming of Age at the End of History—*Sunny* (2011)

In her memoir, *Free: Coming of Age at the End of History*, Lea Ypi recollects her coming-of-age experience at the collapse of communism in Albania and the paradox of freedom.[3] The film *Sunny* could be similarly contextualized. Its title alludes to the song *Sunny* (Boney M), and a group of seven girls take the name for themselves. They are experiencing the welcome consumerism that is appearing after years of a military dictatorship. The box-office success of the film marks a turning point in depicting both girlhood and the democratic political upheaval of South Korea in the 1980s. Instead of girls embodying the victimhood of political traumas, *Sunny* grants a degree of play and idleness to girlhood and a sense of freedom, however limited; the seven girls willfully disregard the political turmoil and disassociate themselves from the political mores of the mid-1980s. The film foregrounds a nostalgia toward the popular culture of the 1980s and a growing consumerism. Despite its specific historical and cultural context—with its flashbacks to a lifting of the school uniform policy (1983–1986) and references to Korean popular culture—it inspired many adaptations in the Asian region: Hong Kong (as a television series, *Never Dance Alone*, 2014), Vietnam (*Go Go Sisters*, 2018), Japan (*Sunny: Strong Mind, Strong Love*, 2018), Indonesia (*Glorious Days*, 2019), and China (*Sunny Sisters*, 2021).[4]

The main plot fondly looks back at the girls' consumer culture set in the 1980s but more specifically in 1986, a year prior to the June Democratic Uprising in 1987. When the police visit Na-mi's home to search for her brother who is a student activist, a close-up of the flyer that he must have composed or disseminated prompts a more specific temporal marker. The signature glimpsed at the bottom of flyer reads 1986, which interestingly coincides with the first year when serial killing began to take place in Hwaseong. In *Memories of Murder* (*Salinui chueok*, Bong Joon-ho, 2003), Joseph Jeon notes, Bong ingeniously uses the document to signal the timeframe: such as when Bak (a.s.a. Park) signs an agreement form required for his sidekick Jo to have his leg amputated, or when the DNA report arrives from the United States.[5] The framing story of *Sunny* takes place in the present, with the protagonist Na-mi, who is now the mother of a teenage daughter. Respecting the dying wish of her friend Chun-hwa, who was the leader of the group in the past, Na-mi contacts each of the group's seven members, most of whom are now financially struggling mothers and almost all working for low wages.

The girls' idle play—going for snacks in the school cafeteria, preparing their dance performance to the song *Sunny*, listening to music, or just hanging out—in the flashbacks is constantly confronted with present reality, often equated with violence in the past, and ultimately, the death of Chun-hwa in the present. The famous girls' fight sequence between two rival "gangs" on the street, in the middle of police suppression of a political demonstration, shows the girls' indifference to the political reality and violence around them (figure 5.2); yet in the girls' own world, their play and fights result in another form of violence.

As O'Connor observes, in the process of self-fashioning—*buildung*—there is a constant tension between self-realization and social usefulness.[6] In the non-religious conception of *buildung*—in contrast to one modeled on a divine being—people's efforts to better themselves or become worthy,

Figure 5.2 Girls fight against the backdrop of police suppressing a political demonstration (*Sunny*, Kang Hyeong-cheol, 2011).

O'Connor notes, are constantly thwarted by usefulness that demands sacrifice. In *Sunny*, the girls' attention to their surroundings increasingly leads to a self-recognition of their lesser selves in the flashbacks. Although the group named after the song *Sunny* presents themselves to be better than their rivals at another school, their difference is only a matter of degree than kind. At the cafeteria during the school's festival, Na-mi and Sang-mi (played by Chun Woo-hee, *Han Gong-ju*) fight each other. Sang-mi was a former member of the gang whom Na-mi has replaced, when she transferred to the school. As the two push and pull, they possibly form a continuum—Sang-mi being a lesser self—despite the perceived differences. The initial shot-reverse-shots of the two characters initially mark their difference and underline their respective timidity and aggressiveness, but such a difference quickly disappears when they are framed in a two-shot, which emphasizes their similarity, having the same bobbed hair style and the same desperation to be accepted as a "legitimate" member of the group (figure 5.3). Sang-mi accidentally slits Su-ji's face with a piece of glass from a broken bottle, when she enters the cafeteria and Su-ji's bleeding face is reflected on the glass panel alongside a magazine cover on which Su-ji is the model. Su-ji's girls (shōjo) comic book-like appearance (long straight hair; large expressive eyes) on the magazine is juxtaposed with Su-ji's scarred face bleeding (figure 5.4).

Even in the present, the adult characters alternate between their dreamed lives in the past and the present reality. The recording of the seven girls' cheerful predictions in high school of what their future selves will be contrasts dramatically with the failure of several of them to achieve this goal. In the present, they are viewed and judged by others in terms of their familial or

Figure 5.3 When Na-mi and Sang-mi struggle with their heads down, their initial difference is less discernible (*Sunny*, 2011).

Figure 5.4 Su-ji's self-reflection on the glass panel further underscores the gap between the idolized self and the violent reality (*Sunny*, 2011).

social worth (or lack thereof). As a mother and wife, Na-mi is rewarded only financially by her husband who offers her money to buy luxury goods for Na-mi and her ill mother; Jang-mi as an insurance salesperson would become the sales queen of the month only with the help of Chun-hwa's support in secret. Some of the adult characters' unpaid or poorly paid labor is dismissed by their family members, in-laws, or employers. Only when Chun-hwa provides money in the present can they enjoy and exercise autonomy briefly again.

The dance sequence of remaining members of the group at Chun-hwa's funeral to the song *Sunny*, is followed by the drawings of their past as well as future selves with Geum-ok and Bok-hui (a.s.a. Bok-hee) having opened their new business thanks to Chun-hwa's generosity. In the epilogue, however, both their present and future are cast in the past tense, as if their future is a delayed completion of their coming-of-age process that began a few decades earlier. One may wonder whether Chun-hwa's death departs from that of a girl in the films discussed in chapter 3 as a form of necro-cinematics (why should she die?), although her death does not escalate a male rivalry but instead brings female characters together and closer. Yet, the "idle play" is granted to Chun-hwa's friends only *at her expense* in the film. Despite the glimpses of their future in the epilogue, idleness would not "prevail as a permanent mode of [their] experience," as O'Connor would describe it, but remains in the past associated with their collective girlhood under the leadership of Chun-hwa.[7]

A critically acclaimed film, *Take Care of My Cat* (*Goyangireul butakhae*, Jeong Jae-eun, 2001) draws a different picture of the idleness of girlhood. It opens with the five girl protagonists playing a skipping game by the harbor of In-cheon, a seaport city west of the capital city Seoul. Despite showing this children's game as the sanctioned end of girlhood, its presentation is slightly unsettling. Shortly before the camera cuts to show the girls smiling and chatting in high-pitched voices, they make a turn along the heavy thick anchor cord placed on the ground. They are singing a military song whose lyrics describe "marching forward over the dead bodies of comrades . . ."

Play, like idleness, is often premised on "freedom from necessity."[8] The girls' play in the opening scene quickly comes to an end with their graduation. As Michele Cho observes, throughout *Take Care of My Cat*, girls' actions are regimented in their everyday spaces and workplaces, underscored by the mise-en-scène: the squares and grids, in particular. The world map in the stock exchange office, where Hye-ju works; the checkered chair in a room where Tae-hui, played by Bae Doona, types for a male poet; the drawings by Ji-yeong—these confine the girls' existence and experience to keep them within their socially defined roles.[9] Even the most "successful" and ambitious character in terms of career, Hye-ju, who works as an office assistant, is constantly denied the opportunity to become a member of the professional world.

Unlike Hye-ju, who is able to move into a new flat near her office with her sister, other protagonists are denied a "shelter" in the sense defined by Fraiman. Earlier in the film, the five girls gather on the rooftop of a building; they end up being locked out on the rooftop—a sign of losing their shelter. The physical collapse of Ji-yeong's poverty-stricken place and Tae-hui's departure from her parents' home further mark the beginning of seeking their own shelter and/or idleness, however temporary it may be. *Take Care of My Cat* ends with Tae-hui, inviting her friend Ji-yeong to join her and begin a new journey together. Although their destination is unclear, the motivation and outcome of Tae-hui's invitation is clear: their desire to prolong their girlhood or liminality a little bit longer.

148   Forever Girls

A shot of Tae-hui and Ji-yeong looking at the information board at the airport, with some time elapsed (as their costumes have changed from winter to spring clothes), signals their departure together to explore possibilities outside their home, family, and country: free from their responsibilities and social existence—their denounced "worthiness." Whether they will leave the country remains ambiguous. But regardless of the reality that awaits them, they seem more determined than resigned, as they appear in the last shot. Instead of offering the girls a form of affordable leisure or idle play, as Chunhwa does in *Sunny*, the director Jeong ends the film with possibly a "beginning" of idleness—free from the pressure from norms or "freedom from opinions of others"—to which they are entitled and which I also see in the film, *Queen of Walking*, discussed in the last section of this chapter.[10]

20 Once Again, or Forever Being a Mom—Miss Granny (2014)

The domestic box office hit *Miss Granny* grabbed regional and global attention for several reasons; it not only inspired several remakes including the Chinese one, *20 Once Again* (*Chong fan 20 sui*, Leste Chen, 2015) but also was available on various platforms as a feature film directed by Hwang Dong-hyuk, after the global success of his Netflix series, *Squid Game* Season 1(*Ojingeo geim*, 2021). Scholars locate the success and significance of *Miss Granny* within its industry context as well as its touch upon the issue of decreasing individual identity. *Miss Granny* earned $53 million US dollars in Korea, which spurred remakes in China, Japan, Vietnam, Thailand, Indonesia, and the Philippines.[11] As a hit with audiences, *Missy Granny* offered a feasible Asian regional co-production strategy that offers a source material, which is easily adaptable to the local needs. It provided the East Asian regional film market with an alternative to the previous attempt at big-budget pan-Asian co-production practices that relied on the transnational narrative with multi-national star casts: *Seven Swords* (*Qi jian*, Tsui Hark, 2005); *The Promise* (*Wu ji*, Chen Kaige, 2005); and *The Myth* (*San wa*, Stanley Tong, 2005). Brian Yecies, in his discussion of the recent co-productions between China and Korea, notes that the Chinese remake, *20 Once Again* by Taiwanese director Leste Chen, follows in the footsteps of *A Wedding Invitation* (*Fen shou he yue*, Oh Ki-hwan, 2013), which provided a successful precedent: "Remove all specifically Korean content from the original film [and] make the film for a Chinese audience."[12] Upon release, both *A Wedding Invitation* and *20 Once Again* set records among the Chinese-Korean co-production films, grossing $31 million US dollars and

$57 million US dollars, respectively. The strategy of film production company CJ E&M, "one source, multiple territory," promotes the flexibility of the source material to be adapted to appeal to local tastes.[13]

Kyung Hyun Kim, in contrast, discusses the films within the recent body of work that he characterizes as "body switch" films, including Korean blockbusters and box office hits, such films as *Masquerade* (*Gwanghae*, Chu Chang-min, 2012) and *The Beauty Inside* (*Beuti insaideu*, Baek Jong-yeol, 2015). In the age of post-dictatorship, Kim observes in this cycle of films a shift from a disciplinary to a "control" society; in the post-trauma Korean society, the notion of individual is replaced by that of "dividual." In the control society, according to Gilles Deleuze, the self is no longer defined in relation to the masses or collectivity, but against or within data and codes.[14] The recent proliferation of body switch films and comedies, Kim claims, both embodies and reconsiders the divide between the self and the external, be it history, society, or the real. Kim assesses that in the case of *Miss Granny*, unlike *Masquerade* or *The Beauty Inside*, the film is incapable of celebrating the disappearance of an authentic body where the self-identity used to be anchored, holding onto a more conservative ontology of the body(soul)/self-identity.

The film further sheds light on an ongoing issue of the aging population of South Korea. The population of the age group between their sixties and seventies increased drastically in the last few decades: it tripled from 5.1 percent in 1975 to 15.7 percent in 2015, while the total population did not quite double—from 35.3 to 50.6 million in the same period.[15] Or it draws attention to related issues of the lack of welfare for and financial vulnerability of the elderly in South Korea. Despite their increased life expectancy, the age group of sixty and above is the country's lowest income group, and they can no longer expect financial support from their children.[16] Other scholars also note "new momism"—a growing re-embracing of traditional family values that focuses on "motherhood as not just a woman's highest vocation but also the key to her own personal happiness"—as the basis of their success across the region.[17]

I sidestep these issues to focus on labor and leisure, shared in all three versions: *Miss Granny*; *20 Once Again*; and the Japanese remake, *Sing My Life* (*Ayashii kanozo*, Mizuta Nobuo, 2016). Instead of discussing and comparing several remakes of *Miss Granny* with the current trend of regional industry and body switch films, I dwell on the juxtaposition of female characters of two different generations, a juxtaposition that pivots on girlhood, where the relived girlhood is shown as an irreality, while the conservative outlook of the patriarchal gender role is endorsed (and even celebrated). My discussion of this aesthetic strategy continues and complements the discussion of films in the previous chapters, including *Spirits' Homecoming* (*Guihyang*, Cho

Jung-rae, 2016) in chapter 2; *Poetry* (*Si*, Lee Chang-dong, 2010); and *A Girl at My Door* (*Do-huiya*, July Jung, 2014) and chapter 3. The pairing of two female protagonists or characters of different generations, with parallel or diverging paths, ironically underscores the perpetuation and replication of the patriarchy regardless of the characters' wish to betray or voluntarily accept it.

Miss Granny and its remakes are based on the narrative premise that the grandmother's seventy-year-old body is swapped with her younger self—when she was about twenty—after she has a photograph taken in a mysterious studio. In the Korean original, O Mal-sun (also spelled as [a.s.a.] Oh Mal-soon) raised her son, Hyeon-cheol (a.s.a. Hyun-chul), as a single mother, after her husband passed away shortly after the child's birth.[18] Mal-sun has dedicated her life to the successful career of her child (a son in the Chinese remake; a daughter in the Japanese version). The narrative closure, however, places the young granny, O Du-ri (a.s.a. Oh Doo-ri, named after Mal-sun's favorite Hollywood star Audrey Hepburn, playing with the Korean pronunciation of Audrey, "*o-deu-ri*"), facing a dilemma. Du-ri must decide whether to let go of her youth once again, for the sake of the life of her grandson who has been injured in a traffic accident. For each film, the gender baggage still exists as the source of "heart-warming" comedies: forever being a mom (or granny).

Miss Granny and the remakes from the People's Republic of China (PRC) and Japan all conclude with the sentimental scene of the granny-turned-young protagonist donating her blood to save the life of her grandchild. Her sacrifice is portrayed as a blood transfusion, which presumably drains her youth out of her body. The Japanese version even starts with the blood transfusion scene, foreshadowing the narrative outcome of the short-lived "holiday" of the grandmother as a young woman. Throughout the Korean source-text, caregiving (family or romantic) is constantly construed as parasitic, inadequately reciprocated or appreciated. Both Mal-sun and Na-yeong (a.s.a. Na-young), Mr. Bak (a.s.a. Park)'s adult daughter, characterize the other's relationship with Bak as "bloodsucking." Earlier in the film, when Mal-sun visits Bak with a bag of peaches, she criticizes Bak's daughter, Na-yeong, for living with her father long after having passed the "appropriate" age for marriage, calling her (financially) parasitic on Bak ("living by bloodsucking the father"); similarly, Na-yeong mistakenly believes the relationship between her father and Du-ri (young Mal-sun) to be a May-December relationship for financial gain. At the thought of public embarrassment, as well as losing her place in Bak's household, Na-yeong bursts into tears, crying that it was the wish of her deceased mother that she look after Bak.

Mal-sun is no longer the principal breadwinner but lives with her son's family, thanks to his filial piety. Mal-sun's transformation into a young woman is on the surface motivated by the fact that she must leave her son's house, as her daughter-in-law collapses due to the stress of living with an overbearing mother-in-law; but underneath, it has more to do with her having no place in the family or society, despite her constant stubbornness and habit of imposing her authority as an elder. Mal-sun's return to her youth and singing performances as Du-ri are set against her increasingly weakened maternal authority in both private and public space. The two major performances, both of which are broadcast live within the film, bear an interesting relationship to her motherhood and girlhood, respectively. Mal-sun's hardship as a young single mother is framed against the 1970s song "White Butterfly (*Hayan nabi*)" that she sings with her grandson's band Semi-basement (*Banjiha*), while her youthful romance with Seung-wu (a.s.a. Seung-woo) is intercut with her final performance of the newly composed song, "One More Time (*Hanbeon deo*)."

During her singing of "White Butterfly," we see the reaction shots of, first, the producer Seung-wu in the studio along with audiences present, then of Mr. Bak outside on the street, and finally of Hyeon-cheol's family at home. Although the cut to Hyeon-cheol's home begins with a shot of the daughter-in-law and a quick appearance of the granddaughter in the frame, the camera quickly focuses on Hyeon-cheol, who is touched by Du-ri's broadcast performance without yet knowing her identity. Du-ri's musical performance, intercut with the flashbacks of her hardship as a single mother, is transformed into a gender performance to be appreciated and re-appreciated by male characters, who stand in different temporal relationships to Mal-sun (her love interest in the present; the lifelong, loyal companion Bak; and the beloved son in the past). The comparison of the woman's role with various ball games and men in the film's opening sequence could be of relevance here. In the pre-credit sequence, the life of a woman is compared to a ball in different kinds of sports: a woman in her teens is comparable to the ball of basketball; in her twenties, that of rugby; in her thirties, that of table tennis; during the middle age, that of golf; and beyond that phase, the fate of a woman is like the ball in dodgeball: everyone wants to avoid her. The status of woman is defined by her relationship to men—as Hyaeweol Choi puts it, a convenient "adjunct" to men: his daughter, his wife, his mother—or, as in the opening sequence, in terms of how men *react* to a woman.[19] Du-ri's performance ends with almost direct exchanges between Hyeon-cheol, whose gaze at Du-ri's televised performance is returned by a cut to Du-ri in the studio, ending her song with tears. It is Hyeon-cheol who in the end must re-appreciate his mother's sacrifice as a single mother.

Through a melodramatic twist, Mal-sun's grandson Ji-ha is injured in a traffic accident shortly before a concert in which the band is to perform on stage a new song, "One More Time," composed by Ji-ha himself. Du-ri insists on playing the song in the absence of Ji-ha. If the previous performance sequence, analyzed above, is about Mal-sun's motherhood, the final performance by Du-ri is about her relived youth. The second verse of the song is accompanied by two montage sequences: one showing her youth since the body swap and the other, her romantic interest in Seung-wu. Although Du-ri's initial voice-over dedicates her performance to Ji-ha, it is only when she is unaccompanied by any family members, that she can be free from the patriarchy and motherly performance of the past. Her short-lived moments of youth—her street performance and her romance with Seung-wu—are celebrated "for the last time (*majimak hanbeon deo*)," despite an inevitable end to both. The staging of the hospital sequence repeatedly has Du-ri blocked by a hospital staff member or Ji-ha in order not to be spotted by Seung-wu, as she is about to resume her previous roles as mother and grandmother. The shot-reverse-shot between Du-ri and Seung-wu underscores the conventional gender asymmetry; Du-ri is momentarily invisible when a staff member of the hospital approaches her bed, blocking Seung-wu's view of her. In the operation room, the object of her gaze is switched from the shot of Seung-wu to that of her grandson, Ji-ha, on the operating table, indicating her willful sacrifice, one more time, for her family.

Motherhood as gender performance, when naturalized, is taken for granted and invisible; only when it is dissociated from the usual (aging) body can it be recognized as performance. The film's rather conservative trajectory could then be reassessed in light of the significance of performance, either gender or creative. Du-ri's singing starts out as a leisure activity at a community center for the elderly but is quickly transformed into "work-play" that becomes instrumental for her to help others. Her street performance with Ji-ha's band gathers enough attention and donations from the crowd that the band can treat themselves a meal afterward; it also—in a somewhat unlikely twist—results in Ji-ha's band being picked by Seung-wu, the producer, who is looking for something new (the assistant producer even criticizes Seung-wu's decision to give Ji-ha's band an opportunity to perform, when they neither have enough experience as a band nor have released an album). Anthony Giddens acknowledges an overlap among various types of activities: work, play, and leisure. He observes, "In societies where the sphere of work and leisure is not clearly delineated, socially or psychologically, it is probably more appropriate to speak only of a continuum between work and play."[20] Nonetheless, Giddens points out the non-instrumental nature of leisure/play and their dissociation from reality; while both play and leisure are "free of social or economic obligation, play as a type of leisure activity entails the temporary creation of a sphere of irreality, which is derived from 'the rules of irrelevance.'"[21]

On the operation table, Mal-sun accepts her short-lived youth as a fun dream—a form of fantasy. Yet, what constitutes irreality is not her singing as leisure but her apparent girlhood. What drives Mal-sun to enjoy her regained youth is her self-recognition of invisibility and indiscernibility as an aging adult; what she achieves through her signing is a social regard and public recognition of her worth, not so much of her idle youth that has been undoubtedly short-lived, or even non-existent. After Mal-sun's initial body switch, her acceptance of the transformation begins with her glancing at an old woman at a *jjimjilbang* (a Korean-style sauna), as well as spotting herself in an elderly crowd whose appearances are indiscernible from behind. Such self-recognition ignites her subsequent shopping sprees, swiftly turning her into a consuming girl in a montage sequence, finally putting frugality—a long-considered and gendered virtue, underscored by her worn-down shoes—behind her.[22]

The film at times raises a light criticism against familism and ageism—possibly outcomes of their occasional selfishness and inconsiderateness. Mal-sun is criticized and even attacked by an old acquaintance for stealing a family recipe to open her own restaurant. When Du-ri critiques a young mother's handling of a crying baby, her remarks go beyond elderly advice and denounce the young mother's physical condition as inadequate for a mother.[23] Conflict still arises from the family hierarchy between women: Mal-sun and her daughter-in-law. When the two prepare the family dinner, their relationship is staged in depth, emphasizing this hierarchy. The framing of the scene visually foregrounds Mal-sun, while the daughter-in-law appears in the background and out of focus. Mal-sun's criticism of her daughter-in-law's fish stew is later repeated when she visits the house as young Du-ri. In the earlier scene, the grandmother comes between the grandson, Ji-ha, and his mother both visually and metaphorically; overbearing Mal-sun dismisses the daughter-in-law's concern that Ji-ha's pursuit of rock music would risk his landing on a secure job.

The generational gap between Mal-sun and her daughter-in-law is reconciled in the end both narratively and visually, but only through the success of Ji-ha's band Semi-basement (*Ban-jiha*, a pun on the name of the grandson, Ban [half] Ji-ha [basement]) thanks to Mal-sun/Du-ri's initial contribution to reshape the band and eventual sacrifice to save the life of Ji-ha. In the film's coda, the visual hierarchy between two women, manifested through the in-depth staging, is now replaced by, first, a three-shot of the women alongside Mal-sun's college professor son, Hyeon-cheol, all rooting for the performance

154 Forever Girls

of Ji-ha's band; then by a two-shot of the women in the ladies' room, reflected in the mirror side by side, both boasting of their part in the talent of Ji-ha or the success of his band. Female value is measured by their sacrifice and the publicly recognized success of their offspring.

In contrast to the Chinese or Japanese remake, the Korean original constantly levels various forms of hierarchy both within family and without.[24] In the Chinese remake, when the grandmother scolds her daughter-in-law for the way she cooks a fish stew, both the grandmother and the mother are literally framed for their shared nurturing roles, guided by the grandson's figure movement in the scene. He is followed by both of the nurturing figures, who are unable to exit the frame of their gender role. What is more interesting is the camera work in the comparable scene in the Japanese remake: the invisibility of the elderly in both public and private space is pronounced. In the opening overhead shot of the public bathhouse, the camera passes the gender divide, along with the voice-over that claims gender matters less when it comes to "seniority." At the breakfast table, through similar camera work, Katsu, the granny, is visually dismissed from the conversation. Katsu constantly interrupts when her daughter, Yukie, wants to inform her mother that she has recently been demoted at work. The camera follows Yukie and leaves the granny outside the frame until the grandson appears. Another character relationship in the Korean film, that between Mal-sun and Mr. Bak, is also construed as formerly a master-servant relationship; Mal-sun was the daughter of the family that Bak had served when he was young, and he still calls her "lady" (*agassi*) in Korean, translated as Ms Mal-sun in the English subtitles. In the Japanese remake, in contrast, Katsu and Jiro grew up together as orphans during the war.

The reconciliation between Katsu and her daughter, Yukie, in the Japanese remake of *Miss Granny*, in the end comes down to their mutual understanding of the shared vulnerability of being single mothers and aging, in addition to the success of the grandson. In *Miss Granny*, the son, Hyeon-cheol, gestures toward saving his mother Mal-sun/Du-ri from making another sacrifice—losing her youth once again—by asking her to reconsider her decision, but the film lacks the level of mutual understanding seen in the Japanese remake. The long-lasting Korean gender baggage and work ethics have pre-dated the post-war economic hardship depicted in the film and have been constructed and reinforced under varying historical contexts and ideologies.[25] Yet the reversing of the linear trajectory of motherhood to (apparent) girlhood then back to (grand-) motherhood in *Miss Granny*, falls short of granting girls a need for idleness. Instead, the film yields her leisure (as well as her maternal sacrifice) as instrumental in earning public cognition and family recognition of her worth. It may be useful to see the continuity in contemporary box office hits, with their narrative trajectory of a female lead's talent for singing or dancing revolving around a competition structure, allowing her to gain or regain her self-worth through passing each stage of the competition. In *Scandal Makers* (*Gwasokseukendeul*, Kang Hyeong-cheol, 2008), a young single mother, Jeong-nam (played by Park Bo-young, *The Silenced*) shows her talent for singing by moving through a series of concerts that eliminate participants in each stage. In *Dancing Queen* (*Daensing qwin*, Lee Seok-hoon, 2012), Jeong-hwa (played by Uhm Junghwa, both the character and actress's names are pronounced the same) enters a talent show, hiding the fact that her husband is running to be mayor of the metropolitan city.

O'Connor underscores a risk with the work-based ethics of leisure that he associates with the tradition of Hegel and Marx, both of whom dismiss idleness as vice for different reasons. If, as Hegel does, one finds self-achievement and worth only in a social world, claims O'Connor, satisfaction comes in degrees only in relation to "the needs of others."[26] Such an ethic would endlessly place one into the world of "recognition" and "opinion."[27] With the lack of an adequate social welfare system within the unspecified "past" of *Miss Granny* (other than the reference to the 1960s guest worker program in West Germany, which Mal-sun's husband joined and where he subsequently died), the mother-manager is responsible for being both the breadwinner and rearing a child; unethical behaviors at times are excused and justified for the well-being of the family or child, which we have seen in Bong's *Mother* in chapter 3, although under crime genre conventions. It is problematic, perhaps, to interrogate the need to grant Mal-sun/Du-ri idleness, when what Mal-sun constantly seeks is "social regard, the opinion of others, and recognition as the most fundamental needs."[28] Leisure (or leisure activity), O'Connor claims, is a goal-directed activity that requires "too much effort to be idle."[29]

If the visibility of performance is to counterbalance and appreciate unpaid or underpaid female labor through leisure, a more nuanced rendition of a transformation of invisibility to visibility through leisure is found in a television documentary, *Dance Sports Girls*, and in indie films *Steel Flower* and *Next Sohee*. In all three films, the filmed subjects and protagonists share a form of leisure in dance, collective or solitary. The documentary film, *Dance Sports Girls* starts and ends with high school girls entering a ballroom dance competition in their final year: the close-ups of the girls' heavy makeup and their bodies in dance costumes resemble the ballerinas in Degas's paintings, in that it is the in-between moments that count. The film concludes with their dance performance at both the competition and in front of their peers back at school. Yet throughout the film, the precarity of both the labor market after the economic

156 Forever Girls

downturn and the girls' unpaid or underpaid labor is constantly underscored. The girls' parents seek new jobs after the layoffs in Geoje Island, known for its heavy industry of shipbuilding, and one is relocated for training needed to begin his own business. The male teacher's attentive caring of each girl extends not only to offering them dance lessons as leisure activity but to learning of their relationships to their parents and siblings; their assisting in a family business, carrying out domestic labor, and caring for their siblings in the absence of their parents. Dance as leisure is to acknowledge both their girlhood that would shortly come to an end when they graduate and their unacknowledged labor.

Indie films, such as *Steel Flower* and *Next Sohee* grant them, however briefly, their solitary leisure of dancing. Homeless Ha-dam in the former film lives from hand to mouth, taking any job offered to her, from handing out flyers to cleaning the restaurant. She is repeatedly exploited by adult characters, unpaid for her work, or unfairly losing a job. Sneaking into the dance studio one night offers her a vicarious leisure. She picks up a pair of shoes for tap dance and leaves the money she saved on the shelf. In the last scene, her safety from the heavy storm by the pier remains ambiguous, yet the sound of her tap dancing remains audible to the spectator as the reminder of last resort allowed literally at the edge of the world, in which she is constantly exploited. *Next Sohee* initially follows So-hui (a.s.a. Sohee)'s employment as a trainee at a telemarketing company, which leads her to death by the middle of the film; the latter half is the investigation of So-hui's death by a female detective, Yu-jin (a.s.a. Yoo-jin, played by Bae Doona). But the narrative is bracketed with sequences of So-hui practicing to cover an idol dance; in the opening she constantly fails with a complicated move, but is seen to succeed retrospectively in the film's coda. The film (or the Korean adult society) grants one last bit of leisure to So-hui, but only after her death.

All the films sketched so far, in different ways, begin to grant leisure, collective or solitary, to girls. Neither So-hui in *Sunday Night and Monday Morning*, the office worker with whom I began this chapter, nor the female protagonists discussed in the first chapter such as Yeong-ja, a domestic helper-turned-sex worker, or Yeong-ok, a bus attendant, can afford adequate leisure or consume as they wish. But when can girls be allowed an idleness of liminal freedom?

Walk into Idleness: *Queen of Walking*

Although O'Connor's monograph advances arguments against the criticisms leveled at idleness, he insightfully notes that the specific form associated with idleness is historically dependent and context sensitive: "Certainly that [idle] freedom is a pleasure, but it is one whose historical context gives it its content."[30] He views idle freedom as a positive freedom, not merely "freedom from," but "positively experienced freedom from specific constraints, in particular those constraints that come from societal norms."[31] Idleness is "an implicit resistance—to specific recommendations about how one ought to live: the need for progress, prestige or success through work."[32] Leisure can renew our capacity to perform, but O'Connor states that "leisure is good not only for the worker but also for the employer."[33] In contrast, "idleness threatens to undermine what that model requires, namely, disciplined goal-oriented individuals."[34] The key difference between leisure and idleness is the latter's non-instrumentality—a non-instrumental break.

Through the girls (*shōjo*) culture in the Japanese context, both during its emergence during the Meiji era and resurgence in the 1970s, as well as through girls' compensated dating (*enjo kosai*, going on dates with older men for money or goods), girls have closely been tied to their unproductivity and consumption.[35] South Korean characters such as Ji-yeong in *Crazy for You* (1977), discussed in chapter 1, could be seen to enjoy leisure and consumption, yet Ji-yeong's tennis practice in the pre-credit sequence of the film merely indicates her middle-class background. Her agency quickly disappears once she begins to help a working-class boy, Jin, who has grown up in an orphanage and has trained for the marathon race at his high school. In the 1974 box office hit, *It Rained Yesterday* (*Eojenaerin bi*, Lee Jang-ho, 1974), underneath college student Min-jeong's cheerful personality and "mindless" behaviors lie her dissatisfaction and anxiety. Her lavish lifestyle merely functions as a charade to avoid any deliberation about serious decisions, moral or otherwise. She finally decides to be with Yeong-hu, a stepbrother to her childhood friend Yeong-uk, who is also infatuated with her. But it leads to the death of both Yeong-uk and herself in a car accident.

Queen of Walking offers an interesting case study with its lead, Shim Eun-kyung, as Shim starred in both *Sunny* and *Miss Granny*. If the girls in *Sunny* are indifferent to the political—the famous girls' fight shown against the suppression of political demonstration—*Queen of Walking* underscores idleness as a form of freedom that one should learn to appreciate. Along with indie hits *The King of Jokgu* (*Jokguwang*, Woo Mun-gi, 2013) and *Microhabitat* (*Sogongnyeo*, Jeon Go-woon, 2018) discussed in chapter 4, which were released before and after *Queen of Walking*, the three could be seen to form an indie youth ("*cheongchun*") film cycle, with a different approach taken to the expectations of youths. The actor An Jae-hong links the films by starring in all as a lead or a supporting character: as the protagonist, Man-seop, in *The King of Jokgu*; as a voice-dub of the cow in *Queen of Walking*; and as a supporting character, the boyfriend to Mi-so, the female protagonist in *Microhabitat*.

158 Forever Girls

The King of Jokgu and *Queen of Walking*, although directed by two different male filmmakers, Woo and Baek, could be seen as companion pieces that challenge the romantic conception of youth. The names of the lead characters—Man-seop and Man-bok—alliterate; the two films mirror some key motifs and narrative structures, revolving around the competition structure; and the protagonists' similar foot injuries create a narrative climax that each of them must overcome to win the tournament or race. Both suggest that youth should be enjoyed and not be consumed with concerns for a future career.

Queen of Walking's opening voice-over, by the actor An, is shortly revealed as that of the cow, *Sossuni*, raised in Man-bok's front yard. It introduces Man-bok's serious childhood trauma. She is plagued by severe vomiting when on any vehicle—whether car, bus, or motorcycle—and can commute long distances only by walking. Since she has begun to attend the current high school, commuting has become even more demanding as it takes her a total of four hours to walk to, and back from, school. Encouraged by her homeroom teacher, Man-bok starts her gym training for race walking, but challenges await her. She not only needs to undergo daily training and the hierarchy of the school's track team but would also place herself at risk if she travels a long distance to attend any out-of-town competitions. She once travels on a bus, but her motion sickness puts her in an extremely poor condition to compete at the race.

Framed between two pregnancies, or better "female" reproductivity, Man-bok's idleness is a source of freedom that she fully embraces only at the end of film. Man-bok's mother is pregnant with her sibling, whereas the cow, Sossuni ("So" means cow in Korean, whereas "suni" is an old-fashioned female name or suffix used to pejoratively refer to girls, as in *gongsuni* [factory girls] and *ppasuni* [girls fandom]), gives birth to a calf in the ending credit, despite the continuing male voice-over attributed to it and its insistence on Man-bok's mistaking its sex. Late for school and seated by the window with no interest in learning, Man-bok is clearly identified as idle. But her idleness does not turn her into a rebel or gangster as in many Korean male coming-of-age films; her heart is filled with passion for walking. Once the teacher completes her mission to help Man-bok to find her talent in the very daily activity of walking, she approaches another doubtful student to imbue her with a musical talent for recorder. The process of false inspiration for the sake of students' finding passion and even hope is ironically rendered when the latter student walks with the teacher to the sound of the off-tune recorder playing Celine Dion's "My Heart Will Go On"—not a great sign of musical talent.

At the final competition, Man-bok gives up the race and looks up toward the sky to frame the airplane with her fingers instead. The initial conflicts between the two female leads, Man-bok and Su-ji, turn into female camaraderie in *Queen of Walking*. The desperation or eagerness that Su-ji criticizes Man-bok for lacking, is what the young Jin in *Crazy for You* embodies, as seen in chapter 1. Man-bok's dream is to walk around the world, not to win the race. Rendered as a dream sequence, she enters a bar in Russia and is recognized as an author of travelogues. In the interview, the director Baek explains that Man-bok's "derailing" from the paths suggested by her teacher or senior in the film should not be seen as a failure; it is her decision and selection to stop, the reason that the director left Man-bok's race unfinished.[36] Desperation is another work ethic imposed from outside, by her senior Su-ji. O'Connor insightfully notes, "The notion of idle freedom entails a life lived without effective interference in our motivations by visions of a superior version of ourselves, especially when that version is indebted to ideas of productivity and restless self-occupation."[37] Unlike other supporting characters such as Su-ji and Jeong-don, whose future occupations are revealed in the film's epilogue—Su-ji becomes a team doctor, while Jeong-don begins his own cleaning business, a service for which he has shown passion as a member of the track team—Man-bok's is left unidentified, as a true idler. Idleness is seen not as a failure, but to put a stop to the logic of "self-advancement" and "self-determination" as markers for "worthlessness" or "virtue" so as not to allow "others to determine their values."[38]

Here the ending of *Queen of Walking* departs from that of its companion piece, *The King of Jokgu*, released earlier. Both films feature the protagonist's foot injury as an obstacle to winning the final race or tournament. Man-bok collapses near the finish line, similar to what happened to Jin in *Crazy for You* discussed in chapter 1—a sign of failure and reason to exclude him from the developing nation-state. But Man-bok quits the race. In contrast, in *The King of Jokgu*, Man-seop wins the final tournament thanks to unexpected help from his dorm roommate. Both Man-seop and Man-bok learn to appreciate the significance of the present non-instrumentally. Yet the male rivalry between Man-seop and Min in *The King of Jokgu* revolves around their entangled romantic relationship with the female lead, An-na, and the additional reward for Man-seop comes with a financial gain instead of romantic union; every member of the team in *The King of Jokgu* sees his or her romantic relationship blossom. Although it is An-na's decision to choose Min over Man-seop, we see Man-seop drive the scenic coast in a Mercedes, which he won in a bet between Min and himself in an earlier one-on-one game. Romance for Man-seop is the process of confession (although he didn't win her heart) yet part of a transaction. Romance does not materialize in *Queen of Walking* either but the result is female solidarity instead of competition over a boy. A similar female solidarity is apparent in the Japanese film, *Linda Linda Linda* (Yamashita Nobuhiro, 2005), which features Bae Doona; three

160 Forever Girls

Japanese girls and a Korean exchange student form a band to play at a school festival—an already liminal time period in which extracurricular activities take the front seat. We see each of the characters romantically involved or approached: one's previous relationship has fallen apart; one prefers to spend time cultivating their female friendship; one wants to confess to a boy she has a crush on. But the film prioritizes their idleness when each member oversleeps and is late for their final performance in the school festival.

Critics praised and located *The King of Jokgu* within the genealogy of "campus" films in the 1970s and through the 1980s, including such works as *March of the Fools* (*Babodeului haengjin*, Ha Gil-jong, 1975) and *Youth Sketch* (*Mi-miwa Cheol-suui cheongchunseukechi*, Lee Kyu-hyung, 1987).[39] The period between one's completing of the military service and landing a secure job, in *The King of Jokgu*, is considered a liminal period, comparable to girlhood, during which one is entitled to enjoy "fun." The ending of the film is accompanied by the song entitled *Youths*. As Kim Suk-young notes, the term "*sampo*," applied to the generation seen to have given up on three things—courtship, marriage, and children—constantly refers to the despair of this generation, "robbed of the ambition that once defined their grandparents' and parents' youth."[40] The notion of youths (*cheongchun*) carries more ambivalence and even irony in the contemporary context, once situated within the local discourses; nostalgic about (or even romanticizing) youth is no longer granted to the current generation, while entertaining the possibility of a form of liminal freedom. A Korean collection of essays, *It's Hurt, So We Are Young*, the title of which is also translated, *Youth It's Painful* (*Apeunikka cheongchunida*, Kim Nan-do, 2010), was a bestseller ranked at the top of the sales charts for over thirty weeks in 2010.[41] The public's embrace of Kim's essays quickly turned sour among the young, and its title was constantly parodied (for instance, "If it hurts, you should get treatment"); the notion of "youth" was deemed almost anachronistic for those who cannot manage to live without juggling several precarious part-time jobs. If in the three youth cycle films—*The King of Jokgu*, *Queen of Walking*, and *Microhabitat*—Mi-so's indifference to social norms and preference for leisure (drinking and smoking) in *Microhabitat* leave her in social isolation (as discussed in chapter 4), Man-bok even finds the self-mastery associated with such autonomy rather onerous and instead remains idle.

Conclusion

I will end this chapter with a brief discussion of actress Shim Eun-kyung, who starred in all three films: *Sunny*, *Miss Granny*, and *Queen of Walking*.

Shim embodied a foul-mouthed teenage girl who emulated her grandmother's coarse language and thick accent to shock girls of her age in *Sunny*; in *Miss Granny*, she carried the manners and wisdom of her old self when she became twenty. It is noteworthy that the first zombie on the train, in *Train to Busan* (*Busanhaeng*, Yeon Sang-ho, 2016), was performed by Shim, although it is hard to even recognize her. Her girl-granny comedic persona, which made her unruly manner permissible, disappears once the industry deems her unprofitable in her subsequent films such as a gender-bending period piece, *The Princess and the Matchmaker* (*Gunghap*, Hong Chang-pyo, 2018)—the least successful entry at the box office among the trilogy of *yeokhak* that includes *The Face Reader* (*Gwansang*, Han Jae-rim, 2013); *Fengshui* (*Myeongdang*, Park Hee-gon, 2018);[42] and *Psychokensis* (*Yeomlyeok*, Yeon Sang-ho, 2018). She has been more active in the Japanese scene since her "serious" performance of a reporter in the Japanese film *The Journalist* (*Shinbun kisha*, Fuji Michihito, 2019). Her final performance in *Miss Granny* could then be seen as the celebration of her short-lived yet distinctive girl persona. It is ironic to spot a hidden sign in Du-ri's final performance that shyly promotes the director, Hwang, who has yet to earn stardom with *Squid Game*: "Bling Bling Hwang Dong-hyuk" (figure 5.5).

Figure 5.5 One of the fan signs in the middle says "Bling Bling Hwang Dong-hyuk" (*Miss Granny*, Hwang Dong-hyuk, 2014) ("Bling bling" refer(s) to flashy jewelleries worn by rappers or the light reflected or sound made while wearing them, but in the Korean context, it possibly means "shiny" and/or "flashy" to adore one of the performers briefly seen in the film, and further to wittily insert the director Hwang' own name).

Afterword

Girlhood, as a subject matter and sensibility, still inspires many Korean directors, coming-of-age films, drama series, and programs, including *The Hill of Secrets* (*Bimileui eondeok*, Lee Ji-eun, 2022), *Soulmate* (*Soulmeiteu*, Min Yeong-keun, 2023), which is a Korean remake of the Chinese original *Soulmate* (*Qi yue yu an sheng*, Derek Tseng, 2016), and *A Girl on a Bulldozer* (*Buldojeoe tan sonyeo*, Park Ri-woong, 2022). There is also an emerging strand of South Korean films concerned with mother-daughter relationships, such as *Missing Yoon* (*Yunsinaega dolawatda*, Kim Jinhwa, 2022) and *The Apartment with Two Women* (*Gateun sokoteul ipneun yeoja*, Kim Se-in, 2021).

Girlhood, adequately contextualized, has helped me to bridge the "nationalizing" and abstract "theorizing" or "philosophizing" of girlhood: as one colleague mentioned to me, examining a national cinema without nationalizing it. The notion of sensibility provided me with the key notion that has run through several pieces of my writing; this book is the last part of my "sensibility" project. Girlhood as a sensibility led me to examine the South Korean horror film series, *The Whispering Corridors*, in a chapter of my first monograph, and several chapters in edited volumes and a few journal pieces afterward. "Ozuesque" was another major sensibility project, focusing on an individual aesthetic sensibility of the Japanese director Ozu Yasujiro as well as the ethical significance of inheriting or sharing a sensibility. I had initially considered writing my "girl book" on the East Asian regional sensibility and aesthetics of girlhood. But I found the topic increasingly challenging due to its extensive scope, which led me to limit it to South Korean films.

I hope this book will encourage more diverse frameworks by which to diagnose, situate, and examine girlhood beyond South Korean cinema. While working on the South Korean case, I have found the notion of sensibility limiting when it comes to discussing some of the principal issues of gender, labor, leisure, and freedom—the major threads and kernels of this book. My goal was to find adequate conceptual tools and theoretical frameworks that pivot around girlhood to discuss the 1970s girls ("reference girl" in chapter 1), survivors of sexual slavery ("the writing subject" in chapter 2), and schoolgirls or young women ("death" in chapter 3; "shelter writing" in chapter 4; "idleness"

Forever Girls. Jinhee Choi, Oxford University Press. © Oxford University Press 2025.
DOI: 10.1093/9780197685822.003.0007

in chapter 5). In doing so, I saw myself reflecting on the self; *my* frustration as a daughter and sister, a schoolgirl, and even as an academic; and a dream or desire for idleness after having fulfilled the expectations and responsibilities imposed on me for a very long time. Writing this book was a journey; the sensing and cultivating of a sensibility and beyond—whether it be as an individual or as a collective—a journey to oneself, and seeking a possibility to connect through the sharing of one's sensibility.

Death is one of the key frameworks of this book: both as a condition ("dead already" in chapter 2 and as a story-telling or industry logic ("to be dead," "mortal economy," and "necro-cinematics" in chapter 3) and I learned of many deaths while writing this book: my PhD supervisor, Professor David Bordwell and Kim Soo-mi (*Girls from Scratch*) in 2024; Lee Sun-gyun (*Parasite*) and Byun Hee-bong (*Barking Dogs Never Bite, Memories of Murder, The Host, Okja*) in 2023; Yoon Jung-hee (*Night Journey, Poetry*) and the director Kim Soo-yong in 2022; Song Jae-ho (*Yeong-ja's Heydays, Girls from Scratch, Memories of Murder*) in 2020; Jeon Mi-seon (*Memories of Murder*) in 2019; some of them took their own lives. This book quickly began to resemble an archaeological undertaking of sorts, in which I followed and examined their performances and traces, which was a novelty and pleasure to me. This book is my excavation as well as my scholarly remembrance of them.

I also saw actresses grow out of their initial character types and roles, successfully maintaining or transforming their star personas: Im Ye-jin (*Crazy for You*), Youn Yuh-jung (*Insect Woman*), Moon Sook (*A Woman Like the Sun*); Park Bo-young (*The Silenced, A Werewolf Boy*), Park So-dam (*The Silenced, Parasite*); Ko Ah-seong (*The Host, Snowpiercer*); Kim Sae-ron (*Snowy Road, A Girl at My Door*); and Shim Eun-kyung (*Sunny, Miss Granny, Queen of Walking*). Some were unable to stay afloat in the South Korean film industry. Regardless, I wish them all well.

One can never remain a girl forever physically—thus the ironic title of this book, *Forever Girls*, refers to something beyond the material body.

Notes

Introduction

1. Jo Hye-young, ed., *Girls: K-pop Screen Square* [*Sonyeodeul: K-pop seukeurin gwangjang*] (Seoul: Yeoiyeon, 2017), 8. In her introduction to the volume, Jo criticizes such a use of girl-image in Im's work as a tendency to retrieve women workers' social significance back to, or replace it with, images of girls, but I would offer a different reading of the film: that it forms a conversation with the reference girl rather than locating the origin of women workers as "girls," 69.

2. Genevieve Yue, *Girl Head: Feminism and Film Materiality* (New York: Fordham University Press, 2021), 8.

3. Yoshimi Yoshiaki, *Comfort Women: Sexual Slavery in the Japanese Military World War II* (New York: Columbia University, 1995), 111–113; Yuki Tanaka, *Japan's Comfort Women: Sexual Slavery and Prostitution during World War II and the US Occupation* (London: Routledge, 2002), 38.

4. Chungmoo Choi, "Nationalism and Construction of Gender in Korea," in *Dangerous Women: Gender and Korean Nationalism*, ed. Elaine H. Kim and Chungmoo Choi (New York: Routledge, 1998), 25.

5. Gooyoung Kim, *From Factory Girls to K-Pop Idol Girls: Cultural Politics of Developmentalism, Patriarchy, and Neoliberalism in South Korea's Popular Music Industry* (New York: Lexington Books, 2019). Kim demarcates the generations of girls across a decade, with 1997 and 2007 as significant temporal markers that divide the cuteness versus ambiguous sexuality of girl groups; by 2011, they become more explicitly sexualized. See his introduction, xxxiii. Gu Ha-ra, a former member of the K-pop group, Kara, committed suicide in 2019 after her former partner threatened to release illicit sexual footage of her; and Sulli from another girl band, ended her life in the same year. "K-Pop Artists Goo Hara Found Dead at Home aged 28," November 24, 2019, https://www.bbc.co.uk/news/world-asia-50535937 (accessed May 18, 2021).

6. I was first introduced to Rhee's work through Chrystal Baek's presentation "Performing Excess, Marking Disposability: Kate-hers Rhee and An Economy of Surplus Feelings," delivered at the workshop "The Affects of Korean Soft Power" hosted by the University of Southern California in February 2016. Rhee is based in Berlin and active through various cultural performances, including Dr. Rhee's Kimchi Shop (2011). The artist's own website is https://katehersrhee.com/project/sex-education-for-finding-face-in-the-21st-century/ (accessed October 28, 2024).

7. Kim Soyoung, for instance, uses the term *sonyeo* to refer to both "factory girls (*yeogong*)" and domestic helpers (*sikmo*), who were exploited for their cheap labor but at the same time were seen as a threat to the middle-class family. See her *The Ghosts of Modernity* [*Geundaeseongui yuryeongdeul*] (Seoul: Ssiateul ppeurineun saramduel, 2000), 212.

166 Notes

8. Kyung Hyun Kim, *The Remasculization of Korean Cinema* (Durham: Duke University Press, 2004); Kyung Hyun Kim, *Virtual Hallyu: Korean Cinema of the Global Era* (Durham: Duke University Press, 2011); Joseph Jonghyun Jeon, *Vicious Circuits: Korea's IMF Cinema and the End of the American Century* (Stanford: Stanford University Press, 2019).

9. KOFIC Kobis, 2011 annual box office data, http://www.kobis.or.kr/kobis/business/stat/offc/findYearlyBoxOfficeList.do (accessed May 7, 2019).

10. Both independent and commercial films, such as *Kuro Arirang* (*Guro arirang*, Park Jong-won, 1989); *The Night before the Strike* (*Paeopjeonya*, Jang Dong-hong, Jang Yun-hyeon, Lee Eun, 1990); *A Petal*; *Peppermint Candy* (*Bakhasatang*, Lee Chang-dong, 1999); *May 18* (*Hwaryeohan hyuga*, Kim Ji-hoon, 2007); *A Taxi Driver* (*Taeksi unjeonsa*, Jang Hoon, 2017); and *1987: When the Day Comes* (*1987*, Jang Joon-hwan, 2017), depict the 1980s with a narrative trajectory that revolves around a political cause.

11. Hee Jeong Sohn, "Feminism Reboot: Korean Cinema under Neoliberalism in the 21st Century," *Journal of Japanese and Korean Cinema* 12.2 (2020): 104.

12. Kathleen Rowe Karlyn, *Unruly Girls, Unrepentant Mothers: Redefining Feminism on Screen* (Austin: Texas University Press, 2011), 78.

13. Karlyn, *Unruly Girls, Unrepentant Mothers*, 98.

14. Hilary Radner, *Neo-Feminist Cinema: Girl Films, Chick Flicks and Consumer Culture* (New York: Routledge, 2011), 53.

15. Jinhee Choi, "A Comedy of Remarriage? *My Love My Bride* (1990)," in *Rediscovering Korean Cinema*, ed. Lee Sang-joon (Ann Arbor: University of Michigan Press, 2019), 260–273; Jinhee Choi, "I'm Not a Girl, Yet Not a Woman: Romance Films," in *South Korean Film Renaissance* (Middletown: Wesleyan University Press, 2010), 85–115.

16. Rosalind Gill, "Postfeminist Media Culture: Elements of a Sensibility," *European Journal of Cultural Studies* 10.2 (2007): 161.

17. Cited in Mirium Ching Yoon Louie, "Minjung Feminism: Korean Women's Movement for Gender and Class Liberation," *Women's Studies International Forum* 18.4 (1995): 428.

18. Rosalind Gill and Elena Herdieckerhoff, "Rewriting the Romance," *Feminist Media Studies* 6.4 (2006): 491.

19. Gill and Herdieckerhoff, "Rewriting the Romance," 499–500.

20. Gill and Herdieckerhoff, "Rewriting the Romance," 497.

21. Jung Min-woo and Lee Na-Young, "Fandom Managing Stars, Entertainment Industry Managing Fandom [Seutareul kwanlihaneun pandeom, pandeomeul kwanlihaneun saneop: '2 sedae' aidol pandeomui munhwasilcheonui teukjing mit hamui]," *Media, Gender & Munhwa* 12 (2009): 191–240.

22. Kim Su-jeong, "When Fandom Meets Feminism: Outcomes and Issue of Fandom Studies from the Feminism Perspective [Paendeomgwa peminiseumdui jou: peminiseum kwanjeomeseo bon paendeom yeonguui seonggwawa jaengjeom]," *Eolronjeongboyeongu* 53.5 (2018): 57; Kang Jun-man and Kang Ji-eun, *What Do Girl Fans Desire? Yes, I'm a Ppasuni!* [*Ppasunineun mueoteul galmanghaneunga? Geurae, naneun ppasunida*] (Seoul: Inmulgwa sasangsa, 2016).

23. Jung and Lee, "Fandom Managing Stars, Entertainment Industry Managing Fandom," 202–203.

24. Ryu Jin-hee, "The Heyday of Girl Group and K-Entertainment [Geolgeurup jeonseongsidaewa 'K-enteoteinteumeonteu]," in *Girls: K-pop Screen Square* [*Sonyeodeul: K-pop seukeurin gwangjang*] ed. Jo Hye-young (Seoul: Yeoiyeon, 2017), 85.

Notes **167**

25. Sarah Banet-Weiser, *Empowered: Popular Feminism and Popular Misogyny* (Durham: Duke University Press, 2018), 13.

26. Karlyn, *Unruly Girls, Unrepentant Mothers*, 27.

27. Mia McKenzie cited in Banet-Weiser, *Empowered*, 31.

28. And interestingly, Park Geun-hye (b. 1952) spent her girlhood in the Blue House in the 1960s and '70s as the daughter of the country's former military dictator and president, Park Chung-hee (1961–1979), and was elected as the first woman president (2014–2017). But she has been constantly dissociated from recognition as a possible feminist icon. See Soo-hyun Mun, " 'Femininity without Feminism': Korea's First Woman President and Her Political Leadership," *Asian Journal of Social Science* 43 (2015): 249–272.

29. Joo Jin-suk and Byun Jae-ran, "The First Women Filmmakers' Association, Yonghuihoe and Women Filmmakers Group, Bariteo [Choechoui yeoseong yeonghwainmoim 'Yeonghuihoe'wa yeoseong yeongsangjipdan 'Barieto']," in *Women Filmmakers Encyclopaedia* [*Yeseong yeonghwain sajeon*] (Seoul: Sodo, 2001), 274; Hyun Seon Park, "South Korean Cine-Feminism on the Movie," *Journal of Japanese and Korean Cinema* 12.2 (2020): 92.

30. Yu Jina and Byun Jae-ran eds, *Feminism/Film/Women* [Peminiseum/Yeonghwa/Yeoseong] (Seoul: Yeoseongsa, 1993); Joo Youshin et al. *Korean Cinema and Modernity* (Seoul: Sodo, 2001).

31. Kwon Kim Hyeon-young, "Young Feminist, Net Feminists' New Challenge: from 1990s to mid-2000s [Yeong peminiseuteu, netpemiui saeroun dojeon: 1990 nyeondae jungbanbuteo 2000 nyeondae jungban kkaji]," in *Net Feminism Her Story*, ed. Kwon Kim Hyeon-young et al., [*Daehanminguk netpemisa*] (Seoul: Namuyeonpil, 2017), 14; Sohn Hee Jeong "Feminism Reboot, the Appearance of New Women Subjects: From mid-2000s to the present" [Peminiseum ributeu, saerowun yeoseong jucheui deungjang: 2000 nyeondae jungbanbuteo hyeonjekkaji], in *Net Feminism Her Story*, ed. Kwon Kim Hyeon-young et al., 80.

32. Ruth Barraclough, *Factory Girl Literature: Sexuality, Violence and Representation in Industrializing Korea* (Berkeley: University of California Press, 2012), 2.

33. Barraclough, *Factory Girl Literature*, 8.

34. Soyoung Kim, "Questions of Woman's Film: *The Maid, Madame Freedom*, and Women," in *South Korean Golden Age Melodrama: Gender. Genre and National Cinema*, ed. Kathleen McHugh and Nancy Abelmann (Detroit: Wayne State University Press, 2005), 189.

35. Kim, *Virtual Hallyu*, 71.

36. Molly Kim, "Film Censorship Policy during Park Chung Hee's Military Regime (1960–1979) and Hostess Films," *IAFOR Journal of Cultural Studies* 1.2 (2016): 39.

37. Park Hyun Seon, "From Secluded Rooms to Streets? Space and Women in Korean Cinema of the 1960s [Milsileseo georiro? 1960nyeondae hanguk yeonghwaui gonggangwa yeoseong]," in *Korean Cinema and Modernity* [*Hangukyeonghwawa geundaeseong*], Joo Youshin et al. (Seoul: Sodo, 2001), 152.

38. Park, "From Secluded Rooms to Streets?" 164.

39. Ha Gil-jong, "*The Road to Sampo* [Sampo ganeungil]," *Sedae* July 1975, cited in Oh Young Sook, "Father and Girl: Representation of Korean Cinema in [the] 1970s [Appawa sonyeo: 70 nyeondae hanguk yeonghwaui pyosang yeongu]," *Yeonghwayeongu* 42 (2009): 438.

40. Joo Youshin, "*Madame Freedom* and *Flower in Hell*: The 1950s Modernity and Female Sexuality as a Signifier [<Jayubuin>gwa <jiokhwa>: 1950 nyeondae geundaeseonggwa

168   Notes

maehokui gipyoroseoui yeoseong seksyueoliti]," in *Korean Cinema and Modernity*, Joo Youshin et al., 38–39.

41. Kathleen McHugh and Nancy Abelmann, eds., *South Korean Golden Age Melodrama: Gender. Genre and National Cinema* (Detroit: Wayne State University Press, 2005); Christina Klein, *Cold War Cosmopolitanism: Period Style in 1950s Korean Cinema* (Berkeley: University of California Press, 2020); Steven Chung, *Split Screen Korea: Shin Sang-ok and Postwar Cinema* (Minneapolis: University of Minnesota Press, 2014).

42. Chris Berry, "Scream and Scream Again: Korean Modernity as a House of Horrors in the Film of Kim Ki-young," in *Seoul Searching: Culture and Identity in Contemporary Korean Cinema*, ed. Frances Gateward (Albany: State University of New York Press), 99–113.

43. Kim, *The Ghosts of Modernity*, 213.

44. Kim Mi-ji, "Why Women Directors Don't Tell the Story of Women [Yeoseong gamdoki yeoseong iyagi anhaneun iyu]," *Gyeongnam domin ilbo*, June 28, 2013, http://www.idomin.com/news/articleView.html?idxno=417852 (accessed August 17, 2020). In the interview, Yim claims that she shied away from making more women-centered films in her earlier features, as she hoped to depict the oppressive nature of Korean society that does not allow diversity. Even if the protagonists are male, her female characters are independent and challenge social norms.

45. Chi-Yun Shin, "Two of a Kind: Gender and Friendship in *Friend* and *Take Care of My Cat*," in *New Korean Cinema*, ed. Chi-Yun Shin and Julian Stringer (Edinburgh: Edinburgh University Press, 2005), 117–131; Jeong, "The Surface of Finance: Digital Touching in *Take Care of My Cat*," in *Vicious Circuits*, 98–122; Michelle Cho, "*Take Care of My Cat* (2001): The Architectonics of Female Subjectivity in Post-crisis South Korea," in *Rediscovering Korean Cinema*, 358-370.

46. 22nd Jeonju International Film Festival Program Event, "Jeonju in Audio with Lee Hwajung (Visible Audio): Your First with Purplay," with Panelists: Yim Soon-rye, Boo Ji-young, and Yoon Ga-eun, https://www.youtube.com/watch?v=-t6YwDZNL8Y (accessed May 3, 2021).

47. Byun Jae-ran notes that the female body in Choi's film is represented here as a site of physical labor, which would contribute to the national development led by the "new leadership" of the third republic, which is allegorized by the young husband. See Byun, "Agents of Modernization: Brassy Women [Geundaehwaui juche: Eoksen yeojadeul]," in *Women Filmmakers Encyclopaedia*, 99.

48. Hyekyong Sim, "Acting 'Like a Woman': South Korean Female Action Heroines," *Journal of Japanese and Korean Cinema* 12.2 (2020): 110–123.

49. Steven Chung, *Split Screen Korea: Shin Sang-ok and Postwar Cinema* (Minneapolis: University of Minnesota Press, 2014); Christina Klein, *Cold War Cosmopolitanism: Period Style in 1950s Korean Cinema* (Berkeley; University of California Press, 2020); Steve Choe, *Sovereign Violence: Ethics and South Korean Cinema in the New Millennium* (Amsterdam: Amsterdam University Press, 2016); Joseph Jonghyun Jeon, *Vicious Circuits: Korea's IMF Cinema and the End of the American Century* (Stanford: Stanford University Press, 2019); and Nam Lee, *The Films of Bong Joon Ho* (New Brunswick, Rutgers University Press, 2020).

50. Lee, *The Films of Bong Joon Ho*, 46–47.

51. Achille Mbembe, "Necropolitics," trans. Libby Meintjes, *Public Culture* 15.1 (2003): 11–40. Jin-kyung Lee, *Service Economies; Militarism, Sex Work and Migrant Labor in South Korea* (Minneapolis: University of Minnesota Press, 2010), 5-6.

Notes   169

52. Mbembe, "Necropolitics," 17.

53. Lee, *Service Economies*, 7.

54. Michele Aaron, "Cinema and Suicide: Necromanticism, Dead-already-ness, and the Logic of the Vanishing Point," *Cinema Journal* 53.2 (2014): 84.

55. Joo Youshin, *Cine-Feminism* [*Sinepeminiseum: Yeoseongui sigakeuro yeonghwareul ikneun 13gaji bangbyeop*] (Busan: Homilbat, 2017), 261–273.

56. Michele Aaron, "Cinema and Suicide," 72.

57. Michele Aaron, *Death and the Moving Image: Ideology, Iconography and I* (Edinburgh: Edinburgh University Press, 2014), 128.

58. Mbembe "Necropolitics," 27.

59. Aaron, *Death and the Moving Image*, 5.

60. Judith Butler, *The Force of Non-Violence: An Ethico-Political Bind* (London: Verso, 2021), 17.

61. Aaron, *Death and the Moving Image*, 5.

62. Bae Gyeong-min, "The Hidden Ideology of Cheerful Classroom: The Prankster Films of the 1970s and Their Hegemonic Reconciliation [Myeongrang gyosil soke gamchueojin ideologi—1970 nyeondae yalgae yeonghwa hyeongseong gwajeongeseo jaehyeondoen hapuie daehan yeongu]," in *Korean Cinema Meets Sexuality* [Hanguk yeonghwa seksyueolitireul mannada], ed. Cho heup and Yu Jina et al. (Seoul: Namusaengak, 2004), 19.

63. Hyunah Yang, "Re-membering the Korean Military Comfort Women: Nationalism, Sexuality, and Silencing," in *Dangerous Women*, ed. Elaine H. Kim and Chungmoo Choi, 133.

64. Kim Su-bin, "20 years of Independent Cinema in Korea," *Hankyoreh*, September 16, 2018, https://english.hani.co.kr/arti/english_edition/e_entertainment/862280.html (accessed, April 15, 2019).

65. Susan Fraiman, *Extreme Domesticity: A View from the Margins* (New York: Columbia University Press, 2017), 18.

66. Brian O'Connor, *Idleness: A Philosophical Essay* (Princeton: Princeton University, 2018), 172, 180.

Chapter 1

1. Molly Hyo J. Kim, *Whoring the Mermaid: The Study of South Korean Hostess Films (1974–1982)*, PhD dissertation, University of Illinois, Urbana-Champaign (2014): 5, footnote 8.

2. Kim, *Whoring the Mermaid*, 81–82; 138–139.

3. Seung-kyung Kim, *Class Struggle or Family Struggle: The Lives of Women Factory Workers in South Korea* (Cambridge: Cambridge University Press, 1997); Soonok Chun, *They Are Not Machines: Korean Women Workers and Their Fight for Democratic Trade Unionism in the 1970s* (London: Routledge, 2003, 2018); Yoo Kyung-soon, ed., *I, Woman Laborer I* [*Na yeoseong nodongja*] (Seoul: Greenbee, 2011); Park Su-jeong, *Women, Speaking of Labor* [*Yeoja, nodongeul malhadaI*] (Seoul: Ehaksa, 2013); Hwasook Nam, *Women in the Sky: Gender and Labor in the Making of Modern Korea* (Ithaca: Cornell University Press, 2021).

4. Ruth Barraclough, *Factory Girl Literature: Sexuality, Violence and Representation in Industrializing Korea* (Berkeley: University of California Press, 2012); Jin-kyung Lee, *Service Economies: Militarism, Sex Work, and Migrant Labor in South Korea* (Minneapolis: University of Minnesota Press, 2010).

170 Notes

5. Mary Ann Doane, *The Desire to Desire: The Woman's Film of the 1940s* (Bloomington, Indiana University Press, 1987), 37.

6. Song Hye-jin, "Has Fallen Ill for 40 years and Woken Up . . . A Girl Who Fell in Love [*40 nyeon alta ileonatda . . . sarange ppajin sonye*]," *Chosun Daily* (April 30, 2016), https://www.chosun.com/site/data/html_dir/2016/04/29/2016042902253.html (accessed June 9, 2022).

7. Lauren Elkin, *Flaneuse: Women Walk in the City, in Paris, New York, Tokyo, Venice and London* (London: Vintage, 2016), 22–23.

8. Genevieve Yue, *Girl Head: Feminism and Film Materiality* (New York: Fordham University, 2021), 3.

9. Yue, *Girl Head*, 101.

10. Yue, *Girl Head*, 17.

11. Yue, *Girl Head*, 8, 11.

12. Oh Young Sook, "Father and Girl: Representations in the 1970s [*Appawa sonyeo—1970 nyeondae hangukyeonghwaui pyosang yeongu*]," *Yeonghwayeongu* 42 (2009): 441.

13. Young Jak Kim, "Park Chung Hee's Governing Ideas: Impact on National Consciousness and Identity," in *Reassessing the Park Chung Hee Era: 1961–1979*, ed. Hyung-a Kim and Clark W. Sorensen (Seattle: University of Washington Press, 2011), 98.

14. Bae Gyeong-min, "The Ideology Underneath the Cheerful Classroom: A Study of the Hegemonic Consensus in the Filmic Representation of Pranksters in the 1970s [*Myeongrang gyosil soke gamchueojin ideologi—1970 yeondae yalgaeyanghwa hyeongseong gwajeongeseo jaehyeondoen hegemonijeok hapuie daehan yeongu*]" in *Korean Films Meet Sexuality* [*Hangukyeonghwa seksyueolitireul mannada*], ed. Yu Jina and Cho Heub (Seoul: Saenggakui namu, 2004), 14.

15. Bae, "The Ideology," 20.

16. Yu Jina, "Women's Body Genre: The Wounds of Modernity—from late 1970s to 1980s [*Yeoseong momui jangreu: Geundaehwaui sangcheo—1970 nyeondae hubaneseo 1980 nyeondae*]," in *Korean Films Meet Sexuality*, 82.

17. Oh, "Father and Girl," 443.

18. Oh, "Father and Girl," 441. As an example of the reverse trajectory from adulthood to girl-hood, she cites *Heavenly Homecoming to Stars*. In the source novel and elsewhere, the author Choi In-ho describes Kyeong-a's incessant habit of chewing gum. But in one flashback in the film, when Kyeong-a is seen working in an office, she is seen carrying herself in a mature manner.

19. All three installments of the series were credited to different screenwriters (first, Seo In-gyeong; second, Kim Ha-rim, Gang Dae-ha, Moon Yeo-song; third, Kim Ji-heon), with only the second and third sharing the same cinematographer, Lee Seok-gi, while Hong Dong-hyeok worked on the first.

20. At one point, Jin is framed by a triangle created between Ji-yeong's legs in the park; or Ji-yeong's father is shot through a space revealed as well as blocked by a table lamp placed in the foreground; Ji-yeong's family is reflected in the circle of a pendulum when she is late one night. The functions of such framings may be merely decorative at times, but they carry a further thematic, ideological weight when it comes to gender.

21. The sick body has been examined as an emblem and common trope employed in colonial literature and in post-war literature and films—see Kyung Hyun Kim, *Virtual Hallyu* (Durham: Duke University Press, 2011), 57. Yet, the significance of Jin's sick body here is different, in that his body does not subvert the Japanese ideology of the hygienic and

Notes **171**

healthy body invoked during the colonial period, especially during wartime; rather, Jin's sick body is a sign of inadequacy in embracing the modernity envisioned by the state.

22. Lee Gil-seong, Lee Ho-geol, and Lee U-seok, *Research on 1970s Exhibition and Film Culture* [*1970 nyeondae Seoului geukjangsanseop mit geukjangmunhwa yeongu*] (Seoul: Korean Film Council, 2004), 52, 88.

23. *Crazy For You*, https://www.kmdb.or.kr/db/kor/detail/movie/K/03116 (accessed July 20, 2022).

24. Lee, Lee and Lee, *Research on 1970s Exhibition and Film Culture*, 55, 88.

25. Nam, *Women in the Sky*, 127; Lee, Lee and Lee, *Research on 1970s Exhibition and Film Culture*, 99.

26. Nam, *Women in the Sky*, 113.

27. Nam, *Women in the Sky*, 126.

28. Yu In-kyung, "Glancing through the 100 years (19): Bus Conductor [Baeknyeoneul yeotboda (19): Bus Conductor]," *Kyunghyang Daily* (March 7, 2010), https://www.khan.co.kr/article/201003071824542 (accessed November 2, 2016).

29. Hwang Gyeong-seo, An Chi-yong, No Su-bin and Park Seo-yun, "Body Search and Beating; What Happened to 18-year old Hui-jin [Almom susaeke maejil, 18 Huijinui jikjangeseo saengginil]," *Oh Mynews* (January 10, 2021). http://www.ohmynews.com/NWS_Web/Series/series_premium_pg.aspx?CNTN_CD=A0002708330&SRS_CD=0000012552 (accessed July 28, 2022).

30. Song Areum, "Censorship as a Social Sanction, the Resistant Voices: The Suspension of the screening of 1981 film, *Maiden Who Went to the City* [Sahoejeok seunginuiroseoui geomyeol, dolchuldoen moksori'deul'ui buleung: '1981'nyeon yeonghwa <Dosiro gan cheonyeo> sangyeongjungji sageonui uimi]," in Korean Film Archive edition, *Censorship in Korean Film History* (Seoul: Korean Film Archive, 2016): 220–221.

31. Hwang, et al., "Body Search and Beating."

32. Song, "Censorship as a Social Sanction, the Resistant Voices," 220–221.

33. Song, "Censorship as a Social Sanction, the Resistant Voices," 220–221.

34. Jin-kyung Lee, *Service Economies: Militarism, Sex Work and Migrant Labor in South Korea* (Minneapolis: University of Minnesota Press, 2010), 84.

35. Cited in Hagen Koo, "Labor Policy and Labor Relations during the Park Chung Hee Era," in *Reasssessing The Park Chung Hee Era 1961–1979: Development, Political Thought, Democracy, and Cultural Influence* ed. Hyung-a Kim and Clark W. Sorensen (Seattle: University of Washington Press, 2011), 131.

36. Barraclough, *Factory Girl Literature*, 73.

37. Barraclough, *Factory Girl Literature*, 73.

38. Kim, *Class Struggle or Family Struggle*, 181.

39. Barraclough, *Factory Girl Literature*, 73.

40. Kim So-hui, "The Korean Cinema Master Selection: *The Maiden Who Went to the City* [Korean cinema geoljakseon: *Dosirogan cheonyeo*]," September 1, 2020, https://www.kmdb.or.kr/story/10/5439 (accessed August 19, 2022).

41. Hwang et al., "Body Search and Beating."

42. Barraclough, *Factory Girl Literature*, 76.

43. Hwang et al., "Body Search and Beating."

44. Barraclough, *Factory Girl Literature*, 60.

45. Barraclough, *Factory Girl Literature*, 16.

172 Notes

46. Barraclough, *Factory Girl Literature*, 2.
47. Kim, *Class Struggle or Family Struggle*, 31.
48. Song, "Censorship as a Social Sanction, the Resistant Voices," 219.
49. Song, "Censorship as a Social Sanction, the Resistant Voices," 239.
50. Song, "Censorship as a Social Sanction, the Resistant Voices," 239.
51. Kim So-hui, "The Korean Cinema Master Selection: *The Maiden Who Went to the City*."
52. Nam, *Women in the Sky*, 176–177.
53. Oh, "Father and Girl," 450.
54. Oh, "Father and Girl," 454.
55. In *Where Is Miss Young?* (*Miseu yeongui hangbang?* Park Nam-su, 1975) in which Moon also stars as the female lead, the character relationship between Nan-hyang (Moon) and the two male characters certainly departs from that of In-yeong and Dong-su. Nan-hyang's actions are partly motivated as a form of rebellion against her mother, and her stay at the two male leads' (Jin-ho and Min-su) place creates situations where her sense of "freedom" is granted due to their "agreement" not to sexually approach her.
56. Sharon Kinsella, "Cuties in Japan," in *Women, Media and Consumption in Japan*, ed. Brian Moeran and Lise Skov (Richmond: Curzon Press, 1995), 244 (italics are mine).
57. Hilary Radner, *Neo-Feminist Cinema: Girly Films, Chick Flicks and Consumer Culture* (London and New York: Routledge, 2011), 53.
58. Radner, *Neo-Feminist Cinema*, 30.
59. Song, "Has Fallen Ill for 40 years and Woken Up . . . A Girl Who Fell in Love."
60. In a horror film, *Svaha: The Sixth Finger* (2019), Moon plays a minor character, Myeong-hui, who has been serving an un-aging cult leader, Kim Dong-su (played by Yu Ji-tae). Dong-su looks younger than Myeong-hui, but prior to his hitting the road for the final quest, he addresses Myeong-hui as if he remembers her girlhood: 'My dear Myeong-hui, you've aged a lot.' In the indie film *Shades of the Heart* (*Amudo eopdeongot*, Kwon Jong-kwan, 2019), Moon's character Mi-yeong, who suffers from dementia, relives the memory of how she met her husband. Her son Chang-seok, pretending to be his father, strikes up a conversation in a cafe with young Mi-yeong (played by Lee Ji-eun [a.k.a. IU]), a Korean singer-song writer/actor, who is loved and known for her girlish look, music, and persona. When Mi-yeong recognizes her son, the camera cuts to Mi-yeong's old self, played by Moon.
61. Susan Fraiman, *Extreme Domesticity: A View from the Margins* (New York: Columbia University Press, 2017).
62. Lee, *Service Economies*, 82.
63. Lee, *Service Economies*, 110.
64. Lee, *Service Economies*, 86.
65. Barraclough, *Factory Girl Literature*, 131.
66. Kim, *Whoring the Mermaid*, 73.
67. Kim, *Whoring the Mermaid*, 83.
68. The state-censorship authority suggested not following the source text, where the district burned down. See Park Yu-hee, "Censorship named Pornography: From *Chunmong* to *Madam Aema*, the Correlation between Censorship of the 'Racy Films' and Their Representation [Geomyeoliraneun poreunograpi: <Chunmong>eseo <Aemabuyin>kkaji 'oeseol' geomyeolgwa jaehyeonui yeokhak]," in *Censorship in Korean Film History*, 181–183.

Notes 173

69. The scene in which her family reads a letter and receives money sent could represent their receiving financial support in the past, but regardless of its temporality, it signals that she sends her family a regular monthly stipend.

70. In the film *The March of Fools*, after Yeong-ja's (a.s.a. Young-ja, played by Lee Young-ok) performance at the theater, there is a shot of her reflected in the mirror. In contrast, after Chang-su attaches the prosthetic arm to Yeong-ja in *Yeong-ja's Heyday*, we see them reflected in the mirror together.

71. Some Korean feminist scholars point out how a similar style is used in the opening sequence and in the sequence of Yeong-ja's sexual assault at the hands of her boss's son, but the shot mentioned signals her gradual internalization of social perception of her as a sex worker.

72. Even in the new family, where Myeong-ja is accepted as a pseudo family member, she is still in the backseat with Dong-sik, an emasculated husband and father to his family. The initial staging of the family members—including Dong-sik and Myeong-ja—seated around the circular dining table for the wife's birthday, breaks up and loosens into two rows of characters, with the wife and two adult children in the foreground, and the husband and Myeong-ja in the background. The film's staging subtly registers how the family may allow the "intrusion" of Myung-ja, due to the husband's extra-marital relationship with her, but will not let her completely take control over Dong-sik or his family.

73. A Korean male filmmaker, Kim Gok, makes an intriguing observation that the relationship between Dong-sik's wife and Myeong-ja is similar to the corporate hierarchy between a contractor and sub-contractor; the husband is exchanged between the two, representing an investment to acquire the "source" of (re)productivity. https://www.kmdb.or.kr/story/177/4785 (accessed June 28, 2022).

74. Doane observes that in the medical melodrama, the female protagonist's apparent agency is often circumscribed by her mental state, such as paranoia and hysteria, and the object of the lead's pursuit (investigation or otherwise) is directed at herself. Once Dong-sik and Myeong-ja move into a new house and a baby mysteriously shows up in their life, the blurred line between reality, dream, and hallucination drive Myeong-ja into a hysterical state, where her fear of not only losing Dong-sik to his wife, but her desire for and fear of pregnancy, dominate the last third of the film. See Doane, *The Desire to Desire*, 45.

75. The strange man's face is not shown, but the censorship script states that this is a sex scene with her teacher; and upon examining the shots closely, it appears that the man is played by the same actor (Joo Hyun) who played the teacher in the earlier flashbacks.

76. Park Yu-hee, "Censorship named Pornography: From *Chunmong* to *Madam Aema*, the Correlation between Censorship of the 'Racy Films' and Their Representation," in *Censorship in Korean Film History*, 187.

77. Kim Soo-yong, *Night Journey* DVD commentary (Korean Film Archive).

78. One may see them as visual spectacles, but throughout the film Hyeon-ju is clearly the subject of sexual frustration as well as fantasy, and Park is repeatedly "ridiculed" through a visual association with a doll with its buttocks exposed.

79. Karen Redrobe (Beckman), *Vanishing Women: Magic, Film and Feminism* (Durham: Duke University Press, 2003).

80. Nam, *Women in the Sky*, 166.

81. Barraclough, *Factory Girl Literature*, 137.

82. Yue, *Girl Head*, 16.

174 Notes

Chapter 2

1. Janet Poole, *When the Future Disappears: The Modernist Imagination in Late Colonial Korea* (New York: Columbia University Press, 2014), 9.
2. "South Korea: Disappointing Japan Ruling Fails to Deliver Justice to 'Comfort Women,'" *Amnesty International*, April 21, 2021, https://www.amnesty.org/en/latest/news/2021/04/south-korea-disappointing-japan-ruling-fails-to-deliver-justice-to-comfort-women/ (accessed July 19, 2021). "Battleship Island—a Symbol of Japanese Progress or Reminder of Its Dark History" *The Guardian*, July 3, 2015, https://www.theguardian.com/world/2015/jul/03/battleship-island-a-symbol-of-japans-progress-or-reminder-of-its-dark-history (accessed July 22, 2021).
3. For the box office success of *Assassination*, see Hyo Won Lee, "South Korea Box Office: Local Action Movie *Assassination* on Top, Becomes Biggest Film of 2015," *Hollywood Reporter*, August 18, 2015, https://www.hollywoodreporter.com/news/general-news/south-korea-box-office-local-815971/ (accessed July 18, 2021); the film gets criticized for its lack of depth in terms of character psychology; see Jason Bechervais, "*Assassination* Review," *Screen Daily*, July 27, 2015, https://www.screendaily.com/reviews/assassination-review/5090978.article (accessed July 18, 2021); for the controversies around *The Battleship Island*, see Jae-heun Kim, "It's Too Early to Discuss Truth of My Battleship Island, says Ryoo," *Korea Times*, August 7, 2017, https://www.koreatimes.co.kr/www/art/2017/08/689_234284.html (accessed July 18, 2021).
4. "Sarah Waters: *The Handmaiden* Turns Pornography into a Spectacle—But It's True to My Novel," *The Guardian*, April 8, 2017, https://www.theguardian.com/film/2017/apr/08/sarah-waters-the-handmaiden-turns-pornography-into-a-spectacle-but-its-true-to-my-novel- (accessed July 22, 2021). In the newspaper article, Claire Armistead states that Park's film is set in the 1930s, but in the actual film the period is not specified.
5. Kyung Hyun Kim, *Virtual Hallyu: Korean Cinema of the Global Era* (Durham: Duke University Press, 2011), 63–64.
6. Jinsoo An, *Parameters of Disavowal: Representation of Colonialism in South Korean Cinema* (Berkeley: University of California Press, 2018), 109.
7. An, *Parameters of Disavowal*, 4, 128.
8. Kim, *Virtual Hallyu*, 58.
9. Eom Mi-ok, *School Girls Encounter Modernity: The Formation of Korean Modern Novel and School Girls* [*Yeohaksaeng, Geundaereul malhada: Hanguk geundae sosoelui hyeongseonggwa yeohaksang*] (Seoul: Yeokrak, 2011), 153, 156. Eom explores the role of writing as a form of community building among girls as both the writing subjects and consumers, when girl readers submit their letters to magazines, as well as a prominent literary style adopted in early women's writing of the 1920s, including in the pioneer woman writer Kim Il-yeop's *Death of a Girl* [*Eoneu sonyeoui sa*] (1920). Also see my "Ribbons and Frills: Shōjo Sensibility and the Transnational Imaginary," in *Routledge Handbook for East Asian Pop Culture*, ed. Koichi Iwabuchi, Chris Berry, and Eva Tsai (London: Routledge, 2017), 178–190.
10. In his coming-of-age drama feature *Like a Virgin* (*Cheonghajangsa Madonna*, 2006), film director Lee Hae-young features a high school protagonist practicing Korean traditional wrestling (*ssireum*) in order to win prize money in a competition so that he can pay for the trans-sexual surgery he so longs for.

Notes **175**

11. Poole, *When the Future Disappears*, 110. In her discussion of Lee Tae-jun (Yi T'aejun)'s work, Poole uses the term to refer to Manchuria.

12. For the hauntology of classical Korean horror of the 1960s such as *The Public Cemetery of Wolhwa* (*Wolhwaui gongdong myoji*, Lee Yong-min, 1967), see Baek Moon-im, *The Sound of Female Ghost under the Moon: A History of Korean Horror and Female Ghost* [*Wolhaui yeogokseong: Yeogwiro ikneun hanguk gongpo yeonghwasa*] (Seoul: Chaeksesang, 2008), 125; Kim, *Virtual Hallyu*, 73.

13. Michele Aaron, "Cinema and Suicide: Necromanticism, Dead-Already-ness, and the Logic of Vanishing Point," *Cinema Journal* 53.2 (2014): 71–92.

14. Aaron, "Cinema and Suicide," 76, 80.

15. Aaron, "Cinema and Suicide," 80.

16. Aaron, "Cinema and Suicide," 73, 745; Aaron contrasts the "life against death" manifest in *A Taste of Cherry* (Abbas Kiarostami, 1997) with the "death-in-life" of *The Seventh Continent* (Michael Haneke, 1989).

17. Aaron, "Cinema and Suicide," 84.

18. Giorgio Agamben, *Homo Sacre: Sovereign Power and Bare Life* (Stanford: Stanford University Press, 1998); Achille Mbembe, *Necro-politics* (Durham: Duke University Press, 2019).

19. Mbembe, *Necro-politics*, 66.

20. Jin-kyung Lee, *Service Economies: Militarism, Sex Work, and Migrant Labor in South Korea* (Minneapolis: University of Minnesota Press, 2010), 82.

21. Kim, *Virtual Hallyu*, 56–57.

22. Dollase, "Girls on the Home Front: An Examination of *Shōjo no Tomo* Magazine 1937–45," *Asian Studies Review* 32 (2008): 326.

23. Dollase, "Girls on the Home Front," 328.

24. Wendy Larson, *Women and Writing in Modern China* (Stanford: Stanford University Press, 1998), 155.

25. Mary Ann Doane, *The Desire to Desire: The Women's Films of the 1940s* (Bloomington: Indiana University Press, 1987), 129.

26. Doane, *The Desire to Desire*, 135.

27. Doane, *The Desire to Desire*, 144.

28. Maggie Lee, "Review: *A Werewolf Boy*," *Variety* (September 20, 2012).

29. Honda Masuko, "The Genealogy of Hirahira: Liminality and the Girl," trans. Tomoko Aoyama and Barbara Hartley, in *Girl Reading Girl in Japan*, ed. Tomoko Aoyama and Barbara Hartley (New York: Routledge, 2010), 20.

30. Honda, "The Genealogy of Hirahira," 20.

31. Margaret D. Stetz and Bonnie B.C. Oh, eds., *Legacies of the Comfort Women of World War II* (London: Routledge, 2015), 9.

32. Asian Women's Fund, "How the Comfort Women Issue Came to Light," http://www.awf. or.jp/e2/survey.html (accessed September 17, 2018).

33. Chunghee Sarah Soh, "The Korean 'Comfort Women' Movement for Redress," *Asian Survey* 36.12 (December 1996): 1230.

34. Soh, "The Korean 'Comfort Women,'" 1226.

35. Yang Hyunah, "Lasting Postcolonial Trauma in [the] Testimony of Korean 'Comfort Women' Survivors [Jeungeoneul tonghae bon hangukin 'gunwiwanbu'deului poseuteu

176 Notes

sikminui sangheun (trauma)]," *Korean Women's Studies* [*Hanguk Yeoseonghak*] 22.3 (2006): 134.

36. Choe Sang-hun, "Japanese and South Korea Settle Dispute over Wartime 'Comfort Women,'" *New York Times,* December 28, 2015, https://www.nytimes.com/2015/12/29/world/asia/comfort-women-south-korea-japan.html (accessed September 17, 2018).

37. Hyonhee Shin, "Victims Absent from South Korea's 'Comfort Women' Rally amid Allegations over Ex-leader," *Reuters,* May 20, 2020, https://www.reuters.com/article/us-southkorea-comfortwomen-idUSKBN22W112 (accessed July 28, 2021).

38. Griselda Pollock, "Art/Trauma/Representation," *Parallax* 15.1 (2009): 42.

39. Pollock, "Art/Trauma/Representation," 45.

40. Pollock, "Art/Trauma/Representation," 46.

41. Pollock, "Art/Trauma/Representation," 45.

42. Pollock, "Art/Trauma/Representation," 46.

43. Pollock, "Art/Trauma/Representation," 51.

44. David Lloyd, "Colonial Trauma/Postcolonial Recovery," *Interventions* 2.2 (2000): 216.

45. Lloyd, "Colonial Trauma/Postcolonial Recovery," 215.

46. Lloyd, "Colonial Trauma/Postcolonial Recovery," 219.

47. Arif Dirlik, "Rethinking Colonialism: Globalization, Postcolonialism and The Nation," *Interventions* 4.3 (2002): 437.

48. Dirlik, "Rethinking Colonialism."

49. Stetz and Oh, "Introduction," in *Legacies of the Comfort Women of World War II*, 14.

50. Soh, "The Korean 'Comfort Women' Movement for Redress," 1230. Yang, "Lasting Postcolonial Trauma," 153, 155.

51. Soh, "The Korean 'Comfort Women' Movement for Redress," 1231.

52. Kim Chung-kang, "The Representations of 'Comfort Women' in Pre-1990 Korean Popular Cinema and the Politics of Memory ['Wianbu'neun eoteoke ithyeojeotna? 1990 nyeondae ijeon daejung yeonghwa sok 'wianbu' jaehyeon]," *Dongasiamunhwayeongu* 71 (2017): 168–169.

53. As the beginning of and shift to the association of wartime sexual slavery with young girls in the cinematic representation, Kim analyzes two films, *Comfort Women* (*Yeojajeongshindae*, Lee Sang-eon/Jeong Jung, 1985), and *Mommy's Name Was Josenpi* (*Emi ireumeun josenpiyeotda*, Ji Yong-ho, 1991), both of which were adaptations of the novel by Yun Jeong-mo, *Mommy's Name Was Josenpi* (Seoul: Dangdae, 1982). Kim, "The Representations of 'Comfort Women,'" 175–177.

54. Robert Eaglestone, "'You Would Not Add to My Suffering, if You Knew What I Have Seen': Holocaust Testimony and African Trauma Literature," *Studies in the Novel* 40.1/2 (Spring Summer, 2008): 79, cited in Katherine Isobel Baxter, "Memory and Photography: Rethinking Postcolonial Trauma Studies," *Journal of Postcolonial Writing* 47.1 (2011): 22.

55. Eaglestone, "'You Would Not Add to My Suffering,'" 82.

56. Joo Youshin, *Cine-Feminism* [*Sinepeminiseum*] (Busan: Homilbat, 2017), 267–268. Sohn Hee Jeong, *Feminism Reboot* [*Peminiseum ribeuteu*] (Seoul: Namuyeongpil, 2017), 249.

57. Zoran Lee Pecic, "Shamans and Nativism: Postcolonial Trauma in *Spirits' Homecoming* (2016) and *Manshin: Ten Thousand Spirits* (2013)," *Journal of Japanese and Korean Cinema* 12.1 (2020): 72–73.

58. Joo, *Cine-Feminism*, 241.

Notes **177**

59. Yang, "Lasting Postcolonial Trauma," 146.
60. Joo, *Cine-Feminism*, 253.
61. Sohn, *Feminism Reboot*, 243.
62. Joo, *Cine-Feminism*, 258.
63. Hyunah Yang, "Finding the Map of Memory: Testimony of the Japanese Military Sexual Slavery Survivors," *Positions* 16.1 (2008): 88–89.
64. Kim mentions that the director of *Mommy's Name Was Josenpi*, Ji Yeong-ho, used to make pornographic films. The producer, Moon Tae-sun, both starred in and produced well-known erotic film cycles of the 1980s: *Red Cherry* (*Ppalganaengdu*, 1982); *Madame Aema* (*Aema Buin*, 1982); and *Uhwudong* (1985). Kim, "The Representations of 'Comfort Women,'" 179–180.
65. Sandra Meiri, "Visual Responses: Women's Experiences of Sexual Violence as Represented in Israeli Holocaust-related Cinema," *European Journal of Women's Studies* 22.4 (2015), 448.
66. Joo, *Cine-Feminism*, 259. Sohn, *Feminism Reboot*, 245.
67. Katherine Isobel Baxter, "Memory and Photography: Rethinking Postcolonial Trauma Studies," *Journal of Postcolonial Writing* 47.1 (2011): 19.
68. Lloyd, "Colonial Trauma/Postcolonial Recovery," 220.
69. Yang, "Lasting Postcolonial Trauma," 151–153.
70. Yang, "Lasting Postcolonial Trauma," 154, footnote 16.
71. Yang, "Lasting Postcolonial Trauma," 154–157.
72. Sohn notes that the sisterhood in *Snowy Road* is something earned rather than something given, as in *Spirits' Homecoming*. Sohn, *Feminism Reboot*, 246.
73. The first Japanese translation of the novel was published in 1927, but, as the Korean translation was not published until the 1960s (1962), it must be an unofficial Korean transcription.
74. Sohn claims that Jong-bun's request in the scene provides Yeong-ae a reason to live on, but I slightly disagree. Sohn, *Feminism Reboot*, 246.
75. Deborah Sahmoon, *Passionate Friendship: The Aesthetics of Girls' Culture in Japan* (Honolulu: University of Hawai'i Press, 2012), 66–67.
76. Roland Barthes, *Camera Lucida* (London: Vintage Classic, 1993), 25–26.
77. Marianne Hirsch, *Family Frames: Photography, Narrative and Postmemory* (New York: Columbia University Press, 1992), 22.

Chapter 3

1. In the Korean thriller *The Neighbours* (*Iutsaram*, Kim Hwi, 2012), Ma plays a supporting character who is a gangster, yet unaware of his neighbor's serial killing. Ma threatens and punishes the killer for taking his usual parking spot.
2. Kyung Hyun Kim, *The Remasculinization of Korean Cinema* (Durham: Duke University Press, 2004).
3. Michele Aaron, *Death and the Moving Image: Ideology, Iconography and I* (Edinburgh: Edinburgh University Press, 2014), 5.
4. Aaron, *Death and the Moving Image*, 5.
5. Joseph Jonghyun Jeon, "Memories of Memories: Historiography, Nostalgia, and Archive in Bong Joon-ho's *Memories of Murder*," *Cinema Journal* 51.1 (Fall 2011): 83.

178   Notes

6. The female victim after whom the film modeled was fourteen when she was murdered in 1990. The film's investigation ends in 1987 and the temporal manipulation of the order of murder victims underscores the film's construction of the narrative climax around the girl's death. Han Seong-gon, "Would the 33 years' Mystery of Hwaseong Serial Killing, Be Solved? [Hwaseong yeonsyeosageon, 33 nyeon misteori pulina?]," *Asia Economy*, September 19, 2019, https://www.asiae.co.kr/article/2019091905025158255 (accessed January 4, 2023).

7. Jeon, "Memories of Memories," 77.

8. Another victim, in whose vagina pieces of peaches were found, was fifty-four years old while the film presents her as though she were in her twenties or thirties. Han, "Would the 33 years' Mystery of Hwaseong Serial Killing, Be Solved?"

9. Jeon, "Memories of Memories," 80.

10. Jeon, "Memories of Memories," 80.

11. Yoonjung Seo and Julia Hollingsworth, "Man Who Confessed to Being One of South Korea's Most-notorious Serial Killers Says He's Surprised He Wasn't Caught Sooner," CNN, 2 Nov, 2020, https://edition.cnn.com/2020/11/02/asia/hwaseong-serial-killer-guilt-intl-hnk/index.html (accessed July 13, 2023).

12. Seo and Hollingsworth, "Man Who Confessed."

13. Nam Lee, *The Films of Bong Joon Ho* (New Brunswick: Rutgers University Press, 2020), 110–111.

14. Ji-yoon An, "The Korean Mother in Contemporary Thriller Films: A Monster or Just Modern," *Journal of Japanese and Korean Cinema*, 11.2 (2019): 167.

15. Lee, *The Films of Bong Joon Ho*, 91.

16. An, "The Korean Mother in Contemporary Thriller Films," 164.

17. An, "The Korean Mother in Contemporary Thriller Films," 164..

18. Mary Ann Doane, *The Desire to Desire: The Woman's Film of the 1940s* (Bloomington: Indiana University Press, 1987), 137.

19. Doane, *The Desire to Desire*, 150–151.

20. An, "The Korean Mother in Contemporary Thriller Films," 165.

21. Judith Butler, *The Force of Non-Violence: An Ethico-Political Bind* (London: Verso, 2020), 17.

22. Lee, *The Films of Bong Joon Ho*, 114.

23. Michele Aaron, "Cinema and Suicide: Necromanticism, Dead-already-ness and the Logic of the Vanishing Point," *Cinema Journal* 53.2 (2014): 79, 86.

24. Wendy Brown, *Undoing the Demos: Neoliberalism's Stealth Revolution* (New York: Zone Books, 2017), 124, 127.

25. Brown, *Undoing the Demos*, 125.

26. Christina Klein, "Why American Studies Needs to Think about Korean Cinema, or, Transnational Genres in the Films of Bong Joon-ho," *American Quarterly* 60.4 (2008): 871–898; Hye Seung Chung and David Scott Diffrient, *Movie Migrations: Transnational Genre Flows and South Korean Cinema* (New Brunswick: Routledge, 2015); Jinhee Choi, *The South Korean Film Renaissance: Local Hitmakers, Global Provocateurs* (Middletown: Wesleyan University Press, 2010).

27. Chin Eun-Kyung and Ann Sang-won, "Ecology and Eco-Feminism as Depicted in the Film *Okja* [Yeonghwa 'Okja'e natanan saengtaehakgwa ecopeminiseum]," *Literature and Environment [Munhwakgwa hwangyeonghoe]* 17.3 (2018): 193–218; Lee Hee-seung, "Signs of Domiciled Motherhood: Focused on *Family Ties*, *The Host*, and *Cruel Winter Blues* [Jeongjuhaneun moseongui gihodeul: <Gajokui tansaeng>,

<Goemul>, <Yeolhyeolnama>reul jungsimeuro]," *Journal of Communication Science* [*Eonlongwahakyeongu*] 13.1 (2013): 359–386; Park Sun-ah, "A Study on Performative Motherhood Identity Represented in *Mother* [Yeonghwa <Madeo>e natanan suhaengjeok moseong jeongcheseonge gwanhan yeongu]," *Hanguk yeonghwahakhoe* 55 (2013): 173–195; Park Jai-in, "The Distorted Father and Mother Epic Given by the Film *Mother* [Yeonghwa <Madeo>eseo jesihan waegokdoen bumoseosa]," *Narration and Literary Therapy Research* [*Seosawamunhakchiryoyeonguso*] 6 (2011): 115–136.

28. Fred Lee and Steven Manicastri, "Not All Are Aboard: Decolonizing Exodus in Joon Ho Bong's *Snowpiercer*," *New Political Science* 40.2 (2018): 211–226.

29. Lee and Manicastri, "Not All Are Aboard," 219, 222.

30. Lee and Manicastri, "Not All Are Aboard," 222.

31. Meera Lee, "Monstrosity and Humanity in Bong Joon-ho's *The Host*," *Positions: Asia Critique* 26.4 (2018): 735.

32. Lee, "Monstrosity and Humanity," 727.

33. Lee, "Monstrosity and Humanity," 727.

34. Lee, "Monstrosity and Humanity," 728.

35. Lee, "Signs of Domiciled Motherhood," 373–374.

36. Lee, "Signs of Domiciled Motherhood," 375.

37. Chin and Ahn, "Ecology and Eco-Feminism," 197; Kim Hyeong-won, "Kim Hyeong-won's Otaku Story [Kim Hyeong-wonui odeok iyagi]," *IT Chosun*, September 14, 2019, http://it.chosun.com/site/data/html_dir/2019/09/13/2019091301124.html?utm_source=daum&utm_medium=original&utm_campaign=it (accessed October 19, 2019).

38. Kelly Oliver, *Hunting Girls: Sexual Violence from the Hunger Games to Campus Rape* (New York: Columbia University Press, 2016), 24, 38.

39. Oliver, *Hunting Girls*, 130.

40. Oliver, *Hunting Girls*, 18, 31.

41. Chin and Ahn, "Ecology and Eco-Feminism," 197.

42. Chin and Ahn, "Ecology and Eco-Feminism," 202.

43. Ha Gil-jong, "*The Road to Sampo* [*Sampo ganeungil*]," *Sedae* July 1975, cited in Oh Young Sook, "Father and Girl: Representation of Korean Cinema in [the] 1970s [Appawa sonyeo: 70 nyeondae hanguk yeonghwaui pyosang yeongu]," *Yeonghwayeongu* 42 (2009): 438.

44. Ed Gonzales, "Poetry," *Slant Magazine*, September 22, 2010, http://www.slantmagazine.com/film/review/poetry (accessed January 28, 2016).

45. Jay Weissburg, "Rotterdam Film Review: 'Han Gong-ju,'" *Variety*, February 9, 2014 (accessed January 26, 2016).

46. Brian Masumi, "The Anatomy of Affect," *Critical Inquiry* 31 (Autumn 1995): 85.

47. Masumi, "The Anatomy of Affect," 85.

48. Paul Griffith, *What Emotions Really Are: The Problem of Psychological Categories* (Chicago: University of Chicago Press, 1997); Carl Plantinga, *Moving Viewers: American Film and the Spectator's Experience* (Berkeley: University of California Press, 2009): 9.

49. Murray Smith, *Engaging Characters: Fiction, Emotion and the Cinema* (Oxford: Oxford University Press, 1995): 98–102.

50. E. Ann Kaplan, "European Art Cinema, Affect, and Postcolonialism: Herzog, Denis, and the Dardenne Brothers," in *Global Art Cinema*, ed. Rosalind Galt and Karl Schnoover (Oxford: Oxford University Press, 2010), 435.

180 Notes

51. Jonathan Flatley, *Affective Mapping: Melancholia and the Politics of Modernism* (Cambridge: Harvard University Press, 2008), 21.
52. Martin Heidegger, *Being and Time*, trans. John Macquarrie and Edward Robinson (San Francisco: Harper and Row, 1962), cited in Flatley, *Affective Mapping*, 21.
53. "Suicide Rate," OECD Data, https://data.oecd.org/healthstat/suicide-rates.htm (accessed November 1, 2023).
54. Elizabeth Kerr, "*Jamsil*: Film Review BFF 2016," *Variety*, October 11, 2016, https://www.hollywoodreporter.com/movies/movie-reviews/jamsil-review-937182/ (accessed November 1, 2023).

Chapter 4

1. Jean Noh, "Korean International Film Sales Up 43% During Rough 2020," *Screen Daily*, February 22, 2021, https://www.screendaily.com/news/korean-international-film-sales-up-43-during-tough-2020/5157292.article (accessed August 2, 2021).
2. Jean Noh, "Korean Film Council Reports Industry Exports up by 17.5% in 2017," *Screen Daily*, February 12, 2018, https://www.screendaily.com/news/korean-film-council-repo rts-industry-exports-up-by-175-in-2017/5126473.article (accessed September 7, 2021).
3. Kim Hyeon-su and Kim So-mi, "10 years of Korean Independent Films with Temporal Markers [Taim raineuro boneun hanguk doklip yeonghwa 10nyeonui yeoksa]" *Cine21*, August 28, 2019, http://m.cine21.com/news/view/?mag_id=93749 (accessed December 17, 2019).
4. Jinhee Choi, *The South Korean Film Renaissance: Local Hitmakers Global Provocateurs* (Middletown: Wesleyan University Press, 2010), 122–124.
5. Kim Min-ji, "Why Women Directors Do Not Tell Women's Stories [Yeoseong gamdoki yeoja iyagi anhaneun iyu]," *Kyeongnam domin ilbo*, June 18, 2013, http://www.idomin.com/news/articleView.html?idxno=417852 (accessed September 8, 2019).
6. Susan Fraiman, *Extreme Domesticity: A View from the Margins* (New York: Columbia University Press, 2017).
7. Fraiman, *Extreme Domesticity*, 18.
8. Fraiman, *Extreme Domesticity*, 29.
9. Fraiman, *Extreme Domesticity*, 25.
10. Fraiman, *Extreme Domesticity*, 18.
11. Fraiman, *Extreme Domesticity*, 19.
12. No Cheol Park, "Undomesticated Vision: A History of South Korean Independent Women's Films, 1974–2004," *Korea Journal* 49.4 (2009): 142.
13. Park, "Undomesticated Vision," 140–142.
14. Park, "Undomesticated Vision," 142.
15. Park, "Undomesticated Vision," 140.
16. Young-a Park, *Unexpected Alliances: Independent Filmmakers, the State and the Film Industry in Postauthoritarian South Korea* (Stanford: Stanford University Press, 2015), 22.
17. Park, "Undomesticated Vision," 146.
18. Maeng Soo-jin, "Study on the Thematics and Aesthetic Diversification of Korean Independent Documentaries [Hanguk doklip dakyumenteoriui juje mit yangsikjeok dayanghwae daehan gochal]," *Cineforum* 18 (2014): 256, 258.

Notes   181

19. Park, *Unexpected Alliances*, 127.
20. Park, *Unexpected Alliances*, 20.
21. Park, *Unexpected Alliances*, 20.
22. Park, *Unexpected Alliances*, 51.
23. Seoul International Women's Film Festival, http://siwff.or.kr/kor/addon/00000002/summa ry_view.asp?summaryYear=1999&QueryYear=1999 (accessed September 7, 2021).
24. Mun Hak-san, "Emptying Screen and Erased History: Tendencies in and History of Korean Independent Films [Biuneun hwamyeongwa biwojin yeoksa: hanguk doklip yeonghwaui gyeonghwanggwa yeoksa]," in *Issues in Korean Independent Short Films: Auteurs, Women, Digital [Hanguk danpyeon yeonghwaui jaengjeomdeul: jakga, yeoseong, digiteol]*, ed. Jeonju Independent Film Festival (Seoul: Sodo, 2003), 45.
25. Lee Ju-hyeon, "Rooting for the Children: The Director of *The World of Us*, Yoon Ga-eun, [Aideulul eungweonhaneun maeumeul damda—<Urideul> Yoon Ga-eun gamdok]" *Cine 21*, June 16, 2016, http://m.cine21.com/news/view/?mag_id=84423 (accessed December 17, 2019).
26. Michael Z. Newman, *Indie: An American Film Culture* (New York: Columbia University Press, 2011).
27. Kim Su-bin, "20 Years of Independent Cinema in Korea," *Hankyoreh*, September 16, 2018, https://english.hani.co.kr/arti/english_edition/e_entertainment/862280.html (accessed April 15, 2019).
28. KOFIC, *Status and Insight: Korean Film Industry 2016*, 36.
29. KOFIC, *Status and Insight: Korean Film Industry 2018*, 45. In footnote 26, the criteria are listed: (1) films that receive the KOFIC's production or distribution support; (2) films that receive production or distribution support from central or regional governments or public organizations (regional film committee); (3) films that are selected through the public in-dependent film festivals hosted in Korean (short and international films).
30. KOFIC, *Status and Insight* (2018), footnote 27. An independent film avoids (1) distribution by majors (10 major distribution companies based on the revenues earned in the previous year) and (2) monopolization of distribution during the opening week.
31. Interview conducted by the author with Jeon Go-woon, November 2, 2018.
32. J. J. Murphy, *Rewriting Indie Cinema: Improvisation, Psychodrama, and the Screenplay* (New York: Columbia University Press, 2019), 10. He traces a tradition of American indie back to the psychodrama form, where priority is given to performers rather than the script. Employing the three categories developed by J. L. Moreno—the spontaneous, the planned, and the rehearsed—Murphy examines some of the American indie staples, including John Cassavetes, where the source of spontaneity comes sometimes from the blurred line be-tween pre-filmic and filmic situations.
33. Lee, "Rooting for the Children."
34. A Special Feature, Park Se-young, in the Korean DVD release of *The World of Us*. She points out the sequence in which Ji-a confides to Seon that her parents were divorced a few years back. Ji-a is having a sleepover at Seon's and the two chat while lying side-by-side on the floor. Park had to pick the best syllable of dialogue, even at the level of suffix such as "ga" or "reul."
35. Director's commentary on the Korean DVD release of *The World of Us*. An example is the interaction between the two leads in the sequence where we learn Jia has just stolen a set of colored pencils from a store. Shortly after the shop owner expresses his annoyance at

182 Notes

Ji-a and Seon as they browse without having anything particular to purchase, they leave the store, running down the hill in one take to land on a bench. In the commentary, Yoon mentions that the scene has been improvised apart from the last cut to Ji-a, who answers a call from her mother with her back to the camera.

36. Fraiman, *Extreme Domesticity*, 59.
37. Fraiman, *Extreme Domesticity*, 73.
38. Fraiman, *Extreme Domesticity*, 25.
39. Lee Ju-hyeon, "Eureka! Yoon Ga-eun's Directorial Debut, *The World of Us*, Depicts the World of Girls [Balgyeon, sonyeodeului segyereul geurin Yoon Ga-eun gamdokui debyu, Urideul]," *Cine 21*, June 16, 2016, www.cine21.com/news/view/?mag_id=84422 (accessed December 17, 2019). It must be added that the truth often elides in the world of girls and the film refuses to verify their words or actions. In the next few shots of the pre-credit sequence, Seon is accused by a member of the opposite team of stepping on the line of a court and is told that she should move to the sideline to play defense instead. Seon defends herself at first but then reluctantly moves to the other end of the court; the camera does not take sides or show who is correct. It instead cuts to black with the sound of girls' talking spilling over the film's title. The last dodgeball scene in *The World of Us*, with which the film ends, draws a parallel between the opening and ending of the film. This time, it is Ji-a who is accused by her peers of having crossed the line. Seon sides with Ji-a, when in fact, Seon was looking at her nails when the dispute took place off-screen. One of the voices—presumably of a boy—questions (although not translated into subtitles) whether Seon in fact saw it.
40. Fraiman, *Extreme Domesticity*, 32.
41. Akira Mizta Lippit, "Hong Sangsoo's Lines of Inquiry, Communication, Defense and Escape," *Film Quarterly* 57.4 (2004): 24. In a different context, Lippit discusses how alcohol and vomit may help Hong Sangsoo's "characters' interiorities reach the outside."
42. Fraiman, *Extreme Domesticity*, 32, 42.
43. Fraiman, *Extreme Domesticity*, 79.
44. Linda C. Ehrlich, "Kore-eda's Ocean View," *Film Criticism* 35.2/3 (2011): 142.
45. Ehrlich, "Kore-eda's Ocean View." *The World of Us* also features a scene by the beach after the death of Seon's grandfather, which functions much like the scene of the father and son in *Still Walking*, through which Ehrlich claims the characters "reach the equilibrium that had evaded them," 140.
46. Fraiman, *Extreme Domesticity*, 37.
47. Fraiman, *Extreme Domesticity*, 42.
48. Fraiman, *Extreme Domesticity*, 119.
49. Fraiman, *Extreme Domesticity*, 31.
50. Yoon in fact wrote a short piece on Ozu's *Ohayo*. She claims that every year on New Year's Day, she watches the film, and adds that she's always fond of Kore-eda's work. See Yoon Ga-eun, "Good Morning by Yoon Ga-eun: A Film That Makes You Happy [Yoon Ga-eunui <Annyeonghaseyo> haengbokhaejineun yeonghwa]," *Cine 21*, January 25, 2017, http://www.cine21.com/news/view/?mag_id=86310 (accessed December 17, 2019).
51. In Ozu's work, conflicts occur between parent(s) and "adult" children, when the latter must leave the house for marriage or other family affairs.
52. Alexander Jacoby, "Why Nobody Knows—Family and Society in Modern Japan," *Film Criticism* 35.2/3 (2011): 77.

Notes **183**

53. Ehrlich, "Kore-eda's Ocean View," 138.
54. Rachel Simmons, *Odd Girl Out: The Hidden Culture of Aggression in Girls* (Boston: Mariner Books, 2011), 21. Simmons cites three types of covert aggression: relational, indirect, and social. Indirect aggression often involves "inflicting pain on a targeted person, by spreading a rumor." In an interview with a Korean film magazine, Yoon mentioned that she read Simmons's book while writing the script of *The World of Us*.
55. Fraiman, *Extreme Domesticity*, 42–43.
56. Fraiman, *Extreme Domesticity*, 43.
57. Shim Hye-kyeong, "Kim Sae-ron: New-Girl or Saeron-Girl [Kimsaeron: Nyu-geol hokeun saeron-sonyeo]," in *Girls: K-pop, Screen, Square* [*Sonyeodeul: K-pop seukeurin gwangjang*], ed. Cho hye-young (Seoul: Yeoyiyeon, 2017), 125.
58. Sohn Dong-joo, "Kim Sae-ron Fined 20 Million Won for Driving under the Influence," *Korea JoongAng Daily*, April 5, 2023, https://koreajoongangdaily.joins.com/2023/04/05/national/socialAffairs/Kim-Saeron-DUI-driving-under-the-influence/20230405111043 373.html (accessed, January 2, 2024).
59. Fraiman, *Extreme Domesticity*, 120.
60. Fraiman, *Extreme Domesticity*, 120, 122.
61. Deborah Shamoon, *Passionate Friendship: The Aesthetics of Girls' Culture in Japan* (Honolulu: University of Hawaii Press, 2012), 37.
62. Jin-kyung Lee, *Service Economies: Militarism, Sex Work, and Migrant Labor in South Korea* (Minneapolis: University of Minnesota Press, 2010), 199.
63. Fraiman, *Extreme Domesticity*, 122.
64. Fiona Handyside, *Sofia Coppola: A Cinema of Girlhood* (London: I. B. Tauris, 2017), 132.
65. Handyside, *Sofia Coppola*, 111, 117.
66. Handyside, *Sofia Coppola*, 117.
67. Soomin Jun, "Korea's 'N-Po' Generation Looks to New Administration for Jobs," *Asia Foundation*, May 31, 2017, https://asiafoundation.org/2017/05/31/koreas-n-po-generat ion-looks-new-administration-jobs/ (accessed September 7, 2021).
68. Gyu-sik Kim, "S. Korea's Unemployment Hits a Record High in 2016 with Highest Jobless Youth Rate," *Pulse*, January 11, 2017, https://pulsenews.co.kr/view.php?year=2017&no= 25912 (accessed September 7, 2021).
69. Fraiman, *Extreme Domesticity*, 164.
70. Fraiman, *Extreme Domesticity*, 158.
71. Jesook Song, *South Koreans in the Debt Crisis: The Creation of a Neoliberal Welfare Society* (Durham: Duke University Press, 2009), 80.
72. Song, *South Koreans in the Debt Crisis*, 76.
73. Fraiman, *Extreme Domesticity*, 165.
74. Fraiman, *Extreme Domesticity*, 166.
75. Fraiman, *Extreme Domesticity*, 166.
76. Yim Su-yeon, "[*Microhabitat*] Mi-so has the Courage that I envision [<Sogongnyeo> Mi-soneun naega saenghakhaneun yonggireul gajeotda]," *Cine 21*, October 30, 2017, http://www.cine21.com/news/view/?mag_id=88549 (accessed January 9, 2020).
77. Fraiman, *Extreme Domesticity*, 44.
78. Fraiman, *Extreme Domesticity*, 164.
79. Kathleen McHugh, "South Korean Film Melodrama: State, Nation, Woman and the Transnational Familiar," in *South Korean Golden Age Melodrama: Gender, Genre and*

184 Notes

National Cinema, ed. Kathleen McHugh and Nancy Abelmann (Detroit: Wayne State University Press, 2005), 31.

80. McHugh, "South Korean Film Melodrama," 32.

81. Fraiman, *Extreme Domesticity*, 170. Interestingly, in her interview with the magazine *Cine 21*, director Jeon characterizes Mi-so as someone who thinks of herself as nobility, which partially explains the Korean title, *Sogongneyo* (*A Little Princess*). See Yim Su-yeon, "[*Microhabitat*] Mi-so Has the Courage That I Envision."

82. Jini Kim Watson, "The Disappearing Woman, Interiority, and Private Space," in *The New Asian City* (Minneapolis: University of Minnesota Press, 2011), 146.

83. Watson, "The Disappearing Woman," 146.

84. Watson, "The Disappearing Woman," 150.

85. Interview conducted by the author with the director Jeon. Also see Jinhee Choi, "Seoul Flaneur? *Breathless* and *Café Noir*," *Journal of Japanese and Korean Cinema* 7.1 (2015): 57–72.

86. Song distinguishes between the "independent homeless" as those who have a "desire to work" or with the "intention to be habilitated" in contrast to "the rootless" [*burangja* in Korean] who lack such desire or capacity, due to their health, either mental or physical. Song, *South Koreans in the Debt Crisis*, 77, 89.

87. Song, *South Koreans in the Debt Crisis*, 89.

88. Jinhee Choi, "Home Is Where the Kitchen Is: *Rinco's Restaurant* (2009) and *Little Forest* (2014, 2018)," *Asian Cinema* 31.2 (2020): 169–185.

89. A similar trend is found for adult female protagonists: *Miss Granny* (*Susanghan geuneyo*, Hang Dong-hyuk, 2014); *Dancing Queen* (*Daensing kwin*, Lee Seok-hoon, 2012); *Scandal Makers* (*Kwasok seukaendeul*, Kang Hyeong-cheol, 2008). All of the female leads in the films pursue singing or dancing career.

90. Kate Taylor, "*Heart* (*Hateu*, 2019)" BFI London International Film Festival Catalog (2019), 46.

Chapter 5

1. Yu Jeong-suk, "From Darkness to the Light [Eodumeseo biteuro]," in *I, Women Labourers* [*Na, Yeoseong Nodongja*], ed. Yu Gyeong-sun (Seoul: Greenbi, 2011), 38–39.

2. Brian O'Connor, *Idleness: A Philosophical Essay* (Princeton: Princeton University, 2018), 172, 180.

3. Lea Ypi, *Free: Coming of Age at the End of History* (London: Allen Lane, 2021).

4. Kim Ji-yeong, "[Movie] *Sunny* . . . A Well-made Comedy for 'the Generation of Free School Uniform Policy' [[Yeonghwa] *Sseoni*, 'gyobokjayulhwa sedae'reul wihan welmeideu komedi]," *Mail Daily*, 26 April 2011. https://www.mk.co.kr/news/culture/4904779 (accessed March 8, 2024).

5. Joseph Jonghyun Jeon, "Memories of Memories: Historiography, Nostalgia, and Archive in Bong Joon-ho's *Memories of Murder*," *Cinema Journal* 51.1 (Fall 2011): 78, 84.

6. O'Connor, *Idleness*, 55.

7. O'Connor, *Idleness*, 56.

8. O'Connor, *Idleness*, 138.

Notes **185**

9. Michelle Cho, "*Take Care of My Cat* (Jeong Jae-eun, 2001): The Architectonics of Female Subjectivity in Post-crisis South Korea," in *Rediscovering Korean Cinema*, ed. Sangjoon Lee (Ann Arbor: University of Michigan Press, 2018), 359, 364–365.

10. O'Connor, *Idleness*, 171.

11. Sonia Kil, "Busan: Asian Market in Flux," *Variety*, October 6, 2015, https://variety.com/2015/film/asia/busan-asian-film-market-in-flux-1201611269/ (accessed November 4, 2024).

12. Brian Yesies, "The Chinese Korean Co-production Pact-Collaborative Encounters," *The International Journal of Cultural Policy* 22.5 (2016): 12.

13. Lee Hyo Won, "South Korean film, 'Miss Granny' to get English and Spanish Language Remakes," *Hollywood Reporter*, November 6, 2016, https://www.hollywoodreporter.com/news/general-news/south-korean-film-miss-granny-get-english-spanish-language-remakes-944612/ (accessed, March 8, 2024).

14. Kyung Hyun Kim, "Dividuated Korean Cinema: Recent Bodyswitch Film in the Overwired Age," in *Surveillance in Asian Cinema: Under Eastern Eyes*, ed. Karen Fang (New York: Routledge, 2017), 181.

15. Min-hua Chiang, *Post-industrial Development in East Asia: Taiwan and South Korea in Comparison* (Singapore: Palgrave Pivot, 2018), 137.

16. Chiang, *Post-industrial Development in East Asia*, 144.

17. Jennifer Coates, Hsin Hsieh, Sung-Ae Lee and Kate Taylor-Jones, "The Pan-Asian 'Miss Granny' Phenomenon," in *East Asian Film Remakes*, ed. David Scott Diffirent and Kenneth Chan (Edinburgh: University of Edinburgh Press, 2023), 278.

18. The death certificate in the film is dated 1963.

19. Hyaeweol Choi, "'Wise Mother, Good Wife': A Transcultural Discursive Construct in Modern Korea," *Journal of Korean Studies* 14.1 (2009): 12. Sung-ae Lee discusses the importance of opening sequences of the three versions in "The Pan-Asian 'Miss Granny' Phenomenon," 274–275.

20. Anthony Giddens, "Notes on the Concept of Play and Leisure," *Sociological Review* 12.1 (1964): 82–83.

21. Giddens, "Notes on the Concept of Play and Leisure," 83.

22. Choi, "'Wise Mother, Good Wife,'" 7.

23. The latter scene is reconfigured in the Japanese remake; Otori, the young Katsu, consoles and praises both a young boy who cries and the mother struggling with an infant as being brave enough to take on a new challenge.

24. Sang-keun Yoo also points out the age-dependent hierarchy manifest in *Squid Game*, directed by Hwang. See "From Patriarchal History to Korean Ethnoformalist Speculative Empathy: *Squid Game* and *The School Nurse Files*," *International Journal of Korean History* 28.1 (2023): 223.

25. Choi, "'Wise Mother, Good Wife,'" 4.

26. O'Connor, *Idleness*, 76.

27. O'Connor, *Idleness*, 76.

28. O'Connor, *Idleness*, 99.

29. J. S. Russell, "Idleness as Play and Leisure: Reflection on Idleness—A Philosophical Essay by Brian O'Connor," *American Journal of Play*, 313.

30. O'Connor, *Idleness*, 4.

31. O'Connor, *Idleness*, 180.

186   Notes

32. O'Connor, *Idleness*, 180.
33. O'Connor, *Idleness*, 7–8.
34. O'Connor, *Idleness*, 8.
35. Sharon Kinsella, *Schoolgirls, Money and Rebellion in Japan* (London: Routledge, 2014), 9.
36. Jeong Seo-hui, "*Queen of Walking* Director, Baek Seung-hwa, 'Hoped to make an adequate film—one that underwent the adequate process in making [<Geotgiwang> Baek Seung-hwa gamdok, 'Jakpumdo, Gwajeongdo olbaruen yeonghwareul mandeulgo sipeotda']," *Maxmovie*, October 31, 2016, https://www.maxmovie.com/news/274648 (accessed, August 7, 2023).
37. O'Connor, *Idleness*, 181.
38. O'Connor, *Idleness*, 20, 27.
39. Choi Han-wook, "As It's Hurt, So You Are Young? Play Jokgu Instead [Apeunikka cheungchun? Charari gokgureul haera]," *Minjungui sori*, Augist 31, 2014, https://vop.co.kr/A00000789054.html (accessed August 7, 2023).
40. Suk-young Kim, "Tragedy Should Force Korea to Consider Despair of Next Generation," *Korea Times*, November 16, 2022, https://www.koreatimes.co.kr/www/opinion/2023/08/137_339939.html (accessed August 7, 2023).
41. Jung Hee-young, " 'Youth, It's Painful,' Offers Hope to Young Koreans," *Korea Herald*, August 17, 2011, https://www.koreaherald.com/view.php?ud=20110817000762; Kim Tae-wan, "[Books] the Most Beloved Books since 1990s and 2000s" [2000nyeondaewa 1990nyeondae ihu gajang sarangbatatdeon chaekeun?], *Monthly Joseon*, August 8, 2023, http://monthly.chosun.com/client/mdaily/daily_view.asp?idx=18135&Newsnumb=20230818135 (accessed August 8, 2023).
42. Bae Seung-hoon, "Moon Chae-won Joins Cast of *Myeongdang*," August 23, 2017, https://koreajoongangdaily.joins.com/2017/08/23/etc/Moon-Chaewon-joins-cast-of-Myeongdang/3037517.html (accessed October 15, 2023).

Selected Filmography

0Shim (*Yeongshimi*, Lee Mi-rye, 1990)
1987: When the Day Comes (*1987*, Jang Joon-hwan, 2017)
20 Once Again (*Chong fan 20 sui*, Leste Chen, 2015)
400 Blows, The (*Les quatre cents coups*, Francois Truffaut, 1959)
Adulthood (*Eoreundogam*, Kim In-seon, 2018)
After My Death (*Joe manheun sonyeo*, Kim Ui-seok, 2017)
Age of Shadows, The (*Miljeong*, Kim Jee-woon, 2016)
Anarchist from Colony (*Park Yeol*, Lee Joon-ik, 2017)
Another Child (*Miseongnyeon*, Kim Yoon-sik, 2018)
Ash Flower (*Jekkot*, Park Seok-yeong, 2014–2016).
Assassination (*Amsal*, Choi Dong-hoon, 2015)
Asura: The City of Madness (*Asura*, Kim Sung-su, 2016)
Bacchus Lady, The (*Jukeoya saneun yeoja*, Lee Je-yong [a.s.a. E J-yong], 2016)
Barking Dogs Never Bite (*Peurandaseuui gae*, Bong Joon-ho, 2000)
Battleship Island, The (*Gunhamdo*, Ryoo Seung-hwan, 2017)
Battleship Potempkin (*Bronenosets Potemkin*, Sergei Eisenstein, 1925)
Beauty Inside, The (*Beuti insaideu*, Baek Jong-yeol, 2015)
Bicycle King Uhm Bok-dong (*Jajeonchawang Eom Bok-dong*, Kim Yu-sung, 2019)
Brand New Life, A (*Yeohaengja*, Ounie Lecomte, 2009)
Breathless (*Ttongpari*, Yang Ik-jun, 2009)
Bridget Jones (Sharon Maguire, 2001)
Burning (*Beoning*, Lee Chang-dong, 2018)
Café Noir (*Kape neuareu*, Jeong Seong-il, 2009)
Call Me by Your Name (Luca Guadignino, 2017)
Cart (*Kateu*, Boo Ji-young, 2014)
Cloud Atlas (the Wachowskis and Tom Tykwer, 2012)
Clueless (Amy Heckerling, 1995)
Coinlocker Girl (*Chainataun*, Han Jun-hee, 2014)
Comfort Women (*Yeojajeongshindae*, Lee Sang-eon/Jeong Jung, 1985)
Confession of a Girl (*Eoneu sonyeoui gobaek*, Park Jong-ho, 1970)
Crazy for You (*Jinjja jinjja joahae*, Moon Yeo-song, 1977)
Crush and Blush (*Misseu hongdangmu*, Lee Kyoung-mi, 2008)
Dance Sports Girls (*Ttanppo geolseu*, Lee Seung-mun, 2017)
Dancing Queen (*Daensing qwin*, Lee Seok-hoon, 2012)
Daughter-in-Law (*Minmyeoneuri*, Choi Eun-hee, 1965)
Dongju: The Portrait of a Poet (*Dongju*, Lee Joon-ik, 2016)
Face Reader, The (*Gwansang*, Han Jae-rim, 2013)
Fengshui (*Myeongdang*, Park Hee-gon, 2018)
Fighter (*Paiteo*, Yun Jero, 2020)
Flower in Hell (*Jiokhwa*, Shin Sang-ok, 1958)
Gangster, the Cop, the Devil, The (*Akinjeon*, Lee Won-tae, 2019)
Ghost Walk (*Bamui muni yeolinda*, Yu Eun-jeong, 2018)
Girl (*Sonyeo*, Choi Jin-seong, 2013)
Girl at My Door, A (*Do-huiya* [a.s.a. *Dohee-ya*], July Jung, 2014)

188   Selected Filmography

Girls from Scratch (*Maenjumeokui sonyeodeul*, Kim Yeong-hyo, 1976)
Girls' High School Days (*Yeogosijeol*, Kang Dae-sun, 1972)
Good Lawyer's Wife (*Baramnan gajok*, Im Sang-soo, 2003)
Guest (*Sonnim*, Yoon Ga-eun, 2011)
Habitual Sadness (*Nateun sumsori 2*, 1997)
Han Gong-ju (Lee Sujin, 2013)
Handmaiden, The (*Agassi* [a.s.a. *Ahgassi*], Park Chan-wook, 2016)
Heavenly Homecoming to Stars (*Byeoldeului gohyang*, Lee Jang-ho, 1974)
Herstory (*Heoseutori*, Min Kyu-dong, 2018)
Homebound (*Gwiro*, Lee Man-hui, 1967)
Host, The (*Goemul*, Bong Joon-ho, 2006)
House of Hummingbird (*Beolsae*, Kim Bora 2018
House of Us, The (*Urijip*, Yoon Ga-eun, 2019)
I Am Really Sorry (*Jinjja jinjja mianhae*, Moon Yeo-song, 1976)
I Can Speak (*Ai kaen seupikeu*, Kim Hyun-seok, 2017)
Insect Woman (*Chungnyeo*, Kim Ki-young, 1972)
Jamsil (*Nuechideon bang*, Lee Wanmin, 2016)
Jane (*Kkumui Jein*, Cho Hyeon-hoon, 2016)
Journalist, The (*Shinbun kisha*, Fuji Michihito, 2019)
King of Jokgu, The (*Jokguwang*, Woo Mun-gi, 2013)
Kuro Arirang (*Guro arirang*, Park Jong-won, 1989)
Last Princess, The (*Deokhyeongju*, Hur Jin-ho, 2016)
Light for the Youth (*Jeolmeuniui yangji*, Shin Su-won, 2019)
Like a Virgin (*Cheonhajangsa Madonna*, Lee Hae-young 2006)
Like Father, Like Son (*Shoshite chichi ni naru*, Kore-eda Hirokazu, 2013)
Linda, Linda, Linda (Yamashita Nobuhiro, 2005)
Love, Lies (*Haeeohwa* [a.s.a. *Haeuhhwa*], Park Heung-sik, 2016)
Madame Aema (*Aema Buin*, Jeong In-yeob, 1982)
Madame Freedom (*Jayubuin*, Han Hyeong-mo, 1956)
Madonna (Shin Su-won, 2015)
Maggie (*Megi*, Yi Ok-seop 2018)
Maiden Who Went to the City, The (*Dosiro gan cheonyeo*, Kim Soo-yong, 1981)
Man from Nowhere, The (*Ajeossi*, Lee Jeong-beom, 2010)
Manshin: Ten Thousand Spirits (*Mansin*, Park Chan-kyong, 2013)
March of Fools, The (*Babodeului haengjin*, Ha Gil-jong, 1975)
Masquerade (*Gwanghae*, Chu Chang-min, 2012)
May 18 (*Hwaryeohan hyuga*, Kim Ji-hoon, 2007)
Mean Girls (Mark Waters, 2004)
Memories of Murder (*Salinui chueok*, Bong Joon-ho, 2003)
Microhabitat (*Sogongnyeo*, Jeon Go-woon 2018)
Midnight Sun, The (*Yeongsi*, Lee Man-hui, 1972)
Minari (Lee Isaac Chung, 2020)
Miss Baek (*Misseu baek*, Lee Ji-won, 2018)
Missy Granny (*Susanghan geunyeo*, Hwang Dong-hyuk, 2014)
Mist (*Angae*, Kim Soo-yong, 1967)
Mommy's Name Was Josenpi (*Emi ireumeun josenppiyeotda*, Ji Yeong-ho, 1991)
Mother (*Madeo*, Bong Joon-ho, 2009)
Murmuring, The (*Nateun sumsori*, Byun Young-joo, 1995)
My Daughter Rescued from a Swamp (*Sureongeseo geonjin naettal*, Lee Mi-rye, 1984)
My Own Breathing (*Sumgyeol, Nateun Sumsori 3*, Byun Young-joo, 1999)
My Sassy Girl (*Yeopgijeokin geunyeo*, Kwak Jae-young, 2001)

Selected Filmography **189**

Myth, The (*San wa*, Stanley Tong, 2005)
Nameless Gangster: Rules of the Time (*Beomjoewaui jeonjaeng*, Yoon Jong-bin, 2012)
Neighbours, The (*Iutsaram*, Kim Hwi, 2012)
New World (*Sinsegye*, Park Hoon-Jung, 2013)
Next Sohee (*Daeum So-hui, a.s.a. Daeum Sohee*, July Jung, 2023)
Night Before the Strike, The (*Paeopjeonya*, Jangsangotmae: Jang Dong-hong, Jang Yun-hyeon, Lee Eun, 1990)
Night Journey (a.k.a. *Night Voyage, Yahaeng*, Kim Soo-yong, 1977)
Nobody Knows (*Dare mo shiranai*, Kore-eda Hirokazu, 2004)
Oh My Ghost (*O naui gwisinnim*, aired on tvN July-August 2015)
Old Boy (*Oldeu boi*, Park Chan-wook, 2003)
Omok Girl (*Omok sonyeo*, Bael Seung-hwa, 2018)
On Your Wedding Day (*Neoui gyeolhonsik*, Lee Seok-geun, 2018)
Our Little Sister (*Umimachi Diary*, Kore-eda Hirokazu, 2015)
Paradise Now (Hany Abu-Assad, 2005)
Parasite (*Gisaengchung*, Bong Joon-ho, 2019)
Park Hwa-young (Lee Hwan, 2017)
Peppermint Candy (*Bakhasatang*, Lee Chang-dong, 1999)
Petal, A (*Kkotnip*, Jang Sun-woo, 1996)
Poetry (*Si*, Lee Chang-dong, 2010)
Priests, The (*Geomeun sajedeul*, Jang Jae-hyun, 2015)
Princess and the Matchmaker, The (*Gunghap*, Hong Chang-pyo, 2018)
Promenade in the Rain (a.k.a. *Walking in the Rain, Ujung sanchaek*, Yim Soon-rye, 1994)
Promise, The (*Wu ji*, Chen Kaige, 2005)
Psychokensis (*Yeomlyeok*, Yeon Sang-ho, 2018)
Queen of Walking (*Geotgiwang*, Baek Seung-hwa, 2016)
Red Cherry (*Ppalganaengdu*, Park Ho-tae, 1982)
Resistance, A (*Hanggeo*, Choi Min-ho, 2019)
Road to Sampo, The (*Sampo ganeungil*, Lee Man-hui, 1975)
Romy and Michele's High School Reunion (David Mirkin, 1997)
Rules of the Game, The (*La regle du jeu*, Jean Renoir, 1939)
Scandal Makers (*Kwasok seukaendeul*, Kang Hyeong-cheol, 2008)
Second Life (*Seon-huiwa Seul-gi*, Park Young-ju, 2018)
Seventh Continent, The (Michael Haneke, 1989)
Seven Swords (*Qi jian*, Tsui Hark, 2005)
Shoplifters (*Manbiki kazoku*, Kore-eda Hirokazu, 2018)
Silenced, The (*Gyeongseonghakgyo: Sarajinsonyeodeul*, Lee Hae-young, 2015)
Sing My Life (*Ayashii kanozo*, Mizuta Nobuo, 2016)
Snowpiercer (Bong Joon-ho, 2013)
Snowy Road (*Nungil*, Lee Na-jeong, 2015)
Spirits' Homecoming (*Gwihyang*, Cho Jung-rae, 2016)
Squid Game Season I (Ojingeo geim, Hwang Dong-hyuk, 2021)
Steel Flower (*Seutil peulawo*, Park Seok-yeong, 2015)
Strong Girl Bong-soon (*Himssen yeoja Do Bong-soon*, aired on tvN February-April 2017)
Sunday Night and Monday Morning (*Ilyoil bamgwa wolyoil achim*, Choe In-hyeon, 1970)
Sunny (*Sseoni*, Kang Hyeong-cheol, 2011)
Sunset on the Sarbin River (*Sareubingange noeul jida*, Chung Chang-hwa, 1965)
Tale of Two Sisters, A (*Janghwa, Hongryeon*, Kim Jee-woon, 2003)
Taste of Cherry (*Ta'm e gilass*, Abbas Kiarostami, 1997)
Taste of Money, The (*Donui mat*, Im Sang-soo, 2012)
Taxi Driver, A (*Taeksi unjeonsa*, Jang Hoon, 2017)

190 Selected Filmography

This Charming Girl (*Yeoja Jeong-hye*, Lee Yoon-ki, 2004)
Uhwudong (*Eo Wu-dong* [*a.s.a. Eowoodong*], Lee Chag-ho, 1985)
Villainess, The (*Aknyeo*, dir. 2017)
Virgin Suicides, The (Sofia Coppola, 1999)
Wedding Invitation, A (*Fen shou he yue*, Oh Ki-hwan, 2013)
Werewolf Boy, A (*Neukdaesonyeon*, Cho Sung-hee, 2012)
Whispering Corridor series, The (*Yeogogoedam*, 1998–ongoing)
Widow (*Mimangin*, Park Nam-ok, 1955)
Wild Flowers (*Deulkkot*, Park Seok-yeong 2014)
Winter Women (*Gyeul yeoja*, Kim Ho-sun, 1977)
Witch Part I, The (*Manyeo*, dir. 2018)
Wives on Parade (*Anaedeului haengjin*, Im Kwon-taek, 1974)
Woman Judge, A (*Yeopansa*, Hong Eun-won, 1962)
Woman Like the Sun, A (*Taeyang dalmeun sonyeo*, Lee Man-hui, 1974)
Woman of Fire (*Hwanyeo*, Kim Ki-young, 1971)
Women Being in Asia (*Asiaeseo yeoseongeuro sandaneun geoteun*, Byun Young-joo, 1993)
World of Us, The (*Urideul*, Yoon Ga-eun, 2015)
Yeong-ja's Heyday (*Yeongjaui jeonseongsidae*, Kim Ho-sun, 1975)
Yongsoon (Shin Joon, 2016)
Young-ju (*Yeong-ju*, Cha Seong-deok, 2018)
Youth Sketch (*Mi-miwa Cheol-suui cheongchunseukechi*, Lee Kyu-hyung, 1987)

Bibliography

"Battleship Island—A Symbol of Japanese Progress or Reminder of Its Dark History." *The Guardian*, 3 July, 2015. https://www.theguardian.com/world/2015/jul/03/battleship-island-a-symbol-of-japans-progress-or-reminder-of-its-dark-history. Accessed July 22, 2021.

"K-Pop Artists Goo Hara Found Dead at Home Aged 28." November 24, 2019. https://www.bbc.co.uk/news/world-asia-50535937. Accessed May 18, 2021.

"Sarah Waters: *The Handmaiden* Turns Pornography into a Spectacle—But it's True to My Novel." *The Guardian*, April 8, 2017. https://www.theguardian.com/film/2017/apr/08/sarah-waters-the-handmaiden-turns-pornography-into-a-spectacle-but-its-true-to-my-novel-. Accessed July 22, 2021.

"South Korea: Disappointing Japan Ruling Fails to Deliver Justice to 'Comfort Women.'" *Amnesty International*, April 21, 2021. https://www.amnesty.org/en/latest/news/2021/04/south-korea-disappointing-japan-ruling-fails-to-deliver-justice-to-comfort-women/. Accessed July 19, 2021.

"Suicide Rate," OECD Data. https://data.oecd.org/healthstat/suicide-rates.htm. Accessed November 1, 2022.

22nd Jeonju International Film Festival Program Event. "Jeonju in Audio with Lee Hwajung (Visible Audio): Your First with Purplay," with Panelists: Yim Soon-rye, Boo Ji-young, and Yoon Ga-eun. https://www.youtube.com/watch?v=-t6YwDZNL8Y. Accessed May 3, 2021.

Aaron, Michele. "Cinema and Suicide: Necromanticism, Dead-already-ness, and the Logic of the Vanishing Point." *Cinema Journal* 53.2 (2014): 84.

Aaron, Michele. *Death and the Moving Image: Ideology, Iconography and I.* Edinburgh: Edinburgh University Press, 2014.

Agamben, Giorgio. *Homo Sacre: Sovereign Power and Bare Life.* Stanford: Stanford University Press, 1998.

An, Ji-yoon. "The Korean Mother in Contemporary Thriller Films: A Monster or Just Modern." *Journal of Japanese and Korean Cinema* 11.2 (2019): 54–169.

An, Jinsoo. *Parameters of Disavowal: Representation of Colonialism in South Korean Cinema.* Berkeley: University of California Press, 2018.

Asian Women's Fund. "How the Comfort Women Issue Came to Light." http://www.awf.or.jp/e2/survey.html. Accessed September 17, 2018.

Bae, Gyeong-min. "The Hidden Ideology of Cheerful Classroom: The Prankster Films of the 1970s and Their Hegemonic Reconciliation [Myeongrang gyosil soke gamchueojin ideologi—1970 nyeondae yalgae yeonghwa hyeongseong gwajeongeseo jaehyeondoen hapuie daehan yeongu]." In *Korean Cinema Meets Sexuality* [Hanguk yeonghwa seksueolitireul mannada], edited by Cho heup, Yu Jina, et al. 11–29. Seoul: Namusaengak, 2004.

Bae, Seung-hoon, "Moon Chae-won Joins Cast of *Myeongdang*," August 23, 2017. https://koreajoongangdaily.joins.com/2017/08/23/etc/Moon-Chaewon-joins-cast-of-Myeongdang/3037517.html. Accessed October 15, 2023.

Baek, Moon-im. *The Sound of Female Ghost under the Moon: A History of Korean Horror and Female Ghosts* [*Wolhaui yeogokseong: Yeogwiro ikneun hanguk gongpo yeonghwasa*]. Seoul: Chaeksesang, 2008.

Banet-Weiser, Sarah. *Empowered: Popular Feminism and Popular Misogyny.* Durham: Duke University Press, 2018.

192 Bibliography

Barraclough, Ruth. *Factory Girl Literature: Sexuality, Violence and Representation in Industrializing Korea*. Berkeley: University of California Press, 2012.

Barthes, Roland. *Camera Lucida*. London: Vintage Classic, 1993.

Baxter, Katherine Isobel. "Memory and Photography: Rethinking Postcolonial Trauma Studies." *Journal of Postcolonial Writing* 47.1 (2011): 18–29.

Bechervais, Jason. "*Assassination* Review." *Screen Daily*, July 27, 2015. https://www.screendaily.com/reviews/assassination-review/5090978.article. Accessed July 18, 2021.

Berry, Chris. "Scream and Scream Again: Korean Modernity as a House of Horrors in the Film of Kim Ki-young." In *Seoul Searching: Culture and Identity in Contemporary Korean Cinema*, edited by Frances Gateward, 99–113. Albany: State University of New York Press, 2007.

Brown, Wendy. *Undoing the Demos: Neoliberalism's Stealth Revolution*. New York: Zone Books, 2017.

Burnett, Frances Hodgson. *A Little Princess*. St. Nicholas Magazine, 1887–1888; Charles Scribner's Sons, 1905.

Butler, Judith. *The Force of Non-Violence: An Ethico-Political Bind*. London: Verso, 2021.

Byun, Jae-ran. "Agents of Modernization: Brassy Women [Geundaehwaui juche: Eoksen yeojadeul]." In *Women Filmmakers Encyclopaedia* [*Yeoseong yeonghwain sajeon*], edited by Joo Jin-suk, 98–99. Seoul: Sodo, 1991.

Chiang, Min-hua. *Post-industrial Development in East Asia: Taiwan and South Korea in Comparison*. Singapore: Palgrave Pivot, 2018.

Chin, Eun-Kyung and Ahn Sang-won. "Ecology and Eco-Feminism as Depicted in the Film *Okja* [Yeonghwa 'Okja'e natanan saengtaehakgwa ecopeminiseum]." *Literature and Environment* [*Munhwakgwa hwangyeonghoe*] 17.3 (2018): 193–218.

Cho, Michelle. "*Take Care of My Cat* (2001): The Architectonics of Female Subjectivity in Post-crisis South Korea." In *Rediscovering Korean Cinema*, edited by Sangjoon Lee, 358–370. Ann Arbor: Michigan University Press, 2019.

Choe, Sang-hun. "Japanese and South Korea Settle Dispute over Wartime 'Comfort Women.'" *New York Times*, December 28, 2015. https://www.nytimes.com/2015/12/29/world/asia/comfort-women-south-korea-japan.html. Accessed September 17, 2018.

Choe, Steve. *Sovereign Violence: Ethics and South Korean Cinema in the New Millennium*. Amsterdam: Amsterdam University Press, 2016.

Choi, Chungmoo. "Nationalism and Construction of Gender in Korea." In *Dangerous Women: Gender and Korean Nationalism*, edited by Elaine H. Kim and Chungmoo Choi, 9–31. New York: Routledge, 1998.

Choi, Han-wook. "As It's Hurt, So You Are Young? Play Jokgu Instead [Apeunikka cheungchun? Charari gokgureul haera]." *Minjungui sori*, August31, 2014. https://vop.co.kr/A00000789054.html. Accessed August 7, 2023.

Choi, Hyaeweol. "'Wise Mother, Good Wife': A Transcultural Discursive Construct in Modern Korea." *Journal of Korean Studies* 14.1 (2009): 1–34.

Choi, Jinhee. "A Comedy of Remarriage? *My Love My Bride* (1990)." In *Rediscovering Korean Cinema*, edited by Lee Sangjoon, 260–273. Ann Arbor: University of Michigan Press, 2019.

Choi, Jinhee. "Home Is Where the Kitchen Is: *Rinco's Restaurant* (2009) and *Little Forest* (2014, 2018)." *Asian Cinema* 31.2 (2020): 169–185.

Choi, Jinhee. "I'm Not a Girl, Yet Not a Woman: Romance Films." In *The South Korean Film Renaissance: Local Hitmakers, Global Provocateurs*, 85–115. Middletown: Wesleyan University Press, 2010.

Choi, Jinhee. "Ribbons and Frills: Shōjo Sensibility and the Transnational Imaginary." In *Routledge Handbook for East Asian Pop Culture*, edited by Koichi Iwabuchi, Chris Berry, and Eva Tsai, 178–190. London: Routledge, 2017.

Choi, Jinhee. "Seoul Flaneur? *Breathless* and *Café Noir*." *Journal of Japanese and Korean Cinema* 7.1 (2015): 57–72.

Bibliography 193

Choi, Jinhee. *The South Korean Film Renaissance: Local Hitmakers, Global* Provocateurs. Middletown: Wesleyan University Press, 2010.

Chun, Soonok. *They Are Not Machines: Korean Women Workers and Their Fight for Democratic Trade Unionism in the 1970s.* London: Routledge, 2003, 2018.

Chung, Hye Seung and David Scott Diffrient. *Movie Migrations: Transnational Genre Flows and South Korean Cinema.* New Brunswick: Routledge, 2015.

Chung, Steven. *Split Screen Korea: Shin Sang-ok and Postwar Cinema.* Minneapolis: University of Minnesota Press, 2014.

Coates, Jennifer, Hsin Hsieh, Sung-Ae Lee and Kate Taylor-Jones. "The Pan-Asian 'Miss Granny' Phenomenon." In *East Asian Film Remakes*, edited by David Scott Diffrient and Kenneth Chan, 272–290. Edinburgh: University of Edinburgh Press, 2023.

Dirlik, Arif. "Rethinking Colonialism: Globalization, Postcolonialism and the Nation." *Interventions* 4.3 (2002): 428–448.

Doane, Mary Ann. *The Desire to Desire: The Woman's Film of the* 1940s. Bloomington, Indiana University Press, 1987.

Dollase, Hiromi Tsuchiya. "Girls on the Home Front: An Examination of *Shōjo no Tomo* Magazine 1937–45." *Asian Studies Review* 32 (2008): 323–229.

Eaglestone, Robert. " 'You Would Not Add to My Suffering, if You Knew What I Have Seen': Holocaust Testimony and African Trauma Literature." *Studies in the Novel* 40.1/2 (Spring Summer, 2008): 72–85.

Ehrlich, Linda C. "Kore-eda's Ocean View." *Film Criticism* 35.2/3 (2011): 127–146.

Elkin, Lauren. *Flaneuse: Women Walk in the City, in Paris, New York, Tokyo, Venice and London.* London: Vintage, 2016.

Eom, Mi-ok. *School Girls Encounter Modernity: The Formation of Korean Modern Novel and School Girls [Yeohaksaeng, Geundaereul malhada: Hanguk geundae sosoelui hyeongseonggwa yeohaksang].* Seoul: Yeokrak, 2011.

Flatley, Jonathan. *Affective Mapping: Melancholia and the Politics of Modernism.* Cambridge: Harvard University Press, 2008.

Fraiman, Susan. *Extreme Domesticity: A View from the Margins.* New York: Columbia University Press, 2017.

Giddens, Anthony. "Notes on the Concept of Play and Leisure." *Sociological Review* 12.1 (1964): 73–89.

Gill, Rosalind. "Postfeminist Media Culture: Elements of a Sensibility." *European Journal of Cultural Studies* 10.2 (2007): 147–166.

Gill, Rosalind and Elena Herdieckerhoff. "Rewriting the Romance." *Feminist Media Studies* 6.4 (2006): 487–504.

Gonzales, Ed. "Poetry." *Slant Magazine.* September 22, 2010.

Griffith, Paul. *What Emotions Really Are: The Problem of Psychological Categories.* Chicago: University of Chicago Press, 1997.

Han, Seong-gon. "Would the 33 years' Mystery of Hwaseong Serial Killing, Be Solved? [Hwaseong yeonsyeosageon, 33 nyeon miseuteori pulina?]" *Asia Economy*, September 19, 2019. https://www.asiae.co.kr/article/2019091905025158255. Accessed January 4, 2023.

Handyside, Fiona. *Sofia Coppola: A Cinema of Girlhood.* London: I. B. Tauris, 2017.

Heidegger, Martin. *Being and Time*, trans. John Macquarrie and Edward Robinson. San Francisco: Harper and Row, 1962.

Hirsch, Marianne. *Family Frames: Photography, Narrative and Postmemory.* New York: Columbia University Press, 1992.

Hwang, Gyeong-seo, An Chi-yong, No Su-bin, and Park Seo-yun. "Body Search and Beating; What Happened to 18-Year Old Hui-jin [Almom susaeke maejil, 18 Huijinui jikjangeseo saengginil]." *Oh Mynews*, January 10, 2021. http://www.ohmynews.com/NWS_Web/Series/series_premium _pg.aspx?CNTN_CD=A0002708330&SRS_CD=0000012552. Accessed July 28, 2022.

194 Bibliography

Jacoby, Alexander. "Simmons—Family and Society in Modern Japan." *Film Criticism* 35.2/3 (2011): 66–83.

Jeon, Go-woon. Interview conducted by Jinhee Choi. November 2, 2018.

Jeon, Joseph Jonghyun. "Memories of Memories: Historiography, Nostalgia, and Archive in Bong Joon-ho's *Memories of Murder*." *Cinema Journal* 51.1 (Fall 2011): 75–95.

Jeon, Joseph Jonghyun. *Vicious Circuits: Korea's IMF Cinema and the End of the American Century*. Stanford: Stanford University Press, 2019.

Jeong, Seo-hui. "*Queen of Walking* Director, Baek Seung-hwa, 'Hoped to make an adequate film—one that underwent the adequate process in making [<Geotgiwang> Baek Seung-hwa gamdok, 'Jakpumdo, Gwajeongdo olbaruen yeonghwareul mandeulgo sipeotda']." *Maxmovie*, October 31, 2016. https://www.maxmovie.com/news/274648. Accessed, August 7, 2023.

Jo, Hye-young, ed. *Girls: K-pop Screen Square* [*Sonyeodeul: K-pop seukeurin gwangjang*]. Seoul: Yeoiyeon, 2017.

Joo, Jin-suk and Byun Jae-ran. "The First Women Filmmakers' Association, Yonghuihoe and Women Filmmakers Group, Bariteo [Choechoui yeoseong yeonghwainmoim 'Yeonghuihoe'wa yeoseong yeongsangjipdan 'Barieto']." In *Women Filmmakers Encyclopaedia* [*Yeseong yeonghwain sajeon*], 274–275. Seoul: Sodo, 2001.

Joo, Youshin. *Cine-Feminism* [*Sine peminiseum: Yeoseongui sigakeuro yeonghwareul ikneun 13gaji bangbeop*]. Busan: Homilbat, 2017.

Joo, Youshin. "*Madame Freedom* and *Flower in Hell*: The 1950s Modernity and Female Sexuality as a Signifier [<Jayubuin>gwa <jiokhwa>: 1950 nyeondae geundaeseonggwa maehokui gipyoroseoui yeoseong seksyueoliti]." In *Korean Cinema and Modernity* [*Hangukyeonghwawa geundaeseong*], Joo Yoshin et al, 13–45. Seoul: Sodo, 2001.

Joo, Youshin et al. *Korean Cinema and Modernity* [*Hangukyeonghwawa geundaeseong*]. Seoul: Sodo, 2001.

Jun, Soomin. "Korea's 'N-Po' Generation Looks to New Administration for Jobs." *Asia Foundation*, May 31, 2017. https://asiafoundation.org/2017/05/31/koreas-n-po-generation-looks-new-administration-jobs/. Accessed September 7, 2021.

Jung, Hee-young, "'Youth, It's Painful,' Offers Hope to Young Koreans." *Korea Herald*, August 17, 2011. https://www.koreaherald.com/view.php?ud=20110817000762. Accessed August 8, 2023.

Jung, Min-woo and Lee Na-Young, "Fandom Managing Stars, Entertainment Industry Managing Fandom [Seutareul gwanlihaneun pandeom, pandeomeul gwanlihaneun saneop: '2 sedae' aidol pandeomui munhwasilcheonui teukjing mit hamui]." *Media, Gender & Munhwa* 12 (2009): 191–240.

Kang, Jun-man and Kang Ji-eun. *What Do Girl Fans Desire? Yes, I'm a Ppasuni!* [*Ppasunineun mueoteul galmanghaneunga? Geurae, naneun ppasunida*]. Seoul: Inmulgwa sasangsa, 2016.

Kaplan, E. Ann. "European Art Cinema, Affect, and Postcolonialism: Herzog, Denis, and the Dardenne Brothers." In *Global Art Cinema*, edited by Rosalind Galt and Karl Schnoover, 285–302. Oxford: Oxford University Press, 2010.

Karlyn, Kathleen Rowe. *Unruly Girls, Unrepentant Mothers: Redefining Feminism on Screen*. Austin: Texas University Press, 2011.

Kerr, Elizabeth. "*Jamsil*: Film Review BFF 2016." *Variety*, October 11, 2016. https://www.hollywoodreporter.com/movies/movie-reviews/jamsil-review-937182/. Accessed November 1, 2023.

Kil, Sonia. "Busan: Asian Market in Flux." *Variety*, October 6, 2015. https://variety.com/2015/film/asia/busan-asian-film-market-in-flux-1201611269/. Accessed November 4, 2024.

Kim, Chung-kang. "The Representations of 'Comfort Women' in Pre-1990 Korean Popular Cinema and the Politics of Memory ['Wianbu'neun eoteokke ithyeojeotna? 1990 nyeondae ijeon daejung yeonghwa sok 'wianbu' jaehyeon]." *Dongasiamunhwayeongu* 71 (2017): 149–193.

Bibliography 195

Kim, Elaine H. and Chungmoo Choi, eds. *Dangerous Women: Gender and Korean Nationalism*. New York: Routledge, 1998.

Kim, Gok. "[Kim Ki-young] Struck by His Film Part 3—*Insect Woman* (1972) [[Kim Ki-young] Geuui yeonghwae kkothida (3)—<Chungnyeo> 1972]." https://www.kmdb.or.kr/story/177/4785. Accessed June 28, 2022.

Kim, Gooyoung. *From Factory Girls to K-Pop Idol Girls: Cultural Politics of Developmentalism, Patriarchy, and Neoliberalism in South Korea's Popular Music Industry*. New York: Lexington Books, 2019.

Kim, Gyu-sik. "S. Korea's Unemployment Hits a Record High in 2016 with Highest Jobless Youth Rate." *Pulse*, January 11, 2017. https://pulsenews.co.kr/view.php?year=2017&no=25912. Accessed September 7, 2021.

Kim, Hyeon-su and Kim So-mi. "10 years of Korean Independent Films with Temporal Markers [Taim raineuro boneun hanguk doklip yeonghwa 10nyeonui yeoksa]." *Cine21*, August 28, 2019. http://m.cine21.com/news/view/?mag_id=93749. Accessed December 17, 2019.

Kim, Hyeong-won. "Kim Hyeong-won's Otaku Story [Kim Hyeong-wonui odeok iyagi]." *IT Chosun*, September 14, 2019. http://it.chosun.com/site/data/html_dir/2019/09/13/201909 1301124.html?utm_source=daum&utm_medium=original&utm_campaign=it. Accessed October 19, 2019.

Kim, Il-yeop. *Death of a Girl [Eoneu sonyeoui sa]. New Woman* [Sinyeoja] April 1920. Reprinted in *Compilation of Kim Il-yeop Writings*, edited by Kim Wu-yeong, 75–89. Seoul: Hyeondae munhak 2012.

Kim, Jae-heun. "It's Too Early to Discuss Truth of My Battleship Island, says Ryoo." *Korea Times* Aug 7, 2017. https://www.koreatimes.co.kr/www/art/2017/08/689_234284.html. Accessed July 18, 2021.

Kim, Ji-yeong. "[Movie] Sunny . . . a well-made comedy for 'the generation of Free School Uniform Policy' [[Yeonghwa] Sseoni, 'gyobokjayulhwa sedae'reul wihan welmeideu komedi]." *Mail Daily*, April 26, 2011. https://www.mk.co.kr/news/culture/4904779. Accessed March 8, 2024.

Kim, Kyung Hyun. "Dividuated Korean Cinema: Recent Bodyswitch Film in the Overwired Age." In *Surveillance in Asian Cinema: Under Eastern Eyes*, edited by Karen Fang, 179–202. New York: Routledge, 2017.

Kim, Kyung Hyun. *The Remasculinization of Korean Cinema*. Durham: Duke University Press, 2004.

Kim, Kyung Hyun. *Virtual Hallyu: Korean Cinema of the Global Era*. Durham: Duke University Press, 2011.

Kim, Min-ji. "Why Women Directors Do Not Tell Women's Stories [Yeoseong gamdoki yeoja iyagi anhaneun iyu]." *Kyeongnam domin ilbo*, June 18, 2013. http://www.idomin.com/news/articleView.html?idxno=417852. Accessed September 8, 2019.

Kim, Molly. "Film Censorship Policy during Park Chung Hee's Military Regime (1960–1979) and Hostess Films." *IAFOR Journal of Cultural Studies* 1.2 (2016): 37–50.

Kim, Molly Hyo J. *Whoring the Mermaid: The Study of South Korean Hostess Films (1974–1982)*. PhD thesis, University of Illinois, Urbana-Champaign, 2014.

Kim, Seung-kyung. *Class Struggle or Family Struggle: The Lives of Women Factory Workers in South Korea*. Cambridge: Cambridge University Press, 1997.

Kim, So-hui, "The Korean Cinema Master Selection: The Maiden Who Went to the City [Korean cinema geoljakseon: *Dosirogan cheonyeo*]." September 1, 2020. https://www.kmdb.or.kr/story/10/5439. Accessed August 19, 2022.

Kim, Soyoung. "Questions of Woman's Film: *The Maid, Madame Freedom,* and Women." In *South Korean Golden Age Melodrama: Gender. Genre and National Cinema*, edited by Kathleen McHugh and Nancy Abelmann, 201–228. Detroit: Wayne State University Press, 2005.

196 Bibliography

Kim, Su-bin. "20 Years of Independent Cinema in Korea." *Hankyoreh*, September 16, 2018. https://english.hani.co.kr/arti/english_edition/e_entertainment/862280.html. Accessed April 15, 2019.

Kim, Su-jeong. "When Fandom Meets Feminism: Outcomes and Issue of Fandom Studies from the Feminism Perspective [Paendeomgwa peminiseumdui jou: peminiseum kwanjeomeseo bon paendeom yeonguui seonggwawa jaengjeom]." *Eolronjeongboyeongu* 53.5 (2018): 47–86.

Kim, Suk-young, "Tragedy Should Force Korea to Consider Despair of Next Generation." *Korea Times*, November 16, 2022. https://www.koreatimes.co.kr/www/opinion/2023/08/137_339939.html. Accessed August 7, 2023.

Kim, Tae-wan, "[Books] the Most Beloved Books since 1990s and 2000s" [2000nyeondaewa 1990nyeondae ihu gajang sarangbatatdeon chaekeun?]. *Monthly Joseon*, August 8, 2023. http://monthly.chosun.com/client/mdaily/daily_view.asp?idx=18135&Newsnumb=20230818135. Accessed August 8, 2023.

Kim, Young Jak. "Park Chung Hee's Governing Ideas: Impact on National Consciousness and Identity." In *Reassessing the Park Chung Hee Era: 1961–1979*, edited by Hyung-a Kim and Clark W. Sorensen, 95–106. Seattle: University of Washington Press, 2011.

Kinsella, Sharon. "Cuties in Japan." In *Women, Media and Consumption in Japan*, edited by Brian Moeran and Lise Skov, 220–254. Richmond: Curzon Press, 1995.

Kinsella, Sharon. *Schoolgirls, Money and Rebellion in Japan*. London: Routledge, 2014.

Klein, Christina. *Cold War Cosmopolitanism: Period Style in 1950s Korean Cinema*. Berkeley: University of California Press, 2020.

Klein, Christina. "Why American Studies Needs to Think about Korean Cinema, or, Transnational Genres in the Films of Bong Joon-ho." *American Quarterly* 60.4 (2008): 871–898.

KOFIC. *Status and Insight: Korean Film Industry*. 2016.

KOFIC. *Status and Insight: Korean Film Industry*. 2018.

Koo, Hagen. "Labor Policy and Labor Relations during the Park Chung Hee Era." In *Reassessing The Park Chung Hee Era 1961–1979: Development, Political Thought, Democracy, and Cultural Influence* ed. Hyung-a Kim and Clark W. Sorensen, 122–141. Seattle: University of Washington Press, 2011.

Kwon, Kim Hyeon-young. "Young Feminist, Net Feminists' New Challenge: From 1990s to Mid 2000s [Yeong peminiseuteu, netpemiui saeroun dojeon: 1990 nyeondae jungbanbuteo 2000 nyeondae jungban kkaji]." In *Net Feminism Her Story* [*Daehanminguk netpemisa*], edited by Kwon Kim Hyeon-young et al., 11–77. Seoul: Namuyeonpil, 2017.

Larson, Wendy. *Women and Writing in Modern China*. Stanford: Stanford University Press, 1998.

Lee, Fred and Steven Manicastri. "Not All Are Aboard: Decolonizing Exodus in Joon-ho Bong's *Snowpiercer*." *New Political Science* 40.2 (2018): 211–226.

Lee, Gil-seong, Lee Ho-geol, and Lee U-seok. *Research on 1970s Exhibition and Film Culture* [*1970 nyeondae Seoului geukjangsanseop mit geukjangmunhwa yeongu*]. Seoul: Korean Film Council, 2004.

Lee, Hee-seung. "Signs of Domiciled Motherhood: Focused on *Family Ties*, *The Host*, and *Cruel Winter Blues* [Jeongjuhaneun moseongui gihodeul: <Gajokui tansaeng>, <Goemul>, <Yeolhyeolnama>reul jungsimeuro]." *Journal of Communication Science* [*Eonlongwahakyeongu*] 13.1 (2013): 359–386.

Lee, Hyo Won. "South Korea Box Office: Local Action Movie *Assassination* on Top, Becomes Biggest Film of 2015." *Hollywood Reporter*, August 18, 2015. https://www.hollywoodreporter.com/news/general-news/south-korea-box-office-local-815971/. Accessed July 18, 2021.

Lee, Hyo Won. "South Korean film, 'Miss Granny' to Get English and Spanish Language Remakes." *Hollywood Reporter*. November 6, 2016. https://www.hollywoodreporter.com/

news/general-news/south-korean-film-miss-granny-get-english-spanish-language-rema
kes-944612/. Accessed, March 8, 2024.

Lee, Jin-kyung. *Service Economies: Militarism, Sex Work and Migrant Labor in South Korea.* Minneapolis: University of Minnesota Press, 2010.

Lee, Ju-hyeon. "Eureka! Yoon Ga-eun's Directorial Debut, *The World of Us*, Depicts the World of Girls [Balgyeon, Sonyeodeului segyereul geurin Yoon Ga-eun gamdokui debyu, *Urideul*]." *Cine 21*, June 16, 2016.

Lee, Ju-hyeon. "Rooting for the Children: The Director of *The World of Us*, Yoon Ga-eun, [Aideulul eungweonhaneun maeumeul damda—<Urideul> Yoon Ga-eun gamdok]." *Cine 21*, June 16, 2016. http://m.cine21.com/news/view/?mag_id=84423. Accessed December 17, 2019.

Lee, Maggie. "Review: *A Werewolf Boy*." *Variety*, September 20, 2012.

Lee, Meera. "Monstrosity and Humanity in Bong Joon-ho's *The Host*." *Positions: Asia Critique* 26.4 (2018): 719–747.

Lee, Nam. *The Films of Bong Joon Ho.* New Brunswick, Rutgers University Press, 2020.

Lippit, Akira Mizta. "Hong Sangsoo's Lines of Inquiry, Communication, Defence and Escape." *Film Quarterly* 57.4 (2004): 22–30.

Lloyd, David. "Colonial Trauma/Postcolonial Recovery." *Interventions* 2.2 (2000): 212–228.

Louie, Mirium Ching Yoon. "Minjung Feminism: Korean Women's Movement for Gender and Class Liberation." *Women's Studies International Forum* 18.4 (1995): 417–430.

Maeng, Soo-jin. "Study on the Thematics and Aesthetic Diversification of Korean Independent Documentaries [Hanguk doklip dakyumenteoriui juje mit yangsikjeok dayanghwae daehan gochal]." *Cineforum* [*Ssineforeom*] 18 (2014): 255–285.

Masuko, Honda. "The Genealogy of Hirahira: Liminality and the Girl," translated by Tomoko Aoyama and Barbara Hartley. In *Girl Reading Girl in Japan*, edited by Tomoko Aoyama and Barbara Hartley, 19–37. New York: Routledge, 2010.

Masumi, Brian. "The Anatomy Affect." *Critical Inquiry* 31 (Autumn 1995): 83–109.

Mbembe, Achille. "Necropolitics," trans. Libby Meintjes. *Public Culture* 15.1 (2003): 11–40.

Mbembe, Achille. *Necro-politics* (Durham: Duke University Press, 2019).

McHugh, Kathleen. "South Korean Film Melodrama: State, Nation, Woman and the Transnational Familiar." In *South Korean Golden Age Melodrama: Gender, Genre and National Cinema*, edited by Kathleen McHugh and Nancy Abelmann, 17–42. Detroit: Wayne State University Press, 2005.

McHugh, Kathleen and Nancy Abelmann, eds. *South Korean Golden Age Melodrama: Gender. Genre and National Cinema*. Detroit: Wayne State University Press, 2005.

Meiri, Sandra. "Visual Responses: Women's Experiences of Sexual Violence as Represented in Israeli Holocaust-related Cinema." *European Journal of Women's Studies* 22.4 (2015): 443–456.

Mun, Hak-san. "Emptying Screen and Erased History: Tendencies in and History of Korean Independent Films [Biuneun hwamyeongwa biwojin yeoksa: hanguk doklip yeonghwaui gyeonghwanggwa yeoksa]." In *Issues in Korean Independent Short Films: Auteurs, Women, Digital* [*Hanguk danpyeon yeonghwaui jaengjeomdeul: jakga, yeoseong, digiteol*], edited by Jeonju Independent Film Festival, 9–55. Seoul: Sodo, 2003.

Mun, Soo-hyun. "'Femininity without Feminism': Korea's First Woman President and Her Political Leadership." *Asian Journal of Social Science* 43 (2015): 249–272.

Murphy, J. J. *Rewriting Indie Cinema: Improvisation, Psychodrama, and the Screenplay.* New York: Columbia University Press, 2019.

Nam, Hwasook. *Women in the Sky: Gender and Labor in the Making of Modern Korea.* Ithaca: Cornell University Press, 2021.

Newman, Michael Z. *Indie: An American Film Culture.* New York: Columbia University Press, 2011.

198 Bibliography

Noh, Jean. "Korean Film Council Reports Industry Exports Up by 17.5% in 2017." *Screen Daily*, February 12, 2018. https://www.screendaily.com/news/korean-film-council-reports-indus try-exports-up-by-175-in-2017/5126473.article. Accessed September 7, 2021.

Noh, Jean. "Korean International Film Sales Up 43% during Rough 2020." *Screen Daily*, February 22, 2021. https://www.screendaily.com/news/korean-international-film-sales-up-43-during-tough-2020/5157292.article. Accessed August 2, 2021.

O'Connor, Brian. *Idleness: A Philosophical Essay*. Princeton: Princeton University Press, 2018.

Oh, Young Sook. "Father and Girl: Representation of Korean Cinema in [the] 1970s [Appawa sonyeo: 70 nyeondae hanguk yeonghwaui pyosang yeongu]." *Yeonghwayeongu* 42 (2009): 435–458.

Oliver, Kelly. *Hunting Girls: Sexual Violence from the Hunger Games to Campus Rape*. New York: Columbia University Press, 2016.

Park, Hyun Seon. "From Secluded Rooms to Streets? Space and Women in Korean Cinema of the 1960s [Milsileseo georiro? 1960nyeondae hanguk yeonghwaui gonggangwa yeoseong]." In *Korean Cinema and Modernity*, Joo Youshin et al., 145–170. Seoul: Sodo, 2001.

Park, Hyun Seon. "South Korean Cine-Feminism on the Movie." *Journal of Japanese and Korean Cinema* 12.2 (2020): 91–97.

Park, Jai-in. "The Distorted Father and Mother Epic Given by the Film *Mother* [Yeonghwa <Madeo>eseo jesihan waegokdoen bumoseosa]." *Narration and Literary Therapy Research* [*Seosawamunhakchiryoyeonguso*] 6 (2011): 115–136.

Park, No Cheol. "Undomesticated Vision: A History of South Korean Independent Women's Films, 1974–2004." *Korea Journal* 49.4 (2009): 135–162.

Park, Su-jeong. *Women, Speaking of Labor* (*Yeoja, nodongeul malhadaI*). Seoul: Ihaksa, 2013.

Park, Sun-ah. "A Study on Performative Motherhood Identity Represented in *Mother* [Yeonghwa <Madeo>e natanan suhaengjeok moseong jeongcheseonge gwanhan yeongu]." *Hangukyeonghwahakhoe* 55 (2013): 173–195.

Park, Young-a. *Unexpected Alliances: Independent Filmmakers, the State and the Film Industry in Postauthoritarian South Korea*. Stanford: Stanford University Press, 2015.

Park, Yu-hee, "Censorship named Pornography: From *Chunmong* to *Madam Aema*, the Correlation between Censorship of the 'Racy Films' and Their Representation [*Geomyeoliraneun poreunograpi: <Chunmong>eseo <Aemabuyin>kkaji 'oeseol' geomyeolgwa jaehyeonui yeokhak*]." In *Censorship in Korean Film History*, 153–209. Seoul: Korean Film Archive, 2016.

Pecic, Zoran Lee. "Shamans and Nativism: Postcolonial Trauma in *Spirits' Homecoming* (2016) and *Manshin: Ten Thousand Spirits* (2013)." *Journal of Japanese and Korean Cinema* 12.1 (2020): 69–81.

Plantinga, Carl. *Moving Viewers: American Film and the Spectator's Experience*. Berkeley: University of California Press, 2009.

Pollock, Griselda. "Art/Trauma/Representation." *Parallax* 15.1 (2009): 40–54.

Poole, Janet. *When the Future Disappears: The Modernist Imagination in Late Colonial Korea*. New York: Columbia University Press, 2014.

Radner, Hilary. *Neo-Feminist Cinema: Girl Films, Chick Flicks and Consumer Culture*. New York: Routledge, 2011.

Redrobe Karen (Beckman). *Vanishing Women: Magic, Film and Feminism*. Durham: Duke University Press, 2003.

Rhee, kh Mirae. https://katehersrhee.com/about/. Accessed May 18, 2021.

Russell, J. S. "Idleness as Play and Leisure: Reflection on Idleness—A Philosophical Essay by Brian O'Connor." *American Journal of Play* 14.3 (2022): 304–326.

Ryu, Jin-hee. "The Heyday of Girl Group and K-Entertainment [Geolgeurup jeonseongsidaewa 'K-enteoteinteumeonteu]." In *Girls: K-pop Screen Square* [*Sonyeodeul: K-pop seukeurin gwangjang*], edited by Jo Hye-young, 79–104. Seoul: Yeoiyeon, 2017.

Bibliography 199

Seo, Yoonjung and Julia Hollingsworth. "Man who confessed to being one of South Korea's most-notorious serial killers says he's surprised he wasn't caught sooner." CNN, 2 Nov, 2020. https://edition.cnn.com/2020/11/02/asia/hwaseong-serial-killer-guilt-intl-hnk/index.html. Accessed July 13, 2023.

Seoul International Women's Film Festival. http://siwff.or.kr/kor/addon/00000002/summary_view.asp?summaryYear=1999&QueryYear=1999. Accessed September 7, 2021.

Shamoon, Deborah. *Passionate Friendship: The Aesthetics of Girls' Culture in Japan.* Honolulu: University of Hawaii Press, 2012.

Shim, Hye-kyeong. "Kim Sae-ron: New-Girl or Saeron-Girl [Kimsaeron: Nyu-geol hokeun saeron-sonyeo]." In *Girls: K-pop, Screen, Square [Sonyeodeul: K-pop seukeurin gwangjang]*, edited by Jo Hye-young, 120–151. Seoul: Yeoyiyeon, 2017.

Shin, Chi-Yun. "Two of a Kind: Gender and Friendship in *Friend* and *Take Care of My Cat*." In *New Korean Cinema*, edited by Chi-Yun Shin and Julian Stringer, 117–131. Edinburgh: Edinburgh University Press, 2005.

Shin, Hyonhee. "Victims Absent from South Korea's 'Comfort Women' Rally Amid Allegations over Ex-leader." *Reuters*, May 20, 2020. https://www.reuters.com/article/us-southkorea-comfortwomen-idUSKBN22W112. Accessed July 28, 2021.

Sim, Hyekyong. "Acting 'Like a Woman': South Korean Female Action Heroines." *Journal of Japanese and Korean Cinema* 12.2 (2020): 110–123.

Simmons, Rachel. *Odd Girl Out: The Hidden Culture of Aggression in Girls.* Boston: Mariner Books, 2011.

Smith, Murray. *Engaging Characters: Fiction, Emotion and the Cinema.* Oxford: Oxford University Press, 1995.

Soh, Chunghee Sarah. "The Korean 'Comfort Women' Movement for Redress." *Asian Survey* 36.12 (December 1996): 1226–1240.

Sohn, Dong-joo. "Kim Sae-ron fined 20 million won for driving under the influence." *Korea JoongAng Daily*, April 5, 2023. https://koreajoongangdaily.joins.com/2023/04/05/national/socialAffairs/Kim-Saeron-DUI-driving-under-the-influence/20230405111043373.html. Accessed, January 2, 2024.

Sohn, Hee Jeong. "Feminism Reboot, the Appearance of New Women Subjects: from Mid-2000s to the Present" [Peminiseum ributeu, saerowun yeoseong jucheui deungjang: 2000 nyeondae jungbanbuteo hyeonjekkagi]. *Net Feminism Her Story [Daehanminguk netpemisa]*, Kwon Kim Hyeon-young et al., 79–145. Seoul: Namuyeonpil, 2017.

Sohn, Hee Jeong. *Feminsm Reboot [Peminiseum ribeuteu].* Seoul: Namuyeongpil, 2017.

Song, Areum. "Censorship as a Social Sanction, The Resistant Voices: The Suspension of the Screening of 1981 Film, *The Maiden Who Went to the City* (Sahoejeok seunginuiroseui geomyeol, dolchuldoen moksori'deul'dui buleung: '1981'nyeon yeonghwa <Dosiro gan cheonyeo> sangyeongjungji sageonui uimi)." In *Censorship in Korean Film History [Hangukyeonghwayeoksa sok geomyeoljedo]*, 211–255. Seoul: Korean Film Archive, 2016.

Song, Hye-jin. "Has Fallen Ill for 40 years and Woken Up. . . . A Girl Who Fell in Love (40 nyeon alta ileonatda. . . . sarange ppajin sonye)," *Chosun Daily*, April 30, 2016. https://www.chosun.com/site/data/html_dir/2016/04/29/2016042902253.html. Accessed June 9, 2022.

Song, Jesook. *South Koreans in the Debt Crisis: The Creation of a Neoliberal Welfare Society.* Durham: Duke University Press, 2009.

Soyoung, Kim. *The Ghosts of Modernity [Geundaeseongui yuryeongdeul].* Seoul: Ssiateul ppeurineun saramdeul, 2000.

Stetz, Margaret D. and Bonnie B. C. Oh, eds. *Legacies of the Comfort Women of World War II.* London: Routledge, 2015.

Tanaka, Yuki. *Japan's Comfort Women: Sexual Slavery and Prostitution during World War II and the US Occupation.* London: Routledge, 2002.

Taylor, Kate. "*Heart (Hateu,* 2019)." BFI London International Film Festival Catalog (2019): 46.

200 Bibliography

Watson, Jini Kim. "The Disappearing Woman, Interiority, and Private Space." In *The New Asian City*, 133–166. Minneapolis: University of Minnesota Press, 2011.

Weissburg, Jay. "Rotterdam Film Review: '*Han Gong-ju*.'" *Variety*, February 9, 2014.

Yang, Hyunah. "Finding the Map of Memory: Testimony of the Japanese Military Sexual Slavery Survivors." *Positions* 16.1 (2008): 79–107.

Yang, Hyunah. "Lasting Postcolonial Trauma in [the] Testimony of Korean 'Comfort Women' Survivors [Jeungeonul tonghae bon hankukin 'wiwanbu'deului poseuteu sikminui sangheun (trauma)]." *Korean Women's Studies* [*Hanguk Yeoseonghak*] 22.3 (2006): 133–167.

Yang, Hyunah. "Re-membering the Korean Military Comfort Women: Nationalism, Sexuality, and Silencing." In *Dangerous Women*, 123–139. New York: Routledge, 1998.

Yesies, Brian. "The Chinese Korean Co-production Pact-Collaborative Encounters." *International Journal of Cultural Policy* 22.5 (2016): 770–786.

Yim, Su-yeon. "[*Microhabitat*] Mi-so has the Courage that I envision [<Sogongnyeo> Mi-sonenn naega saenggakhaneun yonggireul gajeotda]." *Cine 21*, October 30, 2017. http://www.cine21.com/news/view/?mag_id=88549. Accessed January 9, 2020.

Yoo, Kyung-soon, ed., *I, Woman Laborer* [*Na yeseong nodongja*]. Seoul: Greenbee, 2011.

Yoo, Sang-keun. "From Patriarchal History to Korean Ethnoformalist Speculative Empathy: *Squid Game* and *The School Nurse Files*." *International Journal of Korean History* 28.1 (2023): 215–243.

Yoon, Ga-eun. "*Good Morning* by Yoon Ga-eun: A Film That Makes You Happy [Yoon Ga-eunui <Annyeonghaseyo> haengbokhaejineun yeonghwa]." *Cine 21*, January 25, 2017. http://www.cine21.com/news/view/?mag_id=86310. Accessed December 17, 2019.

Yoshiaki, Yoshimi. *Comfort Women: Sexual Slavery in the Japanese Military World War II*. New York: Columbia University, 1995.

Ypi, Lea. *Free: Coming of Age at the End of History*. London: Allen Lane, 2021.

Yu, In-kyung. "Glancing through the 100 years (19): Bus Conductor [*Baeknyeoneul yeotboda (19): Bus Conductor*]." *Kyunghyang Daily*, March 7, 2010. https://www.khan.co.kr/article/201003071824542. Accessed November 2, 2016.

Yu, Jina, "Women's Body Genre: The Wounds of Modernity—from Late 1970s to 1980s [Yeoseong momui jangreu: Geundaehwaui sangcheo—1970 nyeondae hubaneseo 1980 nyeondae]." In *Korean Films Meet Sexuality* [*Hangukyeonghwa seksyueolitireul mannada*], edited by Cho Heup, Yu Jina et al., 77–98. Seoul: Sanggakeu namu. 2004.

Yu, Jina and Byun Jae-ran, eds. *Feminism/Film/Women* [*Peminiseum/Yeonghwa/Yeoseong*]. Seoul: Yeoseongsa, 1993.

Yue, Genevieve. *Girl Head: Feminism and Film Materiality*. New York: Fordham University Press, 2021.

Yun, Jeong-mo. *Mommy's Name was Josenpi* [*Emmy iruemeun josenppiyeotda*]. Seoul: Dangdae, 1982.

Index

Complied by David O'Hara

For the benefit of digital users, indexed terms that span two pages (e.g., 52–53) may, on occasion, appear on only one of those pages.

Figures are indicated by an italic *f* following the page number.

Aaron, Michele, 17, 18, 56–57, 58, 71–72, 81–82, 87–88, 104–5
activism, 4–5, 64–65
    communal activism, 109
    film activism, 107, 108
    labor activism/activist, 24
    political activism, 4–5, 65, 79
    student activists, 4–5, 91, 144
aestheticization, 15, 18, 57, 62–63, 72, 78–79, 81–82, 98, 111–12, 149–50
    aesthetic, 100, 139
    aesthetics, 162
affect, 99, 100
    affective attachment, 100–1
    affective attunement, 100–1
Age of Shadows, The (*Miljeong*), 54–55
agency, 5–7, 8, 11–12
    limited agency, 6, 7, 15, 20
art cinema. *See* cinema
arts, 24, 25–26, 36
Assassination (*Amsal*), 54–56
"at the expense of," 16, 18, 37, 46–47, 51–52, 73, 86–87, 88 (*see also* instrumentality: instrumental)
auteurs, 11–12, 81–82, 84–85
    authorship, 16, 84–85, 88
    male auteurs, 11–12, 15–16, 54–55, 88
authoritarianism (authoritarian), 18, 38, 42–43, 89–90, 108, 109
authority, 14–15, 108, 109, 113, 150–51
    censorship authority, 172n.68
    state authority, 38, 67

Bae, Doona, 91, 106, 123, 124, 130, 147, 156, 159–60
band(s), 1–3, 39, 137, 150–54, 159–60
    boy bands, 7–8
    idol bands, 1–3, 7–8, 127

bargirl(s); hostess (*hoseuteseu*), 12, 33–34, 40–42, 46–47
    bargirl (hostess) films, 10–12, 23–24, 26–27, 29–30, 41–43, 167n.36, 169n.1
    bargirl cycle, 24, 27, 31–32, 35, 42–43
Bariteo, 9, 107–8
Barking Dogs Never Bite (*Peurandaseuui gae*), 88–89, 94–95, 123, 124, 163
Barraclough, Ruth, 9–10, 34–35, 36, 42, 52
bike, 42, 48–49, 49*f*
    bike ride, 48–49, 49*f*
body (bodies, bodily), 5–7, 8, 24, 30, 36, 39, 42, 58, 61, 70, 71–72, 83–84, 85, 86, 90–91, 92–93, 127, 130, 149, 150, 152–53, 163, 170–71n.21
    body (*yukche*) genre, 11–12, 27, 141–42, 170n.16
    body search, 32–33, 35, 36, 37*f*, 37, 171n.29, 171n.31, 171n.41, 171n.43
    body switch (swap) films, 149–50, 151–52, 153
    dead body, 27, 85*f*, 95, 96
    female body (bodies), 6–7, 23–24, 27, 52–53, 54–55, 70–71, 76–78, 89, 90–91, 95, 127, 141–42, 155–56, 168n.47
    sexualized body, 27, 65–66, 70, 71, 92–93
Bong, Joon-ho, 15–16, 20–21, 81, 82–85, 86–87, 88–89, 92–93, 94–95, 139, 144, 155, 171n.28
bus conductor(s), 3–4, 10–11, 19, 26–27, 32–37, 41–42, 43
Butler, Judith, 18, 87
Byun, Young-joo, 13–14, 64–65, 104, 107–8

camera, 28–30, 62–63, 83–84, 85–86, 113, 114, 116, 117*f*, 125, 134–35, 136, 141–42, 147, 151
    camera movement, 5, 13, 38, 43, 45, 47, 70–71, 72, 75–76, 112–13, 118–19, 136, 154

202 Index

camera (*cont.*)
  camera work, 29–31, 37, 43–47, 62–63, 72, 75–76, 81–82, 83–84, 86, 111–13, 116, 125, 144–45, 154
  See also frame/framing
capitalism, 8, 18–19, 36, 101–2
  capital, 34–35
  confucian capitalism, 34–35
  symbolic capital, 108
censorship, 7, 33, 36, 37, 42, 50, 54, 58, 67
cheongchun. See youth
chick flicks (lit), 6–7, 31–32
Choi, Eun-hee (Choe Eun-hui), 12, 14–15
cine-feminism. *See* feminism
cinema, 31–32, 50–51, 130–31, 140, 162
  art cinema, 3, 81–82, 100, 110–11
  independent (indie) cinema, 3, 17, 18–19, 21–22, 81–82, 100, 103–4, 105–6, 107–8, 109–11, 112, 139 (*see also* indie film)
  Korean cinema, 3–5, 9–10, 11–13, 14–16, 18, 19–20, 26, 41, 56, 72, 81–82, 87–88, 101, 103–4, 107–8, 142, 162–63
class, 8–9, 12–13, 24, 26–27, 30, 32, 42, 74–75, 89, 91, 108, 135, 137, 157
  middle-class, 8–9, 13–14, 47–48, 135, 157
  working-class, 17, 24, 30, 31–32, 34–35, 36, 41, 42, 67, 75, 91, 107, 114, 140–41, 157
coloniality (colonial), 16–17, 18, 20, 52–53, 55–57, 64, 65–66, 67, 68–69, 72, 73, 104, 125
  colonial rule, 1–3, 20, 54, 55, 56–57, 64, 65, 66–67, 72, 78–79
  colonial state, 54, 55–57, 59–60, 67–68
  colonial subject, 18, 55–57, 58, 59–62, 67–68, 71–72, 76–79
  postcolonialism (postcolonial), 18, 65, 66–67, 78–79, 80–82, 101
comfort women (*wianbu*), 1–3, 16–17, 56
  See also sex: sexual slave: sexual slavery
commodity (commodities), 1–3, 8, 11–12, 19, 29–30, 92–93, 94–95
  virtual commodity, 19, 25–26, 29–31, 39, 41, 93–94
complicity (complicit), 18, 44–45, 55–57, 85, 86, 101, 126
connectivity, 99, 100
  sonic connectivity, 99, 100–1
consumerism, 4–5, 8–9, 39, 136, 143–44
  consumer(s), 5, 8, 144, 156, 157
Crazy for You (*Jinjja jinjja joahae*), 19, 26–27, 28, 30–32, 33–34, 36, 40–41, 47, 51–52, 157, 158–60

Crush and Blush (*Misseu hongdangmu*), 18–19, 103–4, 139

daughter, 5, 6, 14–15, 33, 46–47, 68, 74–75, 88, 89, 90, 95, 123, 142, 144, 150, 151, 154–55, 162–63
  daughter in-law, 133, 150–51, 153–54
death, 10–11, 12, 16–17, 18–19, 20–21, 30, 32–33, 35, 42–43, 46, 47–48, 51–53, 58, 61, 68, 71, 78–79, 81–86, 87–88, 94, 95, 96, 101–2, 119–20, 125, 126, 128–30, 144, 146–47, 156, 157, 163
  dead-already, 17, 18, 56–57, 58, 61, 72, 76–79, 87–88
  to-be-dead, 17, 18, 57, 61, 63–64, 72, 78–79, 87–88, 104–5
  symbolic death, 10–11, 17, 42, 45, 56, 57, 58, 80–82, 94, 126–27, 136–37
  virtual death, 10–11, 56–57, 63–64, 142
democratization, 4–5, 109
  democratic movement, 143–44
  postdemocratization, 91
  See also Gwangju democratic uprising, The
developmentalism (developmental), 9–10, 12–13, 16, 19, 24, 26–27, 30, 34–35, 80–81, 125, 142, 143
  economic development, 12, 19, 37
  See also nationalistic, developmental ethos
Dirlik, Arif, 67, 69
disappearance (disappearing), 17, 33–34, 52, 54, 56, 59, 61
disposability (disposable), 1–3, 11–12, 16–17, 18, 56–57, 58, 61
documentary, 1, 33–34, 64–65, 104, 107–8, 109, 110–11, 123, 139, 143, 155–56
domesticity (domestic), 14–15, 21, 94–95, 105–6, 112, 113, 133, 134, 135, 137–39
  domestic helper (*sikmo, hanyeo, gasadoumi*), 3–4, 10–11, 13, 34, 41–42, 131–32, 135, 136, 156
  domestic labor, 14–15, 105–6, 133, 135, 155–56
  domestic space, 103–4, 123
  extreme domesticity, 41
  homeless domesticity, 106, 131–32, 137

Eaglestone, Robert, 68–69
empowerment, 6–7, 40–41, 124, 125
ethnicity, 8–9, 89
exteriority (exterior), 62–63, 115
  pure exteriority, 56–57
  See also interiority

Index

Factory Complex (Wirogongdan), 1, 3, 26, 52
factory workers, 3–4, 8–9, 13, 19–20, 24, 37, 52, 82–83
  factory girls (*yeogong* or *gongsuni*), 7, 9–11, 32, 34–35, 36, 158
  women factory workers, 1, 31–32, 34–36
fandom, female (girl), 7–8
  ppasuni, 7, 158
father; 5–6, 14–15, 23, 24, 28–29, 33, 46–48, 55–56, 59–60, 61–62, 63–64, 68, 74, 87, 89–90, 91, 92–93, 98, 114, 115, 118–19, 120–21, 136–37, 150
  stepfather, 123, 124–26, 127–28
  See also patriarchy
feminism, 4–5, 9, 23–24, 26, 27, 35–36, 65–66, 67, 73–74, 105–6
  cine-feminism, 9
  commodity feminism, 8–9
  eco-feminism, 88–89
  feminist criticism, 69, 107–8
  Korean feminism, 5, 7, 8–9, 27, 64, 69
  minjung feminism, 107–8
  neo-feminism, 8, 40–41
  popular feminism, 8–9
  postfeminism, 5–7, 8–9, 130–31
  second wave feminism, 6, 8–9
  third wave feminism, 8–9
  white feminism, 8–9
  young feminism, 9
flaneuse, 25–27, 50–51, 137, 141–42
flashbacks, 10–11, 24, 26–27, 41–42, 43, 48–51, 60–61, 62, 64, 69, 74, 83–84, 98, 99, 134, 143–45, 151
Flower in Hell (Jiokhwa), 12, 27–28
Fraiman, Susan, 21, 105–6, 112–13, 114–15, 116–18, 122, 123, 124–26, 131–35, 137–39, 147
frame/framing, 29, 44–46, 57, 62–63, 71, 75–76, 85–87, 89–90, 99, 100, 112–13, 116, 134–35, 136–37, 151, 153–54, 158–59

Gangster, the Cop and the Devil, The (Akinjeon), 20–21, 80–82, 83–84
gaze, 16, 43, 47–48, 61, 62–63, 70–71, 76, 82–83, 97–98, 114–15, 127, 151–52
  voyeuristic gaze, 27, 70–71
gender
  gender essentialism (expectations), 6, 9, 18, 104–5, 131–32, 134–35

gender in film industry, 5–6, 17, 26, 70–71, 103, 104–5, 107, 108, 111
gender role, 28–29, 47, 63–64, 93–95, 101–2, 124, 125, 131–32, 134–35, 136–37, 149–50, 151–53, 154–55, 160–61
gender ideology (ideologies), 36, 81–82
gender representation in film, 3–4, 9, 10, 11–12, 15–16, 20–21, 27, 60–61, 84–85, 88–89, 91, 92, 93–95, 104–5, 110, 124, 125, 134, 150, 152–53
  See also body: female body
generation, 4–5, 6, 7, 8–9, 10, 11–12, 38, 78, 111, 118–19, 149–50, 153–54, 160
  activist generation, 91
  baby boom generation, 8–9
  n-po generation, 131–32
  sampo generation, 160
genre, 10, 84–85, 86–87, 104–5, 111, 155–56
  body genre, 27
  high school horror, 15, 56–57, 114
  romantic comedies, 5–7
  teen films, 23, 31–32
  youth films, 10
  See also cinema
Gill, Rosalind, 6–7, 8
Girl at My Door, A (Do-huiya; Dohee-ya), 3, 21, 101–2, 103–4, 106, 111, 112, 115, 123, 124–30
girl(s), 1–4, 62–64, 75, 76, 78, 93–95, 103–5, 111, 123, 124, 126–27, 130–31, 137–39, 142, 143–44, 146–47, 149–52, 153, 154–56, 162–63
  bus girl, 32 (*see also* bus conductors)
  factory girls, 9–10, 35
  girl head, 1, 26 (*see also* reference girl)
  girlhood; 1–3, 9, 10–11, 12–13, 14–15, 18–19, 24–25, 26–28, 30, 40–41, 44–45, 46, 47–48, 50–53, 65–66
  girl protagonist(s), 3–4, 5–6, 10–12, 14–16, 19–22, 24, 26–29, 35, 36, 38, 40–41, 46, 51–52, 56–57, 62–63, 64, 73–74, 81, 88–89, 90–91, 93–94, 96–97, 103–6, 112, 113, 114, 119, 121, 130–31, 140–41, 143, 147, 149–50, 155–56, 158
  girly, 5–6, 76, 81, 94–95
  reference girl(s), 3–4, 9–10, 12–13, 19, 21, 24–25, 26, 111
  schoolgirl(s), 3–4, 10, 16, 19, 26–27, 30–31, 46–47, 80, 82–83, 123
Girls from Scratch (Maenjumeokui sonyeodeul), 10–11, 19, 26–27, 33–34, 35, 36, 40–41

204 Index

grievability, 18, 87
Gwangju pro-democracy movement, The 3, 15, 16, 19–20, 80–81

Ha, Gil-jong, 11–12, 95
Han Gong-ju, 17, 20–21, 29, 81, 96–99, 100–1, 103–4, 143
hanyeo. *See* domesticity: domestic helper; *Heavenly Homecoming to Stars* (*Byeoldeului gohyang*), 23–24, 28, 45
holocaust, 65–66, 78
Hong, Sang-soo, 15–16, 109–10, 139
Host, The (*Goemul*), 16, 20–21, 64, 81, 88–89, 90, 91, 92–93
hostess (*hoseuteseu*). *See* bargirls
House of Hummingbird (*Beolsae*), 3, 112, 121, 127, 128–30
House of Us, The (*Urijip*), 21, 101–2, 106, 111–22, 123, 125–26, 128–30, 133, 137–39
Housemaid, The (*Hanyeo*), 12–13, 46
Hwang, Dong-hyuk, 21–22, 142, 148–49
Hwaseong serial killing, 80–81, 82–83, 84, 144

I Can Speak (*Ai kaen seupikeu*), 20, 64, 78–79
identity(-ies)
   gender, 6–7, 8, 9, 107, 126
   identity in film, 74, 76–78, 148–49
   identity through fandom, 6, 7–8
ideology (ideologies), 36, 108
   cold war ideology, 89–90
   gender ideology, 6, 17, 36, 64, 81–82, 155
   state ideology, 12, 17, 18–19, 26–27, 30, 34, 45, 56, 67–68, 73
   utopian ideology, 6
idleness (idle), 17, 21–22, 101–2, 142, 143, 144, 146–47, 148, 153, 154–55, 156–60, 162–63
   idle play, 143, 144, 146–47, 148
idol bands. *See* bands: boy bands
Im, Ye-jin, 10, 23, 27–28, 163
imagination, 17, 23, 48–51, 54, 56, 62–63, 64, 67, 70, 98–99
   imaginary, 18, 50, 62–63, 70, 98–99
   social imaginary, 3–4
immaturity, 26–28, 38
imperialism, 1–3, 16–17, 18, 59, 64, 65–66, 67–68, 78
   imperialist government, 54, 57, 58, 59

indie film, 3, 21–22, 25–26, 103–4, 105–6, 107–8, 109–11, 112, 121, 127, 130–31, 155–56, 157–58 (*see also* cinema: independent (indie) cinema)
industrialization, 4–5, 9–10, 12–13, 32, 42–43, 62
industry, 1, 33–34, 52, 67, 92–93, 149–50, 155–56
   affective industry, 1
   entertainment industry, 1–3, 8
   film industry, 4–5, 9, 13–14, 20–21, 24–25, 56, 64, 71–72, 103, 104, 106, 107, 137–39, 148–49, 163
   service industry, 1, 3, 27, 32
Insect Woman (*Chungnyeo*), 19, 25–27, 46–48
instrumentality (instrumental), 8–9, 17, 20–21, 73, 81, 82, 83–84, 87–88, 152–53, 154–55, 156–57, 159–60
   See also "at the expense of"
interiority, 15, 29, 41, 50–51, 56–57, 62–63, 106, 115
   See also exteriority
irony (ironic), 18, 29–30, 35–36, 47, 50, 56–57, 61–62, 78, 85, 87, 89–90, 91, 93–94, 121–22, 136, 142, 149–50, 158, 160–61, 163

Japanese colonial rule (1910-1945), 1–3, 10, 15, 16–17, 18, 20, 54, 55, 59, 64–66, 67–68
Jeong, Jae-eun, 13–14, 104, 109
Joo, Youshin, 9, 12, 69, 70
Jung, July, 3, 52, 128–30, 139

Karlyn, Kathleen Rowe, 5–6, 8–9
Kim, Ki-young, 12–13, 25–26, 46, 47
Kim, Soyoung, 9, 10, 13, 107–8
King of Jokgu, The, 157–58, 159–60
Kore-eda, Hirokazu, 116–19
Korean war, The, 62, 63, 74

labor, 24–25, 35, 42, 58, 149–50, 162–63
   casualization of labor, 10–11, 107–8, 110
   labor history, 3, 9–10, 24, 32–33, 35–36, 37, 67, 142, 155–56
   labor movement(s), 3, 8–10, 107–8
   labor union(s), 1, 8–9, 107, 142, 143
   low-wage labor, 1–4, 9–11, 12, 13–14, 24, 32, 34–36, 41–42, 52–53, 125, 145–46, 155–56
   sexual labor, 1–3, 10–11, 13, 16–17, 20, 34, 41–42, 58, 65–66, 67–68, 71–72, 75–76,

81–82, 92–93 (*see also* sex: military
    sexual slavery)
unpaid labor, 14–15, 105–6, 132–33, 145–
    46, 155–56
women's labor, 1–4, 8–10, 12–13, 14–15,
    19, 29, 32, 33–36, 37, 52–53, 105–6,
    107–8, 132–33, 135, 142–43, 155–56
    (*see also* domesticity: domestic labor)
Lee, Hae-young, 16–17, 54, 103–4
Lee, Jin-kyung, 16–17, 34, 41, 42, 58, 125
Lee, Kyoung-mi, 18–19, 109–10, 139
Lee, Man-hui, 10–12, 25–26, 27–28, 38, 39,
    40–41, 95
leisure, 3–4, 21–22, 24–26, 48–49, 133, 135,
    136, 139, 140–41, 142–43, 144, 148,
    149–50, 152–53, 154–57, 160
    leisure activities, 31–32, 39, 50–51,
    132–33, 140–41, 142–43, 144, 152–53,
    155–56, 157
Little Princess, A, 75–76, 76*f*, 79
Lloyd, David, 66–67, 69, 73, 78–79

Madame Freedom (Jayubuin), 12–13,
    135, 136
Maiden Who Went to the City, The
    (*Dosirogan cheonyeo*), 26–27, 33, 35–36,
    37, 37*f*, 142–43
masculinity, 3–4, 12–13, 19, 24, 27, 38, 49–50,
    84, 86–87, 134, 135
materiality (material), 26, 52–53, 66–67,
    137, 163
    immateriality, 52
Mbembe, Achile, 16–17, 18, 58
Memories of Murder (Salinui chueok), 16,
    20–21, 80–85, 86, 97, 144
memory (memories), 1–4, 19–20, 23, 30, 50–
    51, 55, 56, 64, 85–86, 99, 100
    post-memory, 78
Microhabitat (Sogongnyeo), 21, 25–26, 75–
    76, 103, 106, 110–11, 121–22, 130–39,
    138*f*, 138*f*, 157–58, 160
military sex slaves. *See* comfort women
    (*wianbu*); sex: military sexual slavery
mimetic, 1, 19, 21, 26, 121
mirror, 44–45, 153–54
    mirror image, 59–60, 61
    mirroring, 29, 44, 48–49, 76, 77*f*, 85–86,
    95, 104, 125, 157–58
misogyny. *See* sexism
Miss Granny (Susanghan geunyeo), 21–22,
    143, 148–53, 154–55, 157–58, 160–61

missing, 94, 162
    missing girls, 60–61
Mist (Angae), 33, 48–49
mobility, 30–31, 38, 61–62
    downward mobility, 10–11, 29–30, 33–34,
    35, 39, 51–52
modernity, 12–13, 31*f*, 32, 41–42, 84, 101–
    2, 142
    colonial modernity, 52–53, 56, 73
    state-led modernity, 24
Moon, Sook (a.s.a. Mun, Suk), 25–26, 27–28,
    38, 39, 40–41, 95, 163
mortal economies, 18, 63–64, 81–82, 163
mother, 43, 46–47, 86–87, 128–30, 151–
    52, 154–55
    motherhood, 5–6, 16, 47, 84–85, 88–89,
    92, 93–95, 101–2, 110, 119–20, 150–51,
    152–53, 154–55
Mother (Madeo), 13, 20–21, 61, 80–82, 84–
    87, 85*f*, 88–89, 96
Murmuring trilogy, The; *The Murmuring*
    (*Nateun sumsori*), 13–14, 64–65, 104

n-po generation. *See* generation
nation, 1, 10, 13–14, 18, 19, 27–28, 30, 42–43,
    52, 73, 88, 123
    cultural nationalism, 67, 69, 73
    nationalism, 1, 26, 30, 55–56 (*see also*
    nationalist ideology)
    nationalistic ethos, 18, 19, 28–29, 34, 41, 56,
    101, 125, 142 (*see also* developmentalism;
    developmental ethos)
    nation-state, 1, 18, 19, 35–36, 52, 67,
    88, 159–60
necro-cinematics, 15–17, 18–19, 20–21, 81–
    82, 87–89, 146–47, 163
necromanticism, 18, 57, 78–79, 81–82,
    87–88
necropolitics, 16–17, 18, 42, 58, 81–
    82, 87–88
neoliberalism (neoliberal), 6–7, 8, 87–88,
    91, 101–2
Never Forget Me (Jinjja jinjja itjima), 19, 23,
    24, 26, 28, 30, 51–52
Next Sohee (Daeum So-hui; Daeum Sohee),
    52, 81–82, 143, 155–56
Night Journey (Night Voyage; Yahaeng,), 19,
    26–27, 46, 48–51, 49*f*
Nobody Knows (Dare mo shiranai), 119–20
normativity (normative), 5–6, 40–41
    heterosexual normativity, 6, 124

206　Index

O'Connor, Brian, 143, 144–45, 146–47, 155, 156–57, 158–59
Okja, 16, 20–21, 81, 88–89, 90–91, 92–95
operative, 1, 19, 26

pair(ing), 16–17, 63–64
　female pairing, 7–8, 13, 16–17, 38, 39, 56, 68, 81, 97, 124, 128–30, 149–50
　See also mirror: mirroring
Paradise Now, 17, 57
Park, Bo-young, 58, 62, 163
Park Chan-wook, 15–16, 55, 105–6
Park Nam-ok, 13–14, 15–16
Park, So-dam, 59–60, 88, 163
patriarchy, 18, 28–29, 47–48, 51–52, 63–64, 67, 70, 74–75, 86–88, 94–95, 101, 110, 124, 125, 126, 127–30, 137, 143, 149–50, 151–52
Petal, A (*Kkotnip*), 3, 19–20, 80–81
play (playing), 28, 30–31, 43–44, 63–64, 112–13, 115, 118–19, 135, 139, 143–44, 146–47, 148, 151, 152–53, 159–60
pleasure
　narrative pleasure, 9, 18, 57
　sexual pleasusre, 6–7, 8, 40–41
Poetry (*Si*), 20–21, 25–26, 81–82, 95, 96–97, 128–30, 149–50
Pollock, Griselda, 66–67
pop idols. *See* bands: idol bands
position(s), 35–36, 39, 61, 65, 70, 99, 136
　moral(istic) position, 37, 80–81
　positionality, 73
　social position(s), 10–11, 19, 26–27, 132–33
post-war, 15, 20, 56, 62, 154–55
protest(s), 36, 37, 64–65, 70
　female protest, 7, 37, 70
　labor protest, 36, 37
　pro-democratic protest, 1–3
　student protest, 4–5 (*see also* activism: student activist)

Queen of Walking (*Geotgiwang*), 21–22, 103–4, 114–15, 143, 156–61, 163

Radner, Hilary, 5–6, 40–41
Really Really (*Jinjja jinjja*) series, The, 19, 26–28, 31–32
recognition, 55, 71, 110–11, 120–21, 158–59
　public recognition, 109, 116, 153–54, 155
　self-recognition 44–45, 60–61, 76–78, 144–45, 153, 158–59

reference image, 1, 19, 24–25, 26. *See also* girl head
Reply series, The, 7–8
Road to Sampo, The (*Sampo ganeungil*), 11–12, 38, 40–41, 95
romantic comedy. *See* genre: romantic comedy

screen, 23, 36, 37, 38, 54–55, 70–71, 113, 119–20, 123, 125–26, 127
　off-screen, 12, 40–41, 43–44, 50–51, 86, 92–93, 113, 116, 120–21, 125, 127
self, 38, 40–41, 44–45, 60–61, 70, 78, 92, 105, 114, 124, 125, 130–31, 137, 144–45, 149, 154–55, 160–61, 162–63
　self-advancement, 21, 155, 159–60
　self-reflexive, 8–9, 29, 60–61, 68–69, 94–95
　self-regard, 39, 48–49, 50–51, 87, 134–35
　See also recognition: self-recognition
sensibility (sensibilities), 15, 24–26, 29–30, 62–63, 65–66, 67, 68–69, 81, 97–98, 100–1, 111, 131–32, 139, 162–63
　postfeminism as sensibility, 6–7, 8–9 (*see also* feminism: postfeminism)
Seoul, 1–3, 23, 31–32, 37, 39–40, 50–51, 92, 107, 136, 137, 140–41
　Seoul Independent Film Festival, 13–14, 103
sex (sex work/sex workers), 3–4, 10–11, 12, 13, 16–17, 24, 25–26, 34, 39, 41–42, 43, 45–46, 47–50, 58, 71–72, 85–86, 96, 132–34, 156, 158
　military sexual slavery (slaves), 1–3, 16–17, 20, 54, 55, 56–57, 58, 64–66, 67–69, 70, 74, 76–79, 104
　sexuality, 3–4, 6–7, 9–11, 12, 13, 15, 19, 23–26, 29–31, 40–41, 50, 51–53, 67–68, 93–94, 112–13, 123, 126, 131–32
　sexual violence, 3, 4–5, 16–17, 73, 81, 96–97, 105–6, 132, 144
Sex and the City, 5–7
sexism, 6, 125
shelter, 21–22, 93–94, 105–6, 111, 112, 114, 115, 122, 123, 124–26, 132, 133–34, 137–39, 147
　shelter writing, 21, 41, 101–2, 105–6, 112–13, 114–15, 116–18, 121–22, 133–34, 137–39
Shoplifters (*Manbiki kazoku*), 110–11, 119
shot-reverse-shot, 89–90, 144–45, 151–52
sikmo. *See* domesticity: domestic helper

Silenced, The (*Gyeongseonghakgyo: Sarajin sonyeodeul*), 16–17, 20, 54, 55, 56–64, 73–74, 76–78, 104, 114

slavery. *See* sex: military sexual slavery

Snowpiercer, 16, 20–21, 81, 88–90

Snowy Road (*Nungil*), 16–17, 20, 54–55, 56, 64–78, 71*f*, 76*f*, 77*f*, 79, 81–82, 130–31

Sohn, Hee Jeong, 5, 69, 70

sonyeo (girl), 1–3, 7, 10–11, 13, 17, 25, 27–28, 62–63, 81–82, 103–4, 143, 162

   sonyeosang (girl statue), 1–3, 2*f*, 68–69, 70
   See also girlhood

sovereignty, 16–17, 18, 58, 70

spectator(ship), 24–25, 26, 29, 56, 72, 81

Spirits' Homecoming (*Gwihyang*), 16–17, 55, 56, 58, 64–78, 71*f*, 149–50

Squid Game (*Ojingeo geim*), 21–22, 148–49, 160–61

subject, 3–4, 10, 16–17, 19–20, 23, 24, 26, 28, 30, 35–36, 47–49, 50–51, 56–57, 58, 59–60, 61, 66–68, 70–71, 76–79
   speaking subject, 20, 64
   viewing subject, 39, 41
   writing subject, 20, 41, 54, 56, 62–63, 73–74, 78

subjectivity, 28, 29, 41–42, 57, 59, 61, 66, 71–72, 76–78, 100–1
   female subjectivity, 7, 9–10, 18, 19, 78–79, 81, 96, 104–5
   male subjectivity, 19, 23–24, 26, 70
   national subjectivity, 23–24, 28, 70

Sunday Night and Monday Morning (*Ilyoil bamgwa wolyoil achim*), 50–51, 140, 141–42, 156

Sunny (*Sseoni*), 3, 4–5, 17, 21–22, 103–4, 143–48, 145*f*, 146*f*, 146*f*, 157–58, 160–61

survivor (survival), 1–3, 16–17, 18, 55, 56, 64–66, 67–69, 70–71, 74, 78, 82–84, 89, 104, 105–6

Take Care of My Cat (*Goyangireul butakhae*), 13–14, 104, 123, 124, 147, 148

teen pictures, 10, 19, 31–32, 41, 104

testimony (-ies), 1, 64–65, 68, 70–71, 74, 82–84, 110

traumas, 3, 4–5, 19–20, 47–48, 64, 65–67, 68–69, 73, 74, 79, 80–81, 96–98, 99, 100, 101–2, 105–6, 158

national traumas, 1–3, 4–5, 16, 67, 73–74, 101, 143–44, 149

urban space, 12, 28, 90–91

vanishing, 4–5, 17, 20, 52, 125–26. *See also* disappearance

victim(s), 1–3, 4–5, 18, 19–20, 36, 55–56, 61, 64–66, 68–69, 70–72, 73, 80–84, 93–94, 96–97, 98–99, 100

victimhood, 1–3, 64, 65–66, 70, 80–81, 84, 85, 87, 100, 104–5, 125, 127, 143–44

violence, 93–94, 104, 105–6, 121, 124–25, 144–45
   See also sex: sexual violence

Virgin Suicides, The, 17, 57

Werewolf Boy, A (*Neukdae sonyeon*), 20, 62–64, 74, 103–4

Whispering Corridors (*Yeogogoedam*), 3, 15, 112, 162

wianbu. See comfort women

Woman Like the Sun, A (*Taeyang dalmeum sonyeo*), 10–11, 19, 21, 25–28, 38, 39–41, 40*f*, 41*f*

Woman of Fire (*Hwanyeo*), 25–26, 47–48

worker. *See* labor: sexual labor; sex worker/workers

World of Us, The (*Urideul*), 3, 18–19, 103–4, 111–13, 114, 115, 120–21

writing, 20, 29, 36, 43, 56–57, 59, 60–61, 62–63, 64, 65–66, 73–74, 78–79, 122. *See also* subject: writing subject

Yang, Hyunah, 20, 74

Yeong-ja's Heydays (*Yeongjaui jeonseongsidae*):
   film, 10–11, 19, 23–24, 26–28, 33, 41–46, 44*f*, 45*f*, 47
   source novel, 42–43

Yim, Soon-rye, 13–14, 104–5, 109, 137–39

Yoon, Ga-eun, 18–19, 103, 109–10, 111–12, 114, 116, 118–19, 120–22, 139

Yoon, Jeong-hee (a.s.a. Yun Jeong-hie), 25–26, 48–49, 50–51, 95

Youn, Yuh-jung, 25–26, 163

Yu, Jina, 9, 27

Yue, Genevieve, 1, 19, 26, 52–53

yukche (body), 11–12, 141–42
   See also body

The manufacturer's authorised representative in the EU for product safety is Oxford
University Press España S.A. of El Parque Empresarial San Fernando de Henares,
Avenida de Castilla, 2 – 28830 Madrid (www.oup.es/en or product.safety@oup.com).
OUP España S.A. also acts as importer into Spain of products made by the manufacturer.

Printed in the USA/Agawam, MA
August 15, 2025

892047.019